Trail of Trees

One family's journey crisscrossing
the USA planting trees and creating
a living Legacy

John and Joyce Jackson

Printing Arts Press
Mount Vernon, Ohio

First Edition, October 2010

Library of Congress Control Number: 2010912698

Jackson, John and Joyce. Trail of Trees - One family's journey crisscrossing the USA
    planting trees and creating a living legacy. John and Joyce Jackson / Publishers
1st Ed. - 261 pages

Request for information should be addressed to:

John and Joyce Jackson
Delaware, Ohio 43015
740-990-9789
JJ1N2@columbus.rr.com
www.thejacksonlegacy.com

ISBN 978-0-615-39714-6

Printed in the United States of America

Book cover design by: Joyce Jackson
Cover photo by: Thinkstock and iStockphoto

Printing Arts Press
8028 Newark Road
Box 431
Mount Vernon, Ohio 43050
740-397-6106
www.printingartspress.com

This book is dedicated

To our parents, Ray and Madge Crooks and
Joe and Helen Jackson for their love and
Support.
To our children, grandchildren and all future
Children added to our family.

The Jackson Legacy

Table of Contents

Table of Contents *(continued)*

The Jackson Legacy

Chronological Table of Planting Sites

PLACE	DATE	TYPE OF TREE	PLACE	DATE	TYPE OF TREE
1. Joyce Washington	2- 5-91	Leyland Cypress	26. Jackson, North Carolina	5-10-95	Crape Myrtle
2. Jackson, California	2-11-91	Scotch Pine	27. Mt.Jackson, Virginia	5-11-95	Cherry and Plum
3. Jackson, Pennsylvania	6-15-91	Blue Spruce	28. Jacksonville, Maryland	5-12-95	Various Species
4. Jackson, New Jersey	8-24-91	Black Pine	29. Jackson, Michigan	9-18-95	Various Species
5. Jackson, South Carolina	1-13-92	Dogwood	30. Jackson, Maine	5- 6-96	White Pine
6. Jackson, Georgia	1-14-92	Yoshina Cherry	31. Jackson, Minnesota	6-10-96	Northwood Maple
7. Jackson, Alabama	1-15-92	Soul Magnolia	32. Jackson Junction, Iowa	6-11-96	Scotch Pine
8. Jacksonville, Florida	1-17-92	River Birch	33. Jackson, Wisconsin	6-12-96	Northwood Maple
9. Jacksonville, New York	6- 4-92	White Dogwood	34. Jacksonville, Illinois	6-14-96	Pin Oak
10. Jacksonville, Vermont	6- 8-92	Dogwood	35. Jackson Place, Honolulu, HI	2-19-97	Silver Trumpet
11. Jackson, New Hampshire	6- 9-92	Hemlock	36. Jacksonport, Arkansas	9-15-97	Flowering Plum
12. Christina River, Delaware	8-16-92	White Pine	37. Jackson Co., Colorado	5-26-98	Aspen
13. Jackson, Texas	2-15-93	Live Oak	38. Jackson Co., Oklahoma	9- 7-98	Mulberry
14. Jackson, Mississippi	2-17-93	Magnolia	39. Jackson Co., Kansas	9- 8-98	Maple and Oak
15. Jackson, Louisiana	2-19-93	Crape Myrtle	40. Jackson, Nebraska	9-10-98	Mayday (choke cherry)
16. Roberts, Massachusetts	5-10-93	White Dogwood	41. Christine, North Dakota	9-11-98	Green Ash
17. Stevens Village, Alaska	6-15-93	White Spruce	42. San Juan Co., New Mexico	6- 7-99	Plum and Pear
18. Jackson, Ohio	6- 5-94	Bradford Pear	43. St. Johns, Arizona	6- 8-99	Red Maple
19. Jackson, Kentucky	6- 6-94	Variety	44. San Juan Co., Utah	6- 9-99	Blue Spruce
20. Jackson, Tennessee	6- 8-94	Willow Oak	45. Jackson Mountains, Nevada	6-11-99	Silver Maple
21. Jackson, Missouri	6- 9-94	Red Oak & Pin Oak	46. Jackson Co., South Dakota	8-30-99	Canada Cherry
22. Jackson Co., Indiana	6-10-94	Tulip Poplar/Red Oak	47. Roberts, Idaho	8-31-99	Aspen
23. Jackson, Rhode Island	10-17-94	Bradford Pear	48. Jackson, Montana	9- 1-99	Pine and Spruce
24. Robertsville, Connecticut	10-18-94	White Pine	49. Jackson, Wyoming	9- 3-99	Aspen
25. Jackson Co., West Virginia	5- 8-95	Crabapple	50. Jacksonville, Oregon	3-20-00	Various Species
The Hermitage, Nashville, Tenn.	6- 7-94	Tulip Poplar	The Capitol, Washington, DC	5- 1-00	Red Oak

<u>Acknowledgments</u>

First of all, we thank God for safely guiding us the many miles we traveled on this journey. Our grateful thanks to the townspeople and officials in the fifty states we visited who so graciously allowed us to beautify their towns.

Many thanks to Tony Cerbo of Cerbo's Greenhouses & Garden Center in Parsippany, New Jersey, whose phenomenal knowledge of trees gave us the foundation for getting the project started along the east coast. Tony's guiding hand helped us in so many ways to better understand what we needed to know about the types of trees best suited to our project.

Kudos to Bailey Nurseries of St. Paul, Minnesota, for helping us out with 25 trees in the upper Midwest.

Our appreciation to all the nurseries who worked with us to select the trees native to their regions.

Our most gracious thanks to the late Virginia Holtry of Roberts, Idaho, for writing us a poem inspired by our visit there.

Thanks to former Governor Jim Florio of New Jersey for arranging the donation of a Wheaton crystal pitcher for our presentation to the native people of Stevens Village, Alaska.

Thanks to author Bill Queen of Newark, Ohio, for offering so many helpful insights on how to write a book and get it printed.

Our appreciation and warm thanks to Chuck Gherman, General Manager of Printing Arts Press in Mount Vernon, Ohio, for helpful suggestions and working with us in the printing of the book.

We are grateful to all the media for putting our story on television in several states and in newspaper articles in almost every state.

To Carolyn Meeker who worked with us in Morristown, New Jersey, at the outset of the project, helped us put our ideas and design into reality and designed a way to re-publish updated lists of our tree planting progress using a greeting-card format, many thanks.

To our families and friends, thank you for always being attentive to our exciting stories; we hope your enjoy the book.

Our special thanks and gratitude to our children, Rob, Chris and Steve, for your support, confidence and companionship during the ten years of planting. To Mike and Debbie, who joined our family through marriage, thanks for your help. To our parents, Joseph and Helen Jackson, Ray and Madge Crooks, our undying love and thanks for always believing in us that this Legacy adventure would be accomplished and become published for others to experience.

To my husband, John, my deep appreciation for your help in digging the many holes for the trees and for your great sense of humor along the American roads.

To my wife, Joyce, whose creativity and indomitable spirit saw this project through to its conclusion, touching so many people in the process.

Introduction

From Maine to Hawaii, Alaska to Florida, and all of the other forty-six states in between, our Jackson family pursued its mission to plant trees as a lasting legacy to our name.

It took us from the cold Atlantic seacoast to the warm currents of the Pacific, through imposing mountains and wide expanses of prairie, the Gulf of Mexico to the Great Lakes, through deserts and verdant green forests, in our ten-year quest to leave behind five trees in each state at a place connected to the name of Jackson and, in the process, to help protect, beautify, cleanse and provide habitat for nature.

Along the way we came to understand our roots better, not only our own ancestry but that of the native peoples whose stewardship of the land is their everlasting gift to us all. The idea for this project came from our desire to celebrate the family name of Jackson in some unique manner that would survive beyond our lifetimes. But, in a way, it began in Ireland many years before.

Family lore has it that Thomas Jackson sailed from an Irish seaport, perhaps Limerick, in 1874 bound for a new life in America. Leaving behind religious persecution and famine, he was one of the large numbers of Irish people who came to the United States throughout the 19th Century. Many challenges awaited them and it wasn't always the perfect haven that they had envisioned. They had to overcome hardships and discrimination and many times they were turned away from jobs or social activities.

Into this environment, Thomas Jackson settled outside of Philadelphia with his wife, Anna, and daughter, Mary. They were modest people who worked the land and were succeeded by descendants who were also working-class people. In this regard, they personified the foundations of the typical American family.

Eighty-seven years after Thomas Jackson's death, his great, great grandson, John Jackson, and wife, Joyce, embarked upon their tree-planting odyssey. The idea occurred to Joyce as she was recuperating from breast cancer in 1987–88. She was trying to think of a project that would help keep her mind off the effects of chemotherapy. The concept of planting trees at a place named Jackson in every state served her on several levels: it commemorated the name of Jackson throughout the country, thereby establishing The Jackson Legacy, it provided opportunities for pursuing our favorite hobby – traveling, and the time devoted to extensive research took her mind off the illness.

Joyce is now a twenty-three year cancer survivor and doing fine. She wishes for anyone who is going through any treatments to have faith in God, love life and listen to music, as it soothes the soul on those not-so-good days.

Planting trees always had a meaningful connection to our lives together. For years we would plant trees to celebrate the birth of a child, a new home or anniversaries. Drawing from this inspiration, our intention became to plant five trees, representing each member of our immediate family, in all fifty states. The research revealed forty states that had significantly-sized communities affiliated with the name Jackson. In order to account for the other ten states, we used the first name of a family member which resulted in such selections as: Joyce, WA, St. Johns, AZ, Roberts, ID, Christine, ND and Stevens Village, AK.

The research also revealed that most Jackson locales were named after Andrew Jackson, seventh President of the United States, Hero of the War of 1812, renowned Indian fighter and responsible for a good deal of formative legislation during his time in Washington, DC. He also had Irish ancestry, his father departing from Carrickfergus, County Antrim, in the north of Ireland in 1765. However, the only bond we have with him is the surname of Jackson. Archivist at The Hermitage, his home outside of Nashville, TN, having assured us that there is no genealogical connection.

It wasn't until later that we discovered so many connections in our story to Native Americans, starting with the fact that half of all state names are derived from Indian words. They inhabited these lands well before the first European ship ever landed on the shores of the New World. For ages, they maintained a pristine living environment without disturbing the balance of nature and with absolute respect for everything their Creator had provided. Even when the Europeans arrived in the 16th and 17th centuries, most Indians were enthusiastic to meet them as they brought new technology like steel knives, copper kettles, swords and other marvels. But, after awhile, it became achingly apparent that the Europeans were excessively possessive and materialistic and didn't respect the land, in contrast to the Native peoples who were melded to the land and imbued with a deep spirit of nature.

Our book explores some of the facts behind the formation of each community named Jackson, including pieces of relevant history pertaining to their involvement with Native Americans. Much of this information was gathered at the source and in research to write the book. We are amazed at how many places possess elements of this story. We decided to weave this background of the American Indians throughout the book as a tribute to the first inhabitants and in appreciation for their stewardship of the land for so many years before we got here.

The story unfolds chronologically starting with our first effort in Joyce, WA, in January, 1991, and ending with the planting ceremony at the Nation's Capital in May, 2000. Along the way, we experienced the effects of hurricanes, tornadoes, drought and other vagaries of travel. All of that was well worth the effort because it enabled us to meet so many interesting people all over America. It enlarged our perspective of this wonderful country and we hope you can take some part of that satisfaction through reading this book.

In retrospect, paying homage to the Jackson name would make our ancestors proud, if they were here today. They would be amazed at the number of namesake communities with their population sizes, modern technological achievements and the beautification that we have lent to each one by the planting of our trees.

One of our trees now stands west of the Capitol Building at Grant's Plaza for all to see. It represents all the people that are living in those fifty places that we visited. It also serves to symbolize the debt that we all owe to Native Americans and our gratitude for what they have passed down to us. We are thankful for our new awareness of their past trials, tribulations and continued courageous love of America.

Our journey is done, now, but we hope that this book might inspire others to do what they can to promote tree planting in their own neighborhoods. Whether you plant one tree or encourage others to do the same, you will experience a little bit of the enjoyment that we had in carrying out this adventure.

John and Joyce Jackson

Doris Pfaff, John and Joyce Jackson, and Leonard Pierce stand along side the newly planted **Cypress** trees outside Joyce General Store.

Joyce, Washington

Washington

"The Beginning"

February 5, 1991

After more than a year of preparation, the opportunity surfaced to put our project plans into action for the first time. Our intention was to accomplish the tree planting activities within the itineraries of our annual vacation trips. Traveling has always been the Jackson family's number one hobby and we had already visited forty-four states even before coming up with the idea of a nationwide tree planting venture. However, we had never been to the Pacific Northwest before, so we thought that February, 1991, might be a good time to do that. The town of Joyce was the only suitable place to visit in the state of Washington since there is no location containing the name of Jackson, which would have been our first preference. It also seemed appropriate to start the project in a place whose name corresponds to the person whose vision launched the whole undertaking – Joyce Jackson.

Joyce, WA, is located in Clallam County in the northwestern part of the state only a few miles from the Strait of Juan de Fuca in Puget Sound. It is at the northern edge of Olympic National Park, approximately 100 miles northwest of Seattle. The moderate climate and unique scenery make it a great spot for visiting any time of the year, especially good for us since some of our vacation time would have to be spent in the winter months.

Joyce had made previous contact with Leonard Pierce and his sister-in-law, Doris Pfaff, who ran the Joyce General Store, which also serves as the Post Office. They extended an invitation to plant our trees outside of the store and provided a general description of the area which would later help us in picking out the trees.

I guess you might say we had finally arrived at the point in our project which could be called the moment of truth – the point at which intentions are turned into action. The long period of preparation had equipped us to go forward but a certain amount of apprehension existed at the outset of an adventure that was wrought with many unknowns: was our mission great enough to achieve support from the people who we were about to encounter; would they accept us and to what degree could we rely upon them for assistance; did we know how to properly select and plant the trees that were appropriate for each of the vastly different locations? It was a lot of fun putting together the planning out of research books that identified the names of places and local contacts, but now it was time to go face to face with them. For lack of a better word, we were a little scared.

We arrived in the area on February 5, 1991. Our first job was to visit the nursery that we had picked out to purchase five trees of the right type. Marge King of Peninsula Nurseries, Inc., in Sequim, WA, was most helpful. She steered us towards the Leyland Cypress (*Cupressocyparis x Leylandii*) which grows to a pyramidal height of twenty feet and is known for quick growth, hardiness, adaptability and grace. It results from the cross-rooting of cypress and Monterrey cypress and is named after Captain Leyland. We chose five trees averaging 2 ½ feet in height and headed for the Joyce General Store.

Leonard and Doris were very interested in our project. They pointed out an area next to the Joyce Depot, about fifty feet from the store. We assembled the five trees into a circle symbolizing our practice of gathering the kids around us at special family times, then, we commenced the planting activities. In less than an hour, five little cypress seedlings stood in a circle spaced about ten feet apart from each other. To commemorate the visit, we provided them with a plaque to be placed at the site attesting to the fact that the trees were *"Planted As a Living Legacy for the Jackson Family."* Photographs were taken before and after the planting. The couple also gave us a tour of the general store and provided some local history. In all we stayed nearly two hours.

After leaving Joyce, WA, we picked up with our tourist activities. One of the memorable excursions was the ferry crossing of the wide Straits of Juan de Fuca between Port Angeles, WA, and the Victorian-like city of Victoria, BC. We enjoyed touring the magnificent Empress Hotel, shopping in quaint stores and having fish and chips at a pub. After returning to the U.S., we drove through the forests of Olympic National Park, arriving by ferry into Seattle and spending a couple of days there touring one of our country's most pleasant cities. Afterward we headed for California to visit with our priest friend, Father Larry Finegan, at his parish in San Francisco.

We were very pleased with the responses of the people in the Joyce, WA, area but one element was missing – we hadn't thought to pursue any reporting of our visit with the local newspaper. Perhaps we were too timid to think that our visit might be newsworthy but the more we thought of how warmly we had been greeted and how interested people were in our project, we decided to notify the local press after the fact and put together the following "Press Release." It's interesting for us to compare this effort with what we later developed but many things in life progress beyond humble beginnings and this is ours:

Dear Editor, Peninsula Daily News,   *February 20, 1991*

The following account may have some news value for your publication. If you decide to publish, we would be very grateful to receive a copy of that edition. The enclosed sum of $1.00 is provided to cover the necessary expenditures.

VISITORS PLANT TREES AS A LIVING LEGACY TO THEIR FAMILY

Mr. and Mrs. John W. Jackson of Madison, NJ, paid a visit to Joyce, Washington on February 5, 1991, for a very special purpose – to plant five trees. The couple plans to do the same thing at one location in each of the states as a living legacy to their family name and future generations. Jackson or the name of some family member will appear in the name of each selected site. Since Mrs. Jackson's first name is Joyce, they chose the nearby town of the same name as the place to begin their project.

The couple's visit to Joyce was not completely unexpected. Several weeks prior to the trip Mrs. Jackson contacted Leonard Pierce and Doris Pfaff who operate the General Store in town. After hearing Mrs. Jackson's story they graciously agreed to provide the location and assistance in planting the trees. There are now five new Leyland Cypress trees next to the Joyce Depot. Each one represents a member of the family: the parents, and their children Robert, Steven and Christine.

Mrs. Jackson was very pleased with the reception she received and was very impressed with the town and its history. "This is a wonderful place to start our project. I hope that every other place we go will be as nice as the people here." .

After leaving the area the couple journeyed to Jackson, California and plan to work their way back to the East Coast in the years to come. But it all started right here in Washington State.

The Peninsula Daily News, published the following story from this press release which appeared in the "*Neighbors*" section on p.A4, issue date unknown but prior to March 5, 1991, reading as follows:

"John and Joyce Jackson, of Madison, N.J., have decided to plant five trees – one for each member of their family – in all of the states, as a living legacy for their family and future generations. "Jackson" or the name of some family member, will appear in the name of each selected site. Joyce, Wash., was their first choice."

The newspaper mailed us a copy on March 5[th.] Joyce picked up the mail on the way out the door of our town house and she read it while we were driving through Madison. We were so excited that we had to pull off the road to read it over and over again while we giggled and basked in the glow of our first success. That little spark was so important to us; it buoyed our confidence for pursuing the rest of the project. There were to be many more stories and adventures ahead.

Five– one foot **Scotch Pine** trees were planted at the Civic
Center. These trees are dedicated to all servicemen and
women in the Desert Storm conflict.

Jackson, California

California

"Gold Rush Country"

It was huge to have that first state planting under our belt but we were still flying an uncertain course as we departed from Washington. It would have been reasonable to consider visiting Oregon while in that part of the country. After all, the research was all done, we knew where Jacksonville, Oregon was located, but the project had not yet reached that level of cohesiveness. We were still acting out of instinct and it told us go slow, to feel our way along, to measure what we had just done and decide the next move. California would be the next stop on our vacation since our high-school friend lives in the Bay Area and the Monterey peninsula has a lasting appeal for us whenever we're on the West Coast.

The prospect of visiting Jackson, California, was there in the background. Joyce had compiled the research data, including the name and contact information for the proper city official. The possibility of going there was not far from our consciousness as we toured the sights of San Francisco. We toyed with the fact that a planting site lay only 130 miles away from where we were, so why not go for it? The pleasant experience in Joyce, WA, gave added promise for a similar occurrence at the next place, so why not get it going while our courage was up and the traveling distance was so near? With all those things coming together, Joyce telephoned for Jim Buell, City Manager of Jackson, CA.

Jim was as nice as he could be as he tried to comprehend why this Mrs. Jackson was calling him. *"You want to come to our city to plant five trees?"* Joyce must have done a good job leading him through all of the details because the invitation was extended and the date set for February 11, 1991. Another round of excitement swept over us, to think that another city official had agreed to our program without any advance notice. It was like making a sale off of a cold call, to put it in salesmen's lingo.

The journey over to Jackson, CA, ascended steadily into the Sierra Nevada foothills. On the way we stopped at the Garden Center in Manteca, CA, to pick out the trees which turned out to be little one-foot Scotch Pine seedlings, then it was back on the trail. Gradually signs along the road started indicating that these surroundings were part of the legendary California Gold Rush, a fact which was confirmed on the sign entering Jackson which proclaimed *"The Heart of the Mother Lode."* Other signs indicated an elevation of 1,200 feet and a population of 3,500 people.

The town traces its founding to 1848 when it was a gold-mining camp. It was named after "Colonel" Alden M. Jackson, a lawyer who helped settle quarrels out of court in the frontier-like environment. The discovery of gold in Coloma along nearby Sutter's Creek is recognized as the start of the California Gold Rush. Jackson quickly expanded due to the influx of prospectors and miners into the area. One of those was Joyce Jackson's great, great, grandfather, according to family lore.

Following Mr. Buell's directions we quickly arrived at the newly-constructed Jackson Civic Center to meet our host. Jim greeted us outside his office where other staff members could also listen in on the story. We didn't have a whole lot of history to recount, at this point; all we could say was that this is the second place we've visited as part of the Jackson Family project to plant trees in all fifty states and where do you want us to plant your trees. Fortunately, the newly constructed Civic Center, in which we were all standing, needed some shrubbery and he directed us to the lower parking lot level. There, next to the driveway alongside a small brook, we planted the little Scotch Pine seedlings, placing a yellow bow on each in commemoration to the nation's armed forces who were engaged in Operation Desert Storm beginning on January 16, 1991.

The planting was not attended by anyone else except us, so there was time to reflect after the little trees were in the ground. Our thoughts turned to each family member represented by the trees, the kindness of the people who went along with our idea and the growing realization that this little endeavor had a good chance of being replayed over and over again in the years to come.

Again, we hadn't thought about publicizing the visit outside of the few people who were personally involved. Just in case we wanted to follow up on that aspect, Jim gave us the name of Carella Guidon, News Editor of the *Amador Ledger Dispatch*. Upon returning home on February 15, 1991, we sent her a press release similar to the one used in Washington from which she published an article. It became our first real newspaper account of the project, appearing on page 3 of the February 25, 1991, edition and covering two columns from the left top of the page to two inches below the fold. Joyce was quoted as saying what a wonderful reception the city provided and how impressed she was with the people and the surroundings.

Two years later, in June, 1993, we were introduced to Gordon and Peggy Winlow of Pleasanton, CA, at the Arctic Circle. We had taken a side trip there after planting trees in Alaska. The Winlows offered to visit the tree planting site in Jackson, CA, which they did and provided pictures of the trees at the Civic Center. However, several years later, in checking back with the City, the sad news surfaced that only one of the trees had survived. Apparently, most of the little seedlings couldn't withstand the elements and the brook beside the site had overflowed, one year, wiping out our dedication plaque and taking out four of the trees. The City sent a picture of the one surviving tree which seemed to be about twenty feet high. From that picture, we resolved to re-visit the city to replace the four trees which didn't make it. That visit took place on September 30, 2008.

By 2008, Jim Buell had retired and his position taken by Mike Daley. Joyce got in touch with him to make arrangements for our visit which would include the purchase of four new trees. Upon arrival we went to the same office as before and Mike introduced us to Terry Watson, Public Works Manager, while staffers Geisel and Sherry also listened in. They had designated a new planting site at the recently-constructed rest area where Mel's Diner used to be. The four of us went out to Lowe's to pick out the trees and wound up with four good-sized trees, pistachio and crape myrtles. We dropped these trees at the rest area for planting by the town crew. The pictures which they later sent to us show all of the trees gracing the grounds of the rest area, where they should stand for many years.

This time the *Amador Ledger Dispatch* was in attendance for an interview with reporter Bethany A. Monk. The story appeared in the October 3, 2008, edition with a picture of the original surviving tree, as well as an account of the project's completion.

Much of this was beyond our comprehension as we departed from Jackson, CA, in February, 1991. However, our pioneering West Coast venture had proven that the concept held real promise and our success with these first two states moved us to conclude that the idea of The Jackson Legacy was becoming a reality.

John And Joyce Jackson planting one of five Blue Spruce trees in June , 1991
Jackson, Pennsylvania

Nameplate left at the trees planted.

The same Blue Spruce tree from the above
photo but eighteen years later in June, 2009

Pennsylvania

"Land of Our Birth"

The nation began its life in Philadelphia and so did John and Joyce Jackson. Both were born in what is today termed the Greater Metropolitan area with Joyce being born in the Germantown section of Philadelphia and John twenty-four miles away in West Chester. Therefore Pennsylvania is our native land, as it is with all three of our children: Robert, Christine and Steven, who were also born in West Chester.

Beginning the tree planting adventure in Washington and California was programmed into a vacation trip to the West Coast that we were taking anyway. It was a fortuitous combination that served as a testing ground for the whole concept, allowing us to learn from actually doing and to discern people's reactions.

We returned home to Madison, NJ, feeling invigorated by the experiences gained in the first two states. We went right to work planning the next places to visit, taking advantage of all the research that Joyce had compiled the previous year. But it only seemed natural that Pennsylvania would be our next point on the map. After all, there's a place named Jackson located only 135 miles from our home and we look for an excuse to visit our native state any chance that we get.

There are several places in Pennsylvania called by some derivative of the name Jackson. Our preference has always been to go with the actual name Jackson, rather than other extensions of the name such as Jacksonville or Jacksonport. That lead us to a village called Jackson, in Jackson Township, Susquehanna County, PA. According to the U.S. Census of 2000, only 200 people reside within Jackson's ZIP code of 18825 and fewer than 800 people in the Township. It's located in the sparsely-settled northeastern corner of the state, 35 miles north of Scranton. The whole settlement consists of little more than a grocery store, gas station, antique store and two churches. It was settled in 1809 and incorporated in 1814, which is the same year that Andrew Jackson led the fight against the British in the Battle of New Orleans.

Joyce made exploratory phone calls to places in the Jackson, PA area which resulted in making contact with Pastor Gary Haskell and wife Joan of the Jackson Baptist Church. Through them, we came upon the names of Ken and Maureen Farr, owners of the Jackson Market, who would likely be acquainted with most of the people in the area and could re-direct us to someone who could help set up our visit. As it turned out, the Farrs, themselves, became very interested in our project to the extent of offering their property as a home for the trees. We gratefully accepted their invitation and mutually agreed to a date of June 8, 1991, for the plantings.

As in all cases, the trees were to be supplied by our family. However, this would be the first time that the site would be within driving distance of our home and we had not yet selected a nursery to work with us on the project. This could involve up to ten states in the northeastern part of the

25

country. Therefore, it was important to select a nursery partner who could advise us about planting locally-indigenous trees and who was also willing to work with us on the costs.

That partner proved to be Tony Cerbo, of Cerbo's Greenhouses and Garden Center in Parsippany, NJ. We met with him one Saturday morning in May, 1991, to explain the overall concept and to arrange trees for our initial planting in Jackson, PA. Tony was very enthused to join forces with us and we were glad to have him, especially after negotiating a wholesale price that coincided with our budget of $50 for all five trees. Cerbo is an environmentally-active supporter; in fact, Tony Cerbo's brother, Joe, operated a farm which provided trees for research to the Delaware Valley College of Horticulture in Doylestown, PA.

On the day before our trip to Jackson, we drove Joyce's Ford Escort hatchback to Cerbo's and loaded up five blue spruces, averaging three to four feet in height. These would be the tallest trees used in our project to date. Even with our relative lack of experience, we correlated increased height to the increased probability of survival. It was also appropriate that blue spruce is one of the tree species that we like best.

For those who don't know the topography, it's amazing to realize that much of our trip from New Jersey to Pennsylvania traversed through verdant forests teeming with wild life, including bears, eventually reaching an elevation of over 1,300 feet. Finally, the two-lane Route 92 deposited us into the village of Jackson where we quickly found the Jackson Market.

Ken and Maureen Farr, and their two children, a boy and a girl, received us warmly. We described the project and showed them the newspaper accounts from the first two states, as well as the letter from President George H. W. Bush, dated May 17, 1991, which states: *"Thank you for telling me about your terrific plan to plant trees in each of our Nation's fifty states. It's a good way to help protect our environment and beautify our country, and I know it will mean a great deal to your family to share in such a special project. I hope others will be inspired by your example."*

Then they led us outside to a prime spot in the backyard which was soon to be sprouting five new trees. The visiting Jacksons, clad in their brand-new tee shirts depicting 25 types of trees, got right to work with the digging, preparation of the holes and positioning of the little, but bushy, blue spruces. The Farr children took the most interest in the activities, asking questions and darting from tree to tree as they were being planted. After all the trees were in the ground, and according to our growing custom, we named each tree after a member of the Jackson family. The kids really got a kick out this and approached each tree saying things like: *"Here's Robbie's tree,"* *"Here's Stevie's tree"* and *"Now I'm hugging Chrissy."* It was very moving for us to see this instance of personal involvement on the part of other people. Joyce described it best *"All of a sudden, I had butterflies in my stomach to know that we are leaving behind a living part of ourselves all around the country."*

The work was completed in little over an hour; we thanked everyone there and departed for the trip back home. Another chapter had been completed, another unique memory took its place alongside the others.

Two weeks later, we sent our write-up of the experience to the *Susquehanna Transcript*. The article ran the entire length of the left column on the front page of this weekly newspaper in the July 3, 1991, issue. It followed the content of our press release, relating the nature of the project, our intention to conclude the plantings in all states by the year 2000, and a note that all five of our family members are natives of Pennsylvania.

We re-visited the spot about ten years later. By then we had moved outside of Buffalo, NY, and our periodic trips to visit relatives in the Philadelphia area took us along I-81, near Jackson, PA. Sadly, it was on one of these visits we discovered that Maureen Farr had passed away and that one of the five trees didn't survive.

Black Pine trees find a safe place to wait out "Hurricane Bob" at the Jackson Department of Public Works. The trees were later planted at the Melvin Cottrell Center for Senior Citizens.

Jackson, New Jersey

New Jersey

"Down the Shore"

Anyone who lives in Pennsylvania or New Jersey within easy driving distance of the Atlantic Ocean refers to the trip as "going down the shore." That's what we planned to do in August, 1991, by scheduling Avon-by-the-Sea, NJ, as the site for the Crooks family reunion. The attendees were mostly from Joyce's side of the family and even though her mother, Madge, and father, Ray, are beloved, would people get the wrong impression to hear that you were going to a gathering of Crooks? Nevertheless, we made up a sign pronouncing the "Crooks Reunion" for placement outside of the Victorian bed and breakfast where we all stayed, called "The Summerplace."

Our three grown children were also coming in from their homes in Ohio and Indiana. Even though they were all born in Pennsylvania, they spent their teenage years in the Midwest and decided to stay behind when their parents, John and Joyce, moved back east to Madison, NJ. We figured it would be a great time to organize a tree-planting event while the whole family was together. That plan was aided by the fact that Jackson, NJ is in Ocean County, only 24 miles from Avon-by-Sea. However, there was one thing we couldn't have taken into account – Hurricane Bob.

Joyce was in contact with Jackson officials in anticipation of our visit. Jackson is actually a fairly unique municipal arrangement, more along the lines of a township. It claims to be the third-largest municipality in the state, behind Newark and Camden. This is similar to the claim of Jacksonville, FL as being the largest municipality in the country, in terms of square miles. It's coincidental that two locations carrying the name Jackson stake claims to being recognized as the biggest in some geographical aspect.

Jackson, NJ is the home of Six Flags Great Adventure Amusement Park which in 2005 had the tallest and fastest roller coaster in the world, called Kingda Ka. This park attracts people from all over the tri-state area and in the summertime swells the Township's normal population of 43,000 people. The population is concentrated in half of the township's 100 square miles with the other half comprised of the Jersey Pinelands, a sort of impenetrable forest known for tales of demons and other nasty critters.

This is also the first site that we can positively state was named for President Andrew Jackson. It was incorporated as Jackson Township on March 6, 1844. Like so many other places we were to visit, it was established during a period of time when the exploits of Andrew Jackson were still well known, such as, his victory in the Battle of New Orleans in 1814 and his service as President from 1829 to 1837.

John Smatusik, Jr., Superintendent of Public Works, was agreeable to our visit. His staff decided that the local Senior Community Center would be a good site for some beautification. Arrangements were set for Sunday, August 18, 1991, which would allow all six people in our family to participate; John, Joyce, Rob, Steven, Chris and her husband, Mike Adams. (Note that our daughter also married into a family with a Presidential name)

Then along came Hurricane Bob. According to Wikipedia, it was the most damaging storm of the season. The hurricane travelled up the east coast of the United States resulting in 17 deaths and an estimated $1.5 billion in damage. It just so happened to hit our part of the New Jersey coastline the weekend of the family reunion.

The brunt of the hurricane hit late Saturday afternoon. Fortunately the main body of the storm was out to sea but its encompassing winds battered everything on the Jersey shore. All anyone could do was watch it bend trees over, stir up vast waves, overflow the storm sewers and hurl debris against the sides of houses. There is a certain attraction in witnessing Mother Nature at her near-worst from safely inside a sturdy building. Our large group made the best of it, even though it seemed to continue endlessly into the night. Needless to say, all of our plans for the next day were set aside. The Jackson Department of Public Works had a lot more important duties to attend to than hosting a family of tree planters.

They made that amply clear when we contacted them on Sunday morning. However, they did invite us to see the site and to store the trees at the Township garage for planting on another day. We had brought five black pines with us from Cerbo's Nursery and innocently set them out in the backyard of the *Summerplace* on Friday night before the storm. These poor little trees, averaging only four feet tall, were out in all the elements as Bob blasted them hither and yon. But they proved to be hardy Jersey trees in keeping with the state's unofficial motto *"New Jersey - only the strong survive."*

It was still raining and blowing as the six of us reached Jackson on Sunday, outfitted in our special tee shirts, to deposit the trees. We located the planting site and the garage where we abandoned the little trees to the elements once again. Our plan was to return to Jackson later in the week, since it's only 62 miles from our home in Madison.

Unfortunately, it meant we would have to do it alone because everyone else had to return to their homes in other states. We would visit many more states before all of us would be together again for a tree planting.

Joyce remained in touch with the Jackson officials and it was decided that we would return on Saturday, August 24rd which we did. The site was between the parking lot and the fence line of the Melvin Cottrell Center for Senior Citizen and the Disabled. The Township provided a crew composed of Tippy Mitchell, foreman of Parks, Grounds and Buildings and his assistant, Tom Picone. They were very helpful resulting in the fact that the trees were soon in the ground. Mr. Smatusik also happened along to supervise during part of the planting. At the conclusion, we showed them our newly-created scrapbook containing pictures and newspaper articles from previous plantings. Then we thanked them, again, and promised to stay in touch in the future.

After they left, we assigned one of our family names to each of the trees and savored the accomplishment of our fourth state planting. The storm had tested our resolve but it also served to bring out the dedication that the project held for us. Similar to the Postal oath, neither wind nor rain nor dark of night was going to stay us from our appointed rounds.

But we still hadn't made much progress with the publicity aspect. Once again we did not alert the local newspaper in advance of the planting date and had to resort to a press release after the fact. This one was addressed to Bonnie Walling, Managing Editor and Reporter of the *Tri-Town News*. Her lead article, reporting on the Jackson Legacy, ran on the front page of the October 17, 1991, edition.

In the Spring of 1993, the *Star-Ledger* of Newark, NJ, the leading newspaper in the state, picked up on our story and assigned reporter Patty Everett to interview us. Her lengthy story appeared in the "In The Towns" section along with four photographs of us with Tony Cerbo.

Then in 1994, Cheryl Baisden, a free-lance writer from Collingswood, NJ, met us in Jackson, NJ, to do a story on our project. Her article, with photographs, appeared in the November / December, 1994, edition of *American Forests* magazine. By that time we had covered twenty-four states, or almost half-way to completion.

The state of New Jersey holds a special place in our hearts. We lived there from 1987 to 1997, and again in 2004, 2005. It was there that Joyce came up with the idea for our project and performed the research. It was the home base for trips to 35 states until a job change took us to Kingwood, TX. The town, in which we lived, Madison, NJ, honored us with a proclamation in 1994. Governor Jim Florio provided us with a letter of introduction and a crystal pitcher for presentation to the people of Steven's Village, Alaska in 1993 and Cerbo's Nursery in Parsippany, NJ, provided fifty of the trees in the initial part of the project.

Mayor Paul K. Greene and John Jackson preparing holes for five **White Dogwood** trees.

Jackson, South Carolina

South Carolina

"The Savannah River Project"

January 13, 1992

The winter of 1991-92 was a time to reflect upon the first year's experiences to see if we could improve upon any of the approaches. We had gained immeasurable confidence by actually doing the work and observing the favorable feedback from people encountered in our initial visits. The four newspaper articles were further encouragement because they revealed reaction from independent sources that were only reporting on how the project occurred to them. Even though we weren't seeking publicity, the media reports were some indication that the story line had some broad appeal.

The main objective had always been to involve as many local people as possible in the endeavor. This would help spread the significance of planting trees to a wider audience and attract more people to get involved. Consequently, for the future, we decided that our notices to the press should go from being released after the fact to being released before the fact to announce the Jacksons' upcoming visit. This would not only alert more people in the community but the actual extent of the reporting would serve as another monitor on the viability of the underlying concept, which is – do people in a place named Jackson really care that a couple from New Jersey is visiting all fifty states to plant trees in places connected to the name of their community.

The geography was another element that we had to contend with. Surprisingly, we never actually drew up a ten-year plan projecting the sequence in which states would be visited. We wanted to keep the year-to-year scheduling flexible as a way to accommodate other travel plans based upon business, family and other considerations. Therefore, beginning with this first winter, and continuing throughout the project, we would sit down to look out over the calendar obligations for the coming year and then decide whether some of the tree-planting states could be worked into it.

There was also the feeling that we needed to build up a cushion of completed states, in the beginning, as a hedge against later years when the greater distances involved and unknown other obligations, might make it more difficult to stay on the schedule of five tree plantings per year. In a way we were already behind. The mathematics of doing all fifty states over a ten-year period works out to an average of five per year. But we had only done four states in the first year of 1991. We resolved that 1992 would necessitate a greater effort than that, which lead us to design one out-of-the area excursion to four states in the Southeast, together with doing as many states in the Northeast that we could handle. It turned out that we covered eight states during the year, bringing us up to a total of twelve states for the project by year end.

Joyce's work schedule required that we use the winter months for part of our annual project timetable. Obviously, that limits the choice of places during that period to the warmer climes in the southern and western parts of the country. That point of view is confirmed by looking at the different dates on which Arbor Day is celebrated around the U.S. It starts as early as the first week in November with the majority of states observing this day during the month of April.

The best month for Joyce to take her vacation was going to be January, 1992, and a group of four neighboring southern states fit nicely into this schedule, with a little squeezing: charts showed that it was alright to plant trees as early as December in South Carolina, and January in Alabama and Florida, but we made a little exception with Georgia which prescribed a planting calendar of early February. In keeping with this timetable, we booked our travel arrangements for the middle of January, flying into Augusta, GA, proceeding to the planting sites in four states and flying out of Tampa, FL, later in the week.

Jackson, SC, is located within 20 miles of Augusta, GA, and less than five miles from the Savannah River site. This site was built in the early 1950's as a place to refine fissionable materials for deployment in nuclear weapons. It has been referenced in several cloak and dagger motion pictures and is famous / infamous around the world, depending upon one's point of view. We knew virtually none of this history in choosing the city of Jackson, SC, for our visit.

Joyce made arrangements with Paul K. Green, the Mayor of Jackson, to come to town on January 13, 1992. It's a place of about 1,600 population situated along state route 125 which also passes by the nuclear site. Several neighboring towns were obliterated in constructing the Savannah River site but Jackson escaped this fate. Aiken County, in which Jackson is located, saw one of the first railroad towns spring up in the mid-1830's when the world's longest railroad was built connecting Charleston and Hamburg on the Savannah River. This town, Aiken, and later the county, were named for the president of that 136 mile-long railroad, William Aiken. One of the other railroad depots which sprang up on this line was named after the foreman of the railroad crew, hence the initial title of Jackson Depot which later became Jackson, SC.

We purchased five White Dogwoods, averaging three to four feet, from Nurseries Caroliniana, Inc. in North Augusta, SC. In keeping within our budget, they kindly honored our requested price of $10 per tree. Then it was off to Jackson to meet Mayor Green. He had selected a site alongside the parking lot of the Jackson Municipal Complex, on the lawn fronting the highway, and actually helped us dig the holes. It was a cool, damp day but the ground was soft allowing the trees to be quickly planted. Mayor Green maintained a constant dialogue with John Jackson as they worked. Joyce participated in some of the planting while showing our scrapbook to Mayor Green's wife, Patty, and a reporter from the Aiken, SC newspaper.

Our advance press release to the *Aiken Standard* resulted in the attendance of Laura Garren, who interviewed us and took photographs. In the article which appeared on page 1B of the January 15, 1992, edition of the newspaper, she called us "*...the Johnny Appleseeds of the 1990's, only with a twist.*" She also quoted Joyce as saying that "*We wanted to leave a legacy to this country, our kids and future generations.*"

After our own personal ceremony we got back into the rented Chevrolet Caprice Classic, one of the last of the big cars, to drive the 158 miles to the next stop in Jackson, GA. It had been a pleasurable visit for us in South Carolina and a great launch to our adventurous four-state junket.

We called Patty Green many years later to inquire about the trees only to learn that her husband, Paul, had passed away in January, 2003. She recounted how it had become necessary to transplant our trees to make room for an expansion in the municipal parking lot and how, unfortunately, the transplanted trees didn't survive. In the same timeframe, we became aware that one of John's former eighth-grade classmates, Craig Chattin, had moved to the Aiken area. He went over to Jackson to investigate the tree situation and, shortly afterwards, on December 5, 2003, a reporter from the *Aiken Standard* named John Moore called us to do a follow-up interview regarding the possibility that the Town of Jackson would replace our trees with five crape myrtles on Arbor Day. Patty Green also indicated this possibility. She said that some of the Garden Club ladies, Tina Sullivan, Susan Brinkley and Sarah Wilson had also taken up the cause. We've been informed that the replacement trees were planted in November, 2009.

Our friend, Patty Green, told us about her daughter opening a restaurant in Jackson in 2008. Patty offered to work one day a week to help get it off the ground, a weekly contribution that is still on-going. It allows her to be there over lunch when many workers come in from the Savannah River site. It is no longer in the nuclear weapons business, which makes for a happy ending to this chapter.

Post hole digging tools made for easier planting for the five **Yoshina Cherry** trees at the Jackson Elementary School.

Jackson, Georgia

Butts County Courthouse—circa 1898 with a monument of two confederate soldiers adjacent to it containing the inscription "Our Hero's."

Georgia

"A Peach of a Place"

January 14, 1992

As measured according to latitude coordinates, Jackson, Georgia, is practically due west of Jackson, South Carolina. The City of Jackson, GA, sits at 33 degrees, 17'37"North and its counterpart in South Carolina sits at 33 degrees, 19'60"North. However, roads are not laid out in a straight line, at least not over the highway distance of 158 miles that separates these two points. Driving west from South Carolina, the terrain rises about 500 feet in elevation as it traverses through the Georgia pines, including the Oconee State Forest. Just south of there, and 17 miles east of Jackson, GA, is Monticello, the seat of Jasper County, GA. We paused there to visit and take photographs of their county courthouse, not realizing that we were experiencing a piece of history because it was in that courthouse and surrounding area that Hollywood made the movie *"My Cousin Vinny."*

You might say "no big deal" about such an event but, in 2008, the members of the American Bar Association voted it their # 3 all-time favorite film, that incorporates a courtroom setting, ranking just behind *"Twelve Angry Men"* and *"To Kill a Mockingbird."* At the time, of our passing through there on January 13, 1992, we just noted the courthouse as an intriguing piece of architecture, along with the nearby statue dedicated to the memory of Confederate soldiers. That was the reason we took time to tour the courthouse, not realizing that it would be the location for a movie only a few months later.

After a brief stop we pushed on to Jackson, GA, arriving in the late afternoon of the same day in which we had already planted trees in another state. This was to be a recurring experience during our project since it was often necessary to plan visits allowing us to plant four states in the course of one-week's vacation time. Sometimes, this constituted a real logistical challenge.

Upon first entering Jackson we stopped to take pictures of the road signs, as is our custom. Often, the welcoming signs tell something about the place, such as the population, the town motto or slogan, or a list of service clubs. In the case of Jackson, GA, attached to the "City of Jackson" standard was a large, colored sign containing the picture of a peach. Georgia is known far and wide as *"The Peach State"* and that source of pride is obviously shared by the people of Jackson.

Purchasing the trees is normally the next thing we take care of upon entering each community. Early on the morning of January 14, 1992, we visited with Ray and Dolly Collier of Collier's Greenhouse and Garden Center who provided trees not only for planting in Jackson, GA, but, planning ahead, also for our next stop in Jackson, AL. Yoshina Cherry (*prunus yedeonsis*) trees were selected for the local planting. This is a graceful, ornamental tree which brings forth fragrant blossoms in early Spring and can grow to a height of forty feet. The trees that we purchased averaged about five feet tall but we packed all ten into the big Chevy Caprice with room to spare for three cubic feet of mulch.

Our visit to the city was arranged between Joyce and Liz Carmichael Jones, Councilwoman, artist, interior designer and member of one of Jackson's more prominent families. Liz was to be our hostess for the entire day. She guided us around the City, making all the proper introductions and insuring that the schedule came off without a hitch. Through her it was arranged to plant the five trees at the Jackson Elementary School which provides education from kindergarten to fifth grade. Little did we know that the turnout for this event was going to be the most extensive that we had experienced so far.

Liz had assembled quite an entourage to attend the ceremony. Those present included another Councilman, Harold Duke, a representative of the Garden Club, Virginia Kelly, the Assistant Principal of the School, Mr. Thompson, a city work crew headed by the foreman, Glenn, a newspaper reporter, Susan Jones, from *The Jackson Progress-Argus*, and a radio DJ from station WJGA, Walter Carmichael, who is Liz's first cousin. But the most memorable attendees were the entire student body from whom four had been selected to assist us in the planting; all of them had the last name of Jackson: DeWon, Ashley, William and Kathy.

The Jackson Progress-Argus published a photograph of our tree planting in the January 22, 1992, edition on page 5B, showing us along with the four children named Jackson. It reminded us of a story that occurred as we were addressing the whole student body with the four children at our side. We had not been informed of their last names when we posed the questioned to the whole group *"How many of you are named Jackson,"* to which one of the four children at our side innocently proclaimed, *"We're all named Jackson."*

The five trees were positioned in a straight line at an angle to the school building. Glenn introduced us to the use of a post-hole digging tool which made excavations a whole lot easier that using the collapsible trenching shovels that we customarily brought to each event. His crew made short work getting the trees into the ground. During the process we addressed the students, keeping it brief so they could return to class. We showed our scrapbook to the others in attendance, in addition to conducting interviews with the newspaper reporter and the radio personality. This was the first time for us to appear on radio or television which added a new dimension to our project experiences.

Liz and Virginia stayed by our side the rest of the time in Jackson. After everyone else had returned to their normal pursuits, they waited while we did our private dedication and then led us off on a tour of the town. We visited the Butts County courthouse, another imposing structure, built in 1898, with a statue of a Confederate soldier adjacent to it containing the inscription *"Our Heroes."* Pride in their hometown was clearly evident, a fact which we encountered over and over again while visiting with other people all across the country. Most people are proud of where they come from, no matter how much or how little the extent of other people's appeal for their hometown.

For lunch they took us to the Fresh Air Barbeque, voted by the WSB-TV audience as the "Best in Georgia." It's been continuously operated by three generations of the G.W. "Toots" Caston family since 1929 and is renowned for its barbequed pork and Brunswich stew. After eating there, it gets our vote, too.

Our hosts provided a running account of Jackson's history during the visit, a past that is steeped in relations with Native Americans and events of the Civil War. Initially we were most interested in the fact that the city had been appointed as the county seat in 1825 and named in honor of President Andrew Jackson, like so many other communities in our project. However its transformation from Native American to a European-dominated society is a story that would resonate with us in many other states.

Most Americans are aware that before our nation could take root and expand we had to force the native peoples off the lands that we wanted. These natives just didn't go willingly in all cases. Wars were one way in which the Indians resisted but they also attempted to control their destiny through the U.S. Court system. The renowned Supreme Court Chief Justice John Marshall was involved in two of these keynote cases. The rulings of the court over which he presided were the foundation for our treatment of the Indians in the early 18th Century and still have reverberations today.

In **Johnson v. M'Intosh**, (1823) the court determined that the United States government had acquired free title to lands in North America based upon the longstanding practices of European colonization under the concept of "Discovery." It wrote that *"Discovery is the foundation of title, in European nations, and this overlooks all proprietary rights in the natives."* It concluded that special treatment of native Americans was not required as they were *"...an inferior race of people, without the privileges of citizens, and under the perpetual protection and pupilage of the government."*

It was under this prevailing national mindset that President Andrew Jackson put through the Indian Removal Act of 1830 which specified the relocation of all Indians from the eastern United States to lands west of the Mississippi River. This was in disregard of treaties that established sovereignty for specific tribes such as the Cherokee Nation situated in northwestern Georgia and parts of Tennessee and Virginia. The Cherokees filed legal actions which culminated in the U.S. Supreme Court decision in **Worcester v. Georgia**, (1832). Here Chief Justice Marshall's court ruled in favor of the Indians stating that they were sovereign nations in which no state could impose their laws. This decision was cited by some as a basis for ignoring the expulsion provisions of the Indian Removal Act to which President Jackson is reputed to have famously remarked, *"John Marshall has made his decision, now let him enforce it."*

Two famous treaties between the Creek Indians and the State of Georgia were signed near Jackson, GA, in 1825, at the Indian Springs Hotel. One of the Creek leaders, William McIntosh, had built the hotel after fighting alongside his people against the new settlers. McIntosh saw some value to peaceful co-existence and he was able to convince most other Indian leaders into signing the treaty, selling their lands and moving to land promised in the west. Unfortunately for him, he was considered a traitor by the leaders of the Upper Creek villages and the Cherokee at New Echota who invaded Chief McIntosh's plantation, killed him, ran off his slaves and burned everything they could. But the treaty stood up and the town began to prosper only to become embroiled in the Civil War less than forty years later. Eventually, Indian Springs became the Nation's oldest state park.

In 1834, the outcome at Indian Springs was replicated upon the Cherokee Nation in New Echota, GA, just over one hundred miles northwest of Jackson. Here a small faction led by an influential leader named Major Ridge also signed away the land rights of the Cherokee in exchange for the promise of land in Oklahoma. Major Ridge and three other leaders met the same fate as William McIntosh. The majority of the Cherokees ignored the Treaty's stipulation to vacate the land by May, 1838. When that time arrived, the U.S. military forcibly compelled the Indians to begin the march to the west which became known as *The Trail of Tears*. Over 4,000 Cherokees died on the way. That number was exceeded by the Creeks, Choctaws, Seminoles and Chickasaws whose forced removal preceded them over the same route.

Over the years we have checked back with Liz Carmichael Jones to see how the trees are doing. In our latest call during February, 2009, she promised to send us photographs of them.

The Jackson Legacy

Shadow box made by the late Joseph Jackson, father of John Jackson, holds our first key to the city.

Jackson, Alabama

Seeing the deep red clay at the planting site gave us a new perspective on the different types of soil we were to dig in across the country. We planted five **Soul Magnolia** trees here.

Alabama

"Key to the City"

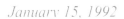

We got off to a late start out of Jackson, Georgia, as a result of their extended hospitality. Usually the planting ceremony would be over well before lunch allowing us to get on the road to the next destination. Now it was past one o'clock and we were looking ahead to a distance of 338 miles to Jackson, Alabama. Fortunately, most of the travel was over Interstate routes 85 and 65 which constituted a fairly direct drive towards southwestern Alabama.

On the way we went near Jacksonville, AL. That would have been a good choice, too, at a distance of only 139 miles from the previous stop. It's a little larger in population (8.404) compared to Jackson, AL (5,419). However, that wouldn't have been in keeping with our preference to visit sites actually named Jackson, as long as they were large enough to carry out the kind of reception we had in mind.

It was beginning to appear that many sites were attempting to make their hosting events a little grander than what we had experienced in other places. Our letters in advance to the town officials and the newspaper press releases may have provided some stimulus for that. These stories pointed out some of the special hosting activities we encountered elsewhere while reinforcing the basic concept underlying the tree project. Up to this stage, it was typical for local people to be present at the plantings but we had not received any special recognition in the form of citations and the like. It just felt like it seemed to be building in that direction.

We arrived in Jackson early on the evening of January 14, 1992. After driving around to get familiar with the town, we settled into the Downtown Inn. Joyce called David Painter, City Engineer of Jackson, AL, who Mayor Norma Beard had designated as our contact in arranging the visit. David informed us that the city was ready to go ahead first thing in the morning and provided us with the feeling that everyone was really looking forward to it. He stated that we were to meet at the City Hall and then proceed to the planting site at the baseball fields in North Jackson Park.

It wasn't necessary to take time to purchase the trees, locally. Five Soul Magnolia trees had accompanied us from Jackson, GA, where we had bought them from Collier's Greenhouse and Garden Center. So we were able to go directly to the City Hall bright and early on the morning of January 15, 1992, where Mayor Beard and others received us warmly. After talking about the project and viewing the scrapbook compiled from previous places, everyone moved out to the ball fields.

The first thing that struck us upon arrival at the site was the deep red color of the soil. A recent rainstorm had turned this rich ground into a mucky condition that we weren't expecting. Fortunately, the city provided two Public Works employees, Emmanuel King and Calvin Stephens, who slogged through the slime to perform most of the digging. They placed the three to five-foot trees into the ground while keeping up a constant banter of local stories laced with humor. Even though we mostly only supervised, it was impossible to avoid getting some of the brilliant, sticky clay on our shoes, clothes and trenching tool. The residue would remain with us the rest of the trip.

Mayor Beard, David Painter and Michael Breedlove, publisher of *The South Alabamian* stayed with us throughout the planting. At the conclusion we all returned to City Hall where the Mayor surprised us with the Key to the City together with a proclamation declaring us honorary citizens of Jackson, Alabama. The kindness and genuine spirit of these awards touched us greatly. It was the first time that we could take away a visible connection to the people of a place who appreciated what we were doing and recognized it in such a special way.

It took upon even more significance after returning home. The project brought special attention to the name Jackson and must have been a source of satisfaction to John's father, Joseph. His Dad had lost both parents by the age of two and was raised by a foster family and in an orphan's school separated from his brother and sister. That environment didn't sustain him with any real sense of family continuity or connection to the family name beyond his own offspring. Without emphasizing it, John and Joyce felt that the Jackson Legacy tree planting project would somehow fill a part of this void in Dad's life, in a way that wouldn't be embarrassing to a very private man. His actions seemed to confirm this. For the first time he joined into our celebration in a way that he knew best. He took the large Key to the City of Jackson, Alabama, with its shiny brass and flowing red, white and blue ribbons and encased it in a shadow box constructed entirely by his own hands. It became one of his last great gifts to us, for he passed away within six months of our tree planting visit to the Southeast.

By the time of his death we had planted in eleven states. He died, unexpectedly, on July 10, 1992, without revealing much of his personal outlook on our venture, as was his nature. It was in our nature to use his remembrance as part of the on-going drive to complete the goal of completing the fifty-state project by the year 2000 and to make a memorable gesture to him in the end.

The people in Jackson, AL, couldn't have been any nicer. This extended to the fine article which Mr. Breedlove published in the January 23, 1992, edition of his newspaper. It appeared on the front page, above the fold over the two left-hand columns, together with a picture taken at the planting site. The story contained many interesting quotes relating to the spirit of our project, with the following from Joyce of particular note: *"It's like leaving a little bit of you in every place that we go."*

For us, it was also starting to bring home the fact that others had preceded over the ground which we were now traveling. You start to appreciate the history of other places when you actually get out there to feel the land, meet the people and make encounters with the stories of their times and place. One of these emerging realizations settled on a connection to the Native American experience. Again and again we encountered some variation of this theme and it would run as a thread throughout our entire adventure.

Having been born in the Northeastern part of the country, the history of Native Americans seems somewhat distant for most Yankees. For many, it's more of an ancient saga that essentially ended with the French and Indian War, an occurrence which preceded the Revolutionary War. However, because of our travels, we were beginning to realize that people outside of the original thirteen colonies had much more contemporary experiences that, in many ways, continue to this day.

Andrew Jackson, the main historical personage connected to our project, played a central role in this emerging awareness. It was he who "subjugated the savages" in ways that are not commendable and much overlooked. Nowhere was this more in evidence than in the American Southeast.

Even before the War of 1812, Jackson made his reputation fighting the Creek Indians, commanding forces against them comprised of the Tennessee militia and rival Indian tribes. During this time, Tecumseh incited the "Red Stick" Creek Indians to war on the white settlements in Northern Alabama and Georgia in order to staunch European expansionism and to gain back Indian control of their lands. They killed four hundred settlers in the Fort Mims Massacre and rampaged throughout this area until Jackson's army arrived, including Davy Crockett and Sam Houston. The American forces finally defeated the Creeks at the Battle of Horseshoe Bend, in east-central Alabama, in 1814, where eight hundred Indians lost their lives. Jackson's force of 2,600 troops overwhelmed the Indian band of 1,000 warriors and paid them no quarter. Jackson imposed the Treaty of Fort Jackson upon the Creeks which appropriated twenty million acres to form white settlements. It was as a result of this service that Andrew Jackson rose to the level of a premier military leader who was entrusted with ultimate command of the army in the south and went on to defeat the British at the Battle of New Orleans in January, 1815.

Jackson, AL, was formed in 1816 and named in memory of Andrew Jackson, more for his leadership in the Creek Indian War than his heroics in The Battle of New Orleans. The area played a part in the War of Southern Independence situated as it is near the navigable Tombigbee River. The largest Confederate cannon ever cast stands outside of Jackson's City Hall having been relocated there from its former position on a bluff protecting the river. Today, Jackson is a place *"where residents enjoy a good life with a stable economy, undergirded by diversified industry, agriculture and forest products. Jackson people are Southern people, which interprets into a warm, caring community."*

David Painter pointed out to us that not far from Jackson stands the Monroe Heritage Museum, where his wife works. This is the site of the Old Courthouse featured in the movie *"To Kill a Mockingbird"* which is based on the book of the same name by Harper Lee. This book is, perhaps, the quintessential expression of changing social values in the Deep South of the mid-20th century and generally recognized as one of the greatest novels in American literary history.

Kevin Smith, Joyce Jackson and Kathy Ellis prepares the holes for planting five
River Birch at the newly designed Botanical Gardens at Florida Community College.
Jacksonville, Florida

Florida

"Community Giving"

January 17, 1992

Three states in three days proved to be a pretty hectic schedule and we were looking forward to a little breather before continuing the tree planting routine in Jacksonville, Florida, on Friday. We had built a day off into the schedule for that reason and also in consideration of the 440-mile drive from Jackson, Alabama, to our next stop. The extra day allowed time for relaxation and a little sight-seeing along the way

The first seventy miles brought us to Mobile, Alabama. The city of Mobile is one of those special Southern places which exudes the charm of the old South. The breezes blow off the Gulf of Mexico gently rustling the trees laden with Spanish moss while the sun glows off the white 19th Century-style buildings and things move at a quieter pace. At least that's the memory that we were expecting from the city and it didn't disappoint as we lingered in its quarters.

Mobile traces its history back to 1702 when it was the first capital of French Louisiana. In the next 100 years it changed hands, first going to the British, then the Spanish and then entering the United States in 1813. Over that time, visitors through its seaport added influences from many other places. The culmination of all that culture has resulted in an atmosphere that is unique among American cities rivaled only in New Orleans. *Tres bien.*

Pleasant as it is, Mobile was still a long way from our ultimate destination so we decided to at least cut the distance in half by proceeding on to Tallahassee, FL, where we stopped for the night. We picked Tallahassee for the additional reason that it is the state capital of Florida and another one of our hobbies is visiting state capitol buildings.

The next morning, upon arriving at the state house, the attendant said there are actually two capitol buildings – the old one and the new one. Either one was available for self-guided touring but we decided to explore the old one which figured to offer more history than the replacement structure erected just across from it. So we climbed the marble stairs to search out history in the upper reaches of the old capitol building, just the two of us, all alone on a sparkling Thursday morning. A commotion outside drew us to the second-floor window which looks out onto a courtyard. There, coming towards where we were peering out, came a mob of people, some carrying what appeared to be campaign signs with someone's name on it. We didn't recognize the name on the signs. For all we knew he was some politician running for local office or maybe an aspirant for the governorship of Florida. Looking closer we noticed that the crowd was growing larger and what appeared to be a media platform had been constructed across from the place where we were standing, on which stood a bevy of photographers and a television camera. Naturally we decided to shoot a few pictures and wait a little while longer to see what was going to develop. In a few more minutes a man emerged out of the entourage below us and ascended to a point just beneath where we were looking out. There he proceeded to make a speech, which we couldn't hear very

47

well through the thick glass windows of the old capitol, but the crowd whooped and hollered, waved their signs and gave this candidate the reception that he must have been looking for. We took a few more pictures and then turned back into the capitol building to continue the tour, leaving the people outside to their own affairs.

On the front cover of the following week's *Time* magazine, in January, 1992, appeared a picture, taken at the Florida State Capitol, of the person who made the speech that day. If they had not cropped the photo so closely, the faces of John and Joyce Jackson would have been identifiable looking out of the window of the old capitol building behind him. It was Bill Clinton, Governor of Arkansas. That was the first time we had ever heard of him and we have the pictures to prove it.

It was ten months too early to realize that we had experienced a snippet of Presidential history. At the time, President Andrew Jackson held our attention as we traveled over ground that he had once trod. In fact we passed through Pensacola, FL, where he had been sworn in as military governor of Florida serving from March to December, 1821. He earned that distinction by once again engaging the Indians at the behest of the U.S. government.

During 1817, the Seminole and Creek Indians of East Florida had been attacking settlements in Georgia from their havens in Spanish-owned Florida. General Jackson was dispatched there to prevent these incursions and his aggressive actions become known as the First Seminole War. In typical style, Jackson went beyond the mandate provided to him by the government. Rather than simply repelling the Indians back into Florida, he reasoned that a more permanent solution would be to take over Florida from the Spanish whom he accused of aiding and abetting the Indians along with the British. He captured and occupied the Spanish capital at Pensicola without any declaration of war. The Spanish government was incensed by this action but it was too weak militarily to defend their possessions in the Americas. The U.S. seized upon this opportunity to exercise its policy of Manifest Destiny by coercing Spain to either defend their territory or cede it to the United States. Spain acceded and that is how Florida became part of our country.

Thanks to Andrew Jackson, we were now traveling towards Jacksonville through a region whose mother tongue is English rather than Spanish.

Just outside of our intended destination, in Glen Saint Mary, FL, we stopped to purchase trees for planting the next day. Joyce's research had discovered a very unique nursery that, in 2003, was placed on the U.S. Register of Historic Places. On January 16, 1992, we met with G. L. (Lin) Taber, III, who is the third-generation owner of the nursery business which was established in 1882. He was very interested in our tree-planting story, especially the historical side of it, because his nursery was participating in a program that grew trees using cuttings from trees at historic landmarks, such as: the Robert E. Lee Sycamore, the Thomas Edison Oleander, the Thomas Jefferson Silver Maple, and so on. There's even a tree cutting taken from the Southern Magnolia that Andrew Jackson had planted at the White House as a memorial to his wife, Rachel, which also happens to be the oldest tree on the White House grounds. Lin escorted us around the nursery to see all of the historic tree choices, as well as trees that would be suitable for downtown Jacksonville. He recommended that we plant River Birch in the city and we decided to buy a Helen Keller Water Oak as a gift for our friends, the Balazeks, in Tarpon Springs, FL. We left

Glen Saint Mary with six trees averaging 3 to 5 feet in height, fitted snugly into the huge trunk of the Chevy Caprice.

We arrived at the Jacksonville City Hall on the morning of January 17, 1992, by invitation of Mayor Ed Austin. The Mayor had arranged for Landscape Architect, Kathy Houston Ellis, project coordinator for "Greenscape," to coordinate the planting of our trees at the Florida Community College, downtown campus. This site was selected by Jackie Eldredge, Director of *"Keep Jacksonville Beautiful."* The rest of the reception committee at the Mayor's office included his secretary, Stella Morse, and receptionist Naomi Glover. After a short visit, we proceeded to the college administration building located between Pearl and Clay Streets.

The reception at the college included Dr. Donald P. Robertson, Director of Administrative and Plant Services, and Kevin Smith, an instructor in landscaping and member of the Botanic Society. They explained that the college, which opened in 1977, was attempting to construct a botanical garden encompassing a living garden for the blind. The planned location was behind the administration building and our trees would be a welcomed first-addition to get this project underway.

Kevin led us out to the planting site, accompanied by Kathy Ellis and joined there by Wilson Bush, an employee of the college who helped dig the holes. It was one of those occasional chilly mornings that occur in northern Florida during January but the ground was pliable and the work went quickly. The five trees were placed in a straight line about twenty five apart from one another. River birch (*bitula nigra*) has beautiful foliage, is heat tolerant and grows quickly to a height of between 25 and 50 feet. We constructed little earthen dams around the base of each tree trunk using the collapsible trenching tool that now accompanied us on every trip. We had also brought along a plaque to mark the occasion displaying the species of tree, the names of all five member s of the Jackson Legacy and the date of our visit.

It's difficult to just up and leave after one of these ceremonies. So much goes into the preparation and the logistics of traveling, acquiring the trees, interacting with people, doing the planting and in ultimately expressing our gratitude to everyone involved. Many times we would come back to the site to be by ourselves after everything else had been attended to and we did that in Jacksonville. This city also had the added significance of being the last stop on the trip. As much as we enjoyed all of the sometimes frenetic activity, it was often a relief to look back on a successful trip and look forward to a little relaxation during the remaining vacation time. We did the latter by visiting with our friends, David and Irene Balazek to help them plant the Helen Keller Water Oak. After a couple of days with them we flew out of Tampa back to New Jersey in time to go to work on Monday.

Jacksonville, FL, is the most populous place we visited, ranking as the 12th largest city in the U.S. It's also the largest city in terms of land area, bigger even than New York and Los Angeles. And, of course, it was named in honor of Andrew Jackson in 1822, the year after he was governor of the territory, Florida not becoming a state until 1845.

The only real shortcoming coming out of this visit was the absence of newspaper coverage. That may have been partially due to our lack of advance notice to the press, although we did send *The*

Florida Times-Union a retrospective account on January 24. 1992. Perhaps the story was published but no one sent us a copy.

John's business traveling allowed him to visit tree planting sites in later years. Subsequent visits to Jacksonville, FL, showed that our plaque had been mounted on a concrete pedestal and two of the original trees had been replaced with other species. But the site is now well established with our trees as the foundation. Many people have probably wandered by this setting, read the plaque and wondered about the story behind this Jackson Legacy. Some of them will now know the answer through this book.

The Jackson Legacy

Jacksonville, New York Post Office was the meeting place for our tree planting connection.
L-R –Councilman Tom Reitz, John Jackson, Barb and Bill Woodams.

May 4,1992

New York

"The Finger Lakes"

May 4, 1992

Jacksonville, New York was the next one on our list to visit due to its proximity of 213 miles from Madison, NJ. We could easily drive there from our home as part of a long weekend. Two months prior to embarking on this trip, the newspaper from our original home town of West Chester, PA, honored us with a substantial story accompanied by photographs. It just so happened that our cousin, Sharon Cosgriff, worked for this paper, *The Daily Local News,* but surely they recognized a good story when they saw one, without her influence.

The story occupied nearly the whole front page of the "Lifestyle" section in the March 5, 1992, edition under the headline "*Routes*" and sub-heading "*This family travels the country spreading a little leafy shade.*" Staff writer Elene C. Brown told the whole story over two long columns of newsprint, describing the motives and goals of our tree-planting treks and emphasizing our roots in West Chester. It more than made up for not gaining any press coverage out of the Florida trip, two months earlier.

We discovered an additional connection to our story in West Chester. It's also the home of another prominent Jackson who helped civilize the Seneca Indians in New York, not far from our tree planting site. Halliday Jackson published his memoirs under the title "*Civilization of the Indian Natives*" (Philadelphia: Marcus T.C. Gould, 1830), which is still available through the Internet today.

The Seneca nation supported the British during the Revolutionary War. As a consequence, the U.S. government appropriated all of their lands for distribution to veterans of our fight for independence, legalizing this through the 1794 Treaty of Stanwix. Two Seneca leaders, the religious prophet and social reformer, Handsome Lake, and the Seneca's chief warrior, Cornplanter, lead the way for a peaceful outcome. Instead of resorting to violent means to protect their lands, these two visionaries urged their people to adopt what they could of the European way of life while retaining their native identity and religion. Cornplanter turned to the Quakers for guidance in helping his people adjust to their new lifestyle. He felt that the Quakers' renowned sincerity and impartiality would help protect tribal members from the charlatans that characterized frontier life.

Responding to a call from the Indian Committee of the Philadelphia Yearly Meeting, three Quaker missionaries, including Halliday Jackson of Pennsylvania, went to live with the Indians from 1798 to 1800. They joined Cornplanter's village along the Allegany River in southern New York to teach school, introduce modern farming methods, improve hygiene and generally anything they could do to help the Indians assimilate more easily. It resulted in one of the few examples where Indians have been able to keep their autonomy, relatively undisturbed, east of the Mississippi River. The Seneca Nation exists in this fashion to this day.

The hamlet of Jacksonville is situated alongside Cayuga Lake, which is the largest of the several Finger Lakes in the state of New York. To the west is Seneca Lake, the next largest, widest and deepest of these lakes. Both are named after Native American tribes, part of the Iroquois Federation indigenous to this region. According to legend, the Great Spirit, in blessing this area, rested His fingers upon the land which left their impressions for all time. Water from springs and tributaries filled in these impressions which became the Finger Lakes.

Jacksonville is located in Tompkins County, whose population, today, is 7% Native American. It is a part of the Township of Ulysses and Councilman Tom Reitz was our primary contact for arranging the tree plantings. He enlisted Barb and Bill Woodams to help out. We met all of them at the Jacksonville, NY, post office on the morning of Monday, May 4, 1992. It was a convenient place to assemble which also allowed us to fulfill another aspect of each visit: obtaining a hand-cancelled "Jackson" postmark on a self-addressed postcard.

From there we traveled to the Jacksonville Community Park which they had selected for the tree plantings. It was still too early for Spring blossoms to appear in that part of the country. Even the five white dogwoods that we had brought along from Cerbo's Nursery in Parsippany, NJ, had not emerged from the bud stage. But we all remarked how pleasing it was going to be for everything to bloom in another few weeks with our little dogwoods heralding the special purpose for their existence.

The Community Park resulted from the efforts of a public-minded group to improve the village's fire protection in the 1950's. The group, comprised of a school, a church and the Grange, pooled their resources to purchase the land. On it they constructed a pond and a hydrant system to distribute water in a fire emergency. The pond attracts ice skaters in the winter time and is used by the community for other recreational purposes the rest of the year.

The three men prepared the holes in a line along the outer edge of the park. As usual, Joyce darted back and forth to help with the trees while displaying the contents of the scrapbook at the same time. In this case she was showing it to Barb Woodams and to the men as they took a break from their efforts. Fortunately they each had their own shovels which meant we could dig multiple holes at the same time. It remained for the Jacksons to position the trees in the holes using the methods learned in our research. This required that the hole had to be twice as wide as the root ball, to avoid compressing the root structure against the base once the tree was planted. In addition, the top of the root ball had to be level with the ground surrounding the hole, which was measured by laying our trenching tool or shovel handle across the hole on top of the ball – if there was room under the handle it meant removing the tree to place additional soil under the root ball until it was level with the handle. Many planters in many places tried to shortcut these procedures but Joyce was ever vigilant to make sure it was done properly.

The trees had to be checked for vertical straightness, with their best side pointing out. The soil had to be mixed with some fertilizer or top dressing and a circular dam built up around the perimeter of the hole to hold in the water. That's always a crucial part of the planting. First, water has to be available from a local supply in order to properly complete the planting procedures but then, perhaps more importantly, someone has to agree to continue watering the trees during the first year to enhance their chances for survival. It was the second part that concerned us more than the first requirement because we were there to insure that the initial water happened, but after that…..who knew what was going to happen.

After the planting was over and the hosts had departed, we gathered as a couple to celebrate one more accomplishment on our journey. It never failed to give us a warm feeling of renewal as if we were doing each one for the first time. Not only did we feel close to our own family but we felt connected to a people and a place that were now a part of something larger than our individual lives. As Joyce put it in the article from our hometown newspaper, *"We want the Jackson Legacy to be part of future generations. These trees will help to provide shade, cut down on noise and pollution, help the environment, and provide a habitat for birds and animals."*

The *Trumansburg Free Press* published an article regarding us in the May 20, 1992, edition, under the headline *"The Jacksons Find Jacksonville."* This time Joyce's quote was, *"This is a wonderful place to include in our project. I hope every place we go will be as nice as this one."*

Our hosts had given us a copy of a book published in connection with the National Bicentennial Celebration of 1976, in which is documented the origin of the town name. Previously the place had been known as Van Courtland Village in memory of the locally-prominent Revolutionary soldier Col. Philip Van Courtland, but in 1815, after the Battle of New Orleans, the name was changed to Jacksonville to honor, would you believe, General Andrew Jackson.

That's not all. In 1878, Halliday Jackson, of West Chester, PA, son of the 1798 missionary of the same name, helped publish a 371-page Jackson family history that traces the Chester County, PA, descendants back to the immigration of Anthony Jackson and his brothers from Lancashire, England to the Province of Ulster, Ireland in 1649. One brother, Richard, married in the city of Carrickfergus, County Antrim. The book goes on to state that General Andrew Jackson is supposed to have been a branch of the same family descended from another brother of Anthony and Richard Jackson who did not connect with the Quaker faith and thus became estranged from his brothers who embraced that religion. The father of Andrew Jackson immigrated to America in 1765 from Carrickfergus which implies the credible possibility of a link between the families. Halliday Jackson, writing in 1878, admits that he cannot produce any other evidence than family tradition but, if true, it does draw our Jackson Legacy story into a closer association with the most famous American Jackson of all.

John and Joyce Jackson plant five **Kousa Dogwoods** in Jacksonville, Vermont.

Vermont

"Upland Vistas"

June 8, 1992

In little more than a month from the previous planting, we were back on the road again. This time the destination would also be within easy driving distance of home, taking advantage of our close proximity to the New England area.

There are six states in the region known as New England. Four of them were part of the original thirteen colonies that formed the United States after achieving independence from England. The two present-day states that were not part of the original colonies are Maine and Vermont; the latter was admitted in 1791, as the fourteenth state, or the first one after Independence.

Vermont is a haven described in the Encyclopaedia Britannica as *"a hilly, upland elevation generally rising to the west."* Over 77% of the state is forested and it is the least populous state in New England. Only one other state in the country, Wyoming, has fewer residents. In fact, Vermont's largest city Burlington, with a population just over 39,000 people, is the smallest size of any state's largest city.

It is the primary state producer of maple syrup in the country. In addition, it possesses some of the most renowned ski resorts on the East Coast and the sixth-largest body of fresh water, Lake Champlain. In the southeastern corner of such a pastoral setting sits the village of Jacksonville. It's bounded on the west by the Green Mountains and on the east by the Connecticut River. It would have been hard for us to select a more worthy residence for the Jackson family's five trees.

Jacksonville is an incorporated village within the Town of Whittingham. Therefore, Joyce's initial contact was with Debbie Doty, the Whittingham Town Clerk. She listened to our story and referred us to Councilperson Susan Johnson who was very happy to provide assistance. In fact she later commented that our project *"became the talk of the town."*

We learned that Jacksonville was originally formed in 1826 near the village of Point Pleasant and named in honor of Andrew Jackson. When the postmaster at Point Pleasant lost his job, he moved his store down the road to Jacksonville and eventually reestablished the post office there. One of the homes in this 19th century village became *"The Engel House"* Bed and Breakfast that we stayed at during our visit. The village was officially incorporated in 1905, although its history predated that event by more than 70 years.

The journey by car from New Jersey to Vermont starts out across the New York City metropolitan area and continues through the state of Connecticut, rising steadily to an elevation of over 1,300 feet. Immediately upon entering Vermont the distinction between the cool, clear air ahead of us and the hazy atmosphere in back of us was clearly apparent.

It was early June in New England, that part of the year when the trees are newly flushed with leaves, the wild flowers waving their blooms in the gentle breeze and the underbrush not yet sprouting sufficiently to spoil the view. The two-lane road from the Interstate to our destination meandered up and over hills, around bends and across streams still surging with run-off from the snows. Ultimately we arrived into the village via a small crossing lined with two concrete abutments into which were placed garden flowers over the sign *"Welcome to Jacksonville, Vermont."*

We headed for the Engel House Bed and Breakfast. Joyce had made reservations with the proprietors, Charles and Charlene Rinaldi. After checking in and expanding upon the purpose of our visit with the owners, we opened the trunk of the car to remove the ten trees that had accompanied us from Cerbo's Nursery in Parsippany, NJ. The five Kousa dogwoods for Vermont and five hemlocks for New Hampshire were placed on the ground to breathe overnight, while we returned inside.

The next morning, Monday, June 8, 1992, dawned unusually warm for that time of year. The temperature outside really didn't occur to us as we lingered over the substantial breakfast served by the Rinaldis and listened as they recounted some of the history of their village. If we hadn't realized it before, we rediscovered the value of close contact with local people to pick up interesting insights regarding their area. Breaking away from breakfast for a moment to make a phone call, Joyce arranged our meeting with Carl Jillson, manager of the water treating plant that Susan Johnson had designated for the tree planting.

Carl was waiting as we arrived at the water treatment facility just outside the village. He quickly showed us where the trees were to go and then hurried off. We were left alone for one of the few tree plantings unaccompanied by people from the community. Planting the white dogwoods proved to be quite an effort. The ground was hard and the temperature steadily rose as we pounded into the soil, which must have contained some backfill or other rocks that characterize a state known for its granite. John removed his shirt due to the exertion while Joyce appeared cool and clean in her trademark white tee shirt with the 25 trees depicted on it.

At last they were in the ground; five three-foot sentinels lined up in a row alongside the driveway of the recently-constructed treatment plant. They represented everything we needed to get out of the trip: another place touched by our hands, another legacy left behind and another testimony to our family love for each other and the world around us.

The Deerfield Valley News covered the story in their June 26, 1992, edition in which reporter Kathy Novy's column, on page 11, accurately adhered to the information in our press release. It was accompanied with a photograph of us taken at the conclusion of the planting.

We've had some contact with Carl Jillson since then to find out that a few of the trees have succumbed to the vagaries of the Vermont climate. However, we take comfort in having been told that our activity inspired others to do likewise in their town. That's the kind of feedback that enriches our vision of The Jackson Legacy.

The Jackson Legacy

John Jackson plants five **Hemlocks** at the newly-constructed Town of Bartlett/ Town of Jackson Transfer Station.

Jackson, New Hampshire

The Jackson covered bridge built in 1876 is a familiar site throughout the area.

New Hampshire

"Just What We Needed"

June 9, 1992

The three states in northern New England are the most heavily forested in the country. In fact, New Hampshire ranks second, behind Maine, in the percentage of land covered by trees. Thick stands of elm, maple, beech, oak, hemlock, and other fir trees formed an almost endless canopy of green as we drove the 200 miles towards Jackson, New Hampshire, from our previous stop in Vermont.

The next planting was scheduled for the following morning at 9:00 o'clock in the home state of the poet Robert Frost. The long trip to get there, over forested country roads, fit in well with the words in one of his most famous poems. In a way, it was a shame that there was no blanketing snowfall to enhance the mood even more.

Our promise to plant in the town was formed by Joyce in numerous preparatory discussions with Diane "Dee" McClave, Selectman of Jackson, NH. Through Dee, we acquired an impression of her hometown as the quintessential New England country village, from its red covered-bridge to its surroundings within a vast panoply of lakes and rivers, mountains and meadows.

We reached there around dinner time and checked into the Ellis River House. This picturesque hostelry lives up to its reputation for elegant accommodations, while still retaining the colonial trappings that guests expect in such a setting. Sitting on the porch as night slowly descended and listening to nature's sounds, unspoiled by the intrusiveness that normally accompanied our daily lives, was as relaxing a mood as we could possibly have hoped to attain.

After all, vacationing was the constant companion to the main objective of spreading *The Jackson Legacy*. Every trip we took was planned around touring local sights before and after taking care of the tree planting. That afforded us plenty of opportunities to enjoy the attractions that make each place we visited so unique, and in New Hampshire, part of the appeal is its isolation.

Morning dawned clear and crisp as befitting an early June day in range of the White Mountains. After a quick breakfast we packed the five hemlocks into the trunk of the car and headed towards the town center for our 9AM meeting with Dee McClave, allowing sufficient time for the brief drive so as not to risk failing the demands of Yankee punctuality.

Dee was waiting for us at the Town Hall in her proper business attire and managerial manner. It didn't take long for the tone to become more relaxed as Joyce recounted the stories of previous state visits while slowly turning the pages of the scrapbook. In turn, Dee described the highlights of living in Jackson, NH, and passed on some reading material for our files. She explained that the planting site was to be the newly-constructed Town of Bartlett / Town of Jackson Transfer Station, just outside of town. For the second time in as many days, we were headed off to the local treatment facility to lend a little of nature's beauty to the surroundings.

Upon arrival it appeared that the land for the facility had been literally carved out the woods. Trees were everywhere, with a heavy concentration of maple and hemlock. Dee was there with a crew from the town's Highway Department that included Michael Clemons. They did a lot of the actual digging while we were removing the four-foot high trees from their containers and setting up their placement. The location that we all agreed upon was a large clearing in front of the facility where the site excavation had removed all of the trees and bushes and which now needed something to re-establish the beautification process. Nevertheless, Dee dryly remarked, in looking over our tree plantings and the adjacent verdant forests, *"Just what we needed, more hemlocks."*

Of course we couldn't have envisioned any such repercussions, as we picked out the tree species at Cerbo's in New Jersey days before. And, in truth, Dee was only spinning some of that laconic humor that is so typical of people in the upper northeast. Her appreciative follow-up letter sent later in the month informed us that our planting of June 9, 1992, had unexpected pleasant consequences. The transfer site attendants were energized to take their nurturing of our planting site very seriously, even to the extent of adding several maple saplings that they had taken out of the woods. A local nursery also donated several flats of annual flowers to the project and the town seeded the hillside with a *"conservative mix."*

The local newspaper, in North Conway, took a keen interest in our visit by noting our upcoming arrival in the June 4, 1991, edition of *The Reporter* and then following that up with a story in the June 11, 1992, edition, subsequent to the planting. The latter article appeared on page 4B over two columns just above the fold with a captioned photograph. The heading above the photo was *"Growing family crest."* Reporter, Nancy Waldron, identified us in the picture along with Michael Clemons of the highway crew, indicating that New Hampshire was the eleventh state during our *"cross-country odyssey to plant trees in every town bearing their family name."*

Her slight overstatement is understandable; we were not visiting every place named Jackson, only one in each state. Many states, in fact, have several locations named after some variant of the name Jackson, using suffixes like –ville or –port and prefixes like Mount. But most of them have a common relationship to the one and only Andrew Jackson. Even the entire state of New Hampshire, itself, was considered a stronghold of Jacksonian Democracy and supported him in his two successful presidential campaigns. Much of his appeal to the general electorate was based on the fact that Jackson was the first President to be considered a man of the people. Much was made of his frontier background and hard-nosed approach to routing the British, removing the threat of Indian confrontation and opposing the efforts of the Eastern gentry to construct an America more aligned to their interests than those of the common people. Consequently, depending upon differing points of view, he was perceived either as a dangerous outsider or heroic protector of the masses. The town of Adams, NH, named after John Adams, a founding father and President from Massachusetts, changed its name to Jackson, NH, in 1829, with only one opposing vote.

After leaving Jackson, we drove up Mount Washington, at 6,288 feet the highest point on the East Coast and we have the certificate confirming it. There's nothing benign about this peak in the White Mountains. It is recognized as having the highest sustained wind velocity in the world, once hitting over 215 miles per hour. Many climbers, hikers, and motorists test its dangers each year and some don't live to tell about it. We count driving up and down this mountain as one of those things that's only going to happen once in our lifetime.

Besides, it was over 400 miles back to our home in New Jersey and we had to get back to resume our plans for the next round of tree plantings. You might say that we had promises to keep.

Christine (Jackson) Adams holding the
newly planted **White Pine** tree on August
17, 1992 in Banning Park, located by the
Christina River, Delaware

Joyce Jackson mother of Christine Adams
standing in front of the same **White Pine**
tree as above but seventeen years later in
August, 2009.

Banning Park, Delaware

64

Delaware

"Close to Home"

Joyce looked throughout the state of Delaware for the name of a suitable community in which to plant our trees. According to the standards that we established for the overall project, the primary choice required "Jackson" in its name or, if none existed, the alternate was to use the first name of one of our five family members. Failing to find any place names that fit either rule, we turned to geographic features and there, near the state boundary adjoining the county of our youth, was the Christina River. Its name matched one of the pet names for our daughter Christine, although she wouldn't want us to list the others in public. In fact, the river, itself, has been called all kinds of different names over the years, one of which was the Christine River. So it seemed like a proper match for our purposes.

The headwaters of the Christina River rise in Chester County, Pennsylvania, where our particular Jackson clan has resided as far back as we can trace. Its entire length is less than 30 miles, entering Delaware through New Castle County, skirting the city of Newark and the town of Newport, before receiving the Brandywine Creek and then contributing its flow to the mighty Delaware River at Wilmington. We welcomed the Town of Newport as our planting site because it's here that the Christina widens significantly and because some of John's relatives live in the immediate area. Also the Brandywine Creek has great personal meaning in our lives, running as it does through the lands of our youth.

The Christina was named after Queen Christina of Sweden. Fort Christina was the first permanent European settlement in Delaware, established by the Swedes at the confluence of the Brandywine Creek and Christina River in 1638. An earlier settlement had been attempted in 1631, on what was called the Delaware Bay, named in honor of Sir Thomas West, Lord de la Warr, but the entire population was killed by the Indians and their settlement wiped out. The name Delaware was shaped out of the English nobleman's surname and was applied in naming the Bay, the River, the State and the tribe of American Indians living in the area.

The name Delaware was attached to the Lenape Indians living near the Delaware River. They were among the first to encounter the Europeans during the first half of the 17th Century, similar to the experiences of the Powhatans in 1607 at Jamestown, Virginia and the Wamanpoags in 1620 at Plymouth, Massachusetts.

Continued expansionism by the white settlers in the 18th Century drove the Delaware tribes farther west where they settled in Ohio, becoming a powerful force against the relentless European encroachment. Eventually their resistance was ended, through The Indian Removal Act of 1830, spearheaded by Andrew Jackson's efforts to resettle all Indians, and the Delaware Indians were pushed across the Mississippi River, along with many other tribes. Ironically, the authors of this book, John and Joyce Jackson, live in the city of Delaware, Ohio, today.

Since most of the Christina River is within New Castle County, Joyce initiated her visit request with the County Executive Dennis Greenhouse. He embraced the concept and referred us to Robin Lucas, Public Relations Specialist for the County's Department of Parks and Recreations. The events that later transpired were largely due to her efforts. She arranged with Jonathan Husband, Park Development Planner and landscape architect to use the 155-acre Banning Park, in Newport, because the Christina River runs alongside it. She organized a reception committee, invited the press and a television reporter from the Wilmington TV station. Then, subsequent to our visit, she nominated us for an award from the state of Delaware.

The visit was scheduled for Monday, August 17, 1992, at 9:30AM in Banning Park. We picked up five white pines at Cerbo's in Parsippany, NJ, and drove the 120 miles to spend the weekend with our relatives before proceeding to the site on Monday morning. It was a short drive of 20 miles from our hometown of West Chester, PA. We headed directly to the park in a misty rain, following the directions provided to us. Immediately upon entering the park we noticed a band of people which proved to be our reception committee, along with our children Robert and Christine and her husband Mike Adams.

Dennis Greenhouse, the County Executive, made a welcoming speech and gave us a certificate proclaiming August 17, 1992, as "Jackson Family Day" in New Castle County. Also present were Robin Lucas and Jonathan Husband who had made the actual arrangements for the planting. Other park visitors were attracted to the gathering, undoubtedly by the TV crew and reporters. After the opening ceremonies, we followed them over to the designated site at the baseball fields along the southern edge of the park.

It was very exciting to realize that all of these people had come together in this place because of us and the appeal of wanting to be a part of what we were trying to accomplish around the country. They all helped us carry the trees and the equipment across two ball fields to the far end of the property. There we lined up the trees in a straight line, approximately twenty-five apart, following Tony Cerbo's advice that the pines would quickly fill up the space in between as they grew to over forty feet in height.

Our family of five did all of the digging and placement of the trees. It was truly a family experience as we shuttled from hole to hole, encouraging each other with constant chatter and admiring our work. The rain-softened ground aided in our digging. Occasionally, we would be startled by the passing of an Amtrak passenger train on the main line just behind the nearby vine-covered fence that bordered the park. On the other side of those tracks ran the Christina River.

Once the tree planting was finished, we exchanged departing remarks of appreciation with the local people and after they left, the five of us lingered at the site for awhile. We stood alongside the particular tree that was appointed to represent each of us. Since our son Steven was not present, we placed a raincoat over his tree to represent him. Christine hugged her tree as we all thanked God for the wonderful family that he had created and the blessings he had given that allowed us to pursue the dream of planting these trees everywhere.

The News Journal of Wilmington, DE, had printed our story in that day's edition on page A5 as reported by Phil Milford, staff reporter and accompanied with a photograph taken by Fred Comegys. *The Post* of Newark, DE, also ran a story on August 21, 1992, accompanied by a picture of us planting the trees over the headline *"Tree planters on natl. trek."* We always enjoyed newspaper coverage and encouraged their coverage through press releases prior to the visit, but we had never dreamed of appearing on television. That night on station WDEL-TV, we watched videotape of Dennis Greenhouse's speech to our gathered family, some remarks by us stating that we had already planted in seven states during the year and a shot of us unloading the trees in Banning Park. That was a thrill which we would only experience in a few other places.

However, Delaware wasn't done with us yet. Robin Lucas' nomination resulted in us being honored as *"Friends of Recreation"* awarded by the Delaware Recreation and Park Society. We were invited to the state capital of Dover to receive the award at a banquet on February 19, 1993. Joyce's parents, Ray and Madge Crooks, attended in our place and in their acceptance speech mentioned that *"We were unable to attend because we were away planting trees in Texas, Mississippi and Louisiana."* The Fall, 1992, issue of *Pathways* also featured an article and photographs of our visit to Banning Park in Newport, DE.

We have been back to re-visit the planting site many times, due to its proximity to where our relatives live. In August, 2000, we were invited back by Linda Gould, New Castle County Department of Special Services and *The News Journal* ran a follow-up story reported by Robin Brown in the August 15, 2000, edition. We also used the occasion to hold a family picnic attended by Joyce's sister, Barbara Coffey, our high-school friend, Bunny Dunleavy and Chris Marlow, of Elmhurst, DE, who was Helen Jackson's mail carrier.

The latest visit was in 2008 and the trees are doing exactly what Tony Cerbo had predicted. They are healthy forty-footers whose girth will soon join with each other into a living wall of pine needles. And behind them, beyond the Amtrak railroad tracks, still flows the beautiful, historic Christina River.

Charles Page, owner of Page Nursery, Shirley and Virgil Melton, residents of Canton stand by a newly – planted **Live Oak** tree.

Jackson, Texas

Texas

"A Visit to East Texas"

February 15, 1993

Covering eight states in one year was a real confidence builder for us. It confirmed that we had developed a workable approach towards the project, one that could accomplish what we had set out to do within the time frame envisioned. However, it was the reaction of the people with whom we came in contact that buoyed our hopes the most. They gave us a feeling that we weren't just doing this project for ourselves, that others were being touched in a special way, too. Those feelings influenced us to set another adventurous schedule for the year of 1993.

The program for the start of the year was designed to combine Joyce's time off from work in February with the fact that the conditions for tree-planting were confined to mostly southern states during that time of year. We decided to go as far south as possible which meant visiting the rest of the states bordering on the Gulf of Mexico. Having already done Florida and Alabama the previous year, we set our sights on Texas, Louisiana and Mississippi.

To make it even more exciting, we decided to visit with our son, Rob, in Iowa, before proceeding to Texas. Rob was living in Clear Lake, IA, and working at the Winnebago plant in Forest City, from which he managed the delivery of newly-manufactured motor homes. Not far from there is Mason City, IA, which is where rock and roller Buddy Holly lost his life in a plane crash after performing at the Surf Ballroom in Clear Lake. It was this occurrence that Don McLean immortalized in his song *"American Pie,"* with the words *"the day the music died."* We visited the shrine at the Surf Ballroom, stopped by the airport in Mason City and then proceeded to Minneapolis for our flight to Dallas, TX.

We weren't due in Jackson, TX, until Monday, February 15, 1993. It's a drive of less than 60 miles from Dallas which allowed us to visit the site of John F. Kennedy's assassination, J. R. Ewing's Southfork Ranch and other interesting sites around "Big D" on Sunday.

Initially, Joyce had selected Jacksonville, TX, as our planting site and had already made contact with the community leaders there. But then one day she happened to be looking at a Texas map only to discover that a place with the actual name of Jackson existed in Van Zandt County, approximately 60 miles west of Jacksonville. Further investigation resulted in an invitation to plant our trees at a place actually named Jackson, which is always our first choice of a name when one is available. The people of Jacksonville were very disappointed at our change of plans.

Jackson, TX, is a very small place that was more prominent in the late 19th century than it is today. Van Zandt County was actually part of the Republic of Texas upon its independence from Mexico in 1836 to its admission as the 25th state in 1845. Parts of the county saw battles between the Texas army and the Western branch of the Cherokee Indians. The Cherokee had been ordered out of Arkansas into Oklahoma by the Indian Removal Act of 1830. Instead of complying, they took refuge in East Texas which was not a part of the United States at the time. However, the Texans had already laid claims here and they were not about to share the land with a band of displaced Indians, especially after they had secured the area from the original inhabitants, the Caddoan Indians. The Battle of the Neches ensued in 1839, with the Texas army decisively defeating and dispersing the Cherokees, opening the way for Anglo-American settlement. By the early 1880's, the early settlers of Union Hill had established a community of homes, schools, churches and businesses. Dr. Jackson Kennedy led the cause for a post office and when it was secured the community changed its name to Jackson in his honor. It was to be a short-lived prosperity. In 1907, the post office was discontinued and mail was routed from the county seat of Canton, six miles away. Few structures remain standing in Jackson, today, other than two churches and the old school building.

Joyce approached officials in the county seat of Canton for guidance since there was no municipal organization to contact in Jackson. Rita Ragsdale, at the Canton City Hall, was instrumental in putting us in touch with Shirley and Virgil Melton, lifelong residents of Canton. They not only invited us to plant our trees at the Jackson Missionary Baptist Church but also put us in touch with Charles Page, the proprietor of the local nursery. This group made all the arrangements for our visit which included notifying Linda Brown, reporter for *The Canton Herald*. We sent her a press release in advance of our visit and another one subsequent to the event. The advance notice resulted in a preview article that appeared on February 4, 1993, one of the first such notices that ever heralded our coming.

The night before the event was spent in Canton. It's a typical old East Texas town, with the court house in the center square and the stores across the street still looking as if the wood-plank sidewalks and hitching rails haven't been gone for too long. We went to the movie theater which could have passed for the one used in the movie *"The Last Picture Show."* The town is famous for its "First Monday Trade Days," reputed to be one of the three largest flea markets in the world. All in all, we thoroughly liked our stay there, so much in fact, that we went back into town for another visit after the planting in Jackson.

Charles Page had already decided that live oak would be the proper species of tree to plant. He had five of them waiting for us when we arrived at his nursery in the morning and gave the five-foot beauties to us for a total of $45, well within our budget. Not only did he provide the trees but he loaded them into his pickup truck, along with his assistant, and they did most of the planting at the church site.

The temperature was 60 degrees, with rain pouring down and tornado warnings in the area, as we pulled into the church parking lot. The Meltons were waiting for us under the roof in front of the church, along with Mr. Barrier, a nearby resident of 57 years. Linda Brown, the reporter, was also present. Joyce spent most of the time showing them the contents of our "traveling" scrapbook as she related the background behind the project. The newspaper clippings and photographs from the first twelve states were proving to be too much to carry around. So Joyce put together a scaled-down version for the first time using duplicate material while the originals remained safely at home. This "traveling" version is what we packed for each trip to show the people we came in contact with.

Meanwhile, the other men, including John, set the trees out in a straight line near the fence in back of the church building and began digging. The rain pounded off their rain suits as they maneuvered the trees into the holes. On cue, Joyce would come out to help form the dams at the base of the trees using the collapsible trenching shovels that were part of our standard tree-planting kit brought from home. The kit also included knee pads for John, gloves and other planting accessories, assembled with the hope, at least from John's point of view, that our hosts would sympathize with the paltry collection of tools and be moved to provide us with as much assistance as possible.

After the planting was done, the driving rain caused us to head for cover inside the church, instead of lingering alongside the trees as we normally did. Everyone chatted away oblivious to the conditions outside. Too bad that Linda's interview wasn't caught on tape because her questions captured the essence of what we were trying to do in a way that held the attention of the others around us. A lot of good quotes flowed from that. As an example, Charles Page remarked *"Their project promotes good will and gives them an opportunity to meet new people."* But it was Linda's own later reporting that supplied one of the most memorable comments that we've ever encountered during the project. In her February 18, 1993, article which covered a good deal of the front page of *The Canton Herald*, she lead with the following paragraph, *"John and Joyce Jackson of Madison, New Jersey, are making the world a better place to live – five trees at a time."*

We could end on that note but there is another story that marks the trip to Texas. It was the first time that we used a tape recorder to capture our thoughts as they occurred at the time. Like most people, we started off with uncertainty, not knowing quite what to record or how to go about it and we didn't even bring out the tape recorder until returning to the car after the tree planting ceremony. The first taped conversation between Joyce and John starts out with: *"You go first; no, you go first,"* but eventually it gave way to more substantive content. In fact, we've discovered that there is more on the tapes than anyone would want to know, in the context of a book narrative. Maybe we'll publish them separately as *"The Jackson Legacy Tapes."*

At the end of the week we passed through the area, again, on the way back to the Dallas airport. We used the opportunity to re-visit the trees in Jackson. This time the climate was a lot more agreeable than the previous Monday. It felt good to come back, on a quiet Saturday morning, to confirm that everything turned out well with the plantings despite the arduous weather conditions in which we had worked. It also gave us a chance to privately dedicate the trees to our family and to express thanks for another successful tree-planting trip. Moving on to Canton, we saw ourselves on the front page of *The Canton Herald* in passing by a newspaper dispensing machine. Naturally we bought a few copies and lingered for awhile to see if anyone would recognize the celebrities in town. Probably the few people who walked by were too timid to approach us, because no one did. We figured they'll probably recognize us when we appear on *The Oprah Winfrey Show*, someday.

Some years later, our former neighbors from when we lived in Kingwood, TX, Jeff and Denise Lochore, stopped in Jackson on their way through the area. They confirmed that our trees are growing along the fence line in back of the church and provided us with pictures of them.

State Capitol Of Mississippi.

Jackson, MS

Mississippi

"A Capital Place"

The rain continued to beat down on our car like a drum as we crossed Louisiana. Our plan was to plant trees every other day in each of the three states. This timetable encompassed time to do some sight-seeing in the area surrounding Vicksburg, MS, but it meant continuous driving in order to stay on schedule.

The rain and hail, wind and cold didn't let up for eight hours, finally forcing us off the road 35 miles west of Vicksburg. We had driven over 300 miles from Texas in the most trying of conditions, to practically the limits of our endurance. In Joyce's case, it actually was the end of her endurance.

Vicksburg National Military Park is one of the country's best preserved memorials of the Civil War. It was certainly worth the effort in getting there. We drove along the 16 ½ mile tour road through the park listening to an audio tape that provided the history of the engagement and its importance in the overall conflict. Later we took in other period places in downtown Vicksburg, including the gunboat USS Cairo. On the lighter side, we visited the Biedenharn Candy Company where Coca-Cola was first bottled in 1894.

After a relaxing day we drove on to Jackson, MS, and checked into the Edison Waithall Hotel in the center of the city. Our hosts had made arrangements for us to stay at one of their finer hotels, built in 1928 and renovated just prior to our visit. When we got to the room there was an invitation to breakfast waiting from George Norris, whose responsibilities for the city included downtown landscape management. He would be revealing the site of the tree plantings to us then. That initial contact when we arrive in a new place always fuels our excitement.

The evening was spent driving around to get more familiar with the city. Jackson is the state capital of Mississippi, the only state capital in the country so named. It manifests an aura of importance through its imposing capitol building, the governor's mansion and other structures of government. That's further evidenced in the history associated with this place. It was appointed the state capital in 1821, at a time when Andrew Jackson was still celebrated as the hero of The Battle of New Orleans, which concluded the War of 1812 with Great Britain. He became the city's namesake and a large statue of "Old Hickory" stands outside of City Hall today. The city carries a prominent record of involvement in the Civil War and in the civil rights movement. It was a major manufacturing and railroad center for the Confederacy which resulted in its complete destruction by Union forces, under the command of General William Tecumseh Sherman, in July, 1863. Over the next one hundred years it typified the Deep South's resistance to integration. As the state capital, it witnessed many civil rights demonstrations and unrests including the freedom riders, the death of Medgar Evers and the terminus of the James Meredith March led by the first black person to be registered at the University of Mississippi. No place named Jackson that we went to can claim as much importance to American history as Jackson, Mississippi.

George Norris came to us through Joyce's contact with Allyne Evans, City Clerk, who referred it to the Department of Public Works, Building and Grounds Division. They agreed with the notion that it would be a worthy activity and enlisted Mr. Norris, a landscape architect from the Department, to be our coordinator. On the morning of February 17, 1993, this tall, cowboy-booted gentleman met us at breakfast. He provided directions where to meet him after we had picked up the trees at Harper's Nursery. Bob Harper recommended magnolia trees which we purchased and then loaded the four-foot trees into the trunk of our rental car.

The planting site was alongside the Mississippi State Fairgrounds Complex at the entrance to the city along a wide expanse of East Pearl Street. George brought workmen, including Calvin Hudson, from his department who actually had the holes dug before we arrived. Someone had also alerted the local media who appeared in the form of three television crews, a radio reporter and a newspaper photographer. That assembly of people, along with George Norris and his associates, made for quite a gathering stretched out along the busy street.

The work crew had left two trees for us to plant as part of the ceremony. We went about the usual process of getting down on our knees to round off the holes, position the trees for straightness and then backfilling the space around the little tree trunks leaving an earthen dam to hold in the water. All of this provided good action for the TV cameras to videotape with occasional pauses for us to give them sound bites. The stations were WLBT, WJTV, and WAPT, channels 3, 12 and 16, respectively. After the TV people had finished, a man named Scott, in a pickup truck, motioned us to get in the cab with him, thrust a microphone at us and proceeded to broadcast a live FM radio remote from the scene. It seemed to go on for a long time but actually only lasted about three minutes. It was our first time on live radio during the project. Joyce recalls it primarily for John's talking so much which furthered his reputation as being "a ham," when it came to grabbing the spotlight.

Throughout all the activities, photographer Greg Jensen of *The Clarion Ledger* was clicking away. We had sent an advance press release to the newspaper's environmental editor, Sharon Spallworth, which must have resulted in the photographer's assignment. However, we were never able to establish whether an article or photograph ever appeared in their newspaper. We have to count it as one of the few places for which no newspaper coverage is known to have occurred.

Jackson, MS, has to go down as one of the better receptions accorded us. The people were enthusiastic, the city was impressive and the feedback was exceptional. Early that evening, we had just settled into our room at the antebellum Monmouth Plantation in Natchez, MS, and switched on the television to Channel 12 only to encounter quite a surprise on the six o'clock news. First came a brief promo announcement showing us as the coming attraction later in the news program, then the whole piece ran at the end of the show. It mostly featured Joyce talking away as they showed pictures of the tree planting. This time "the ham" got very little air time. It only lasted a couple of minutes on the screen but it has lasted infinitely in our minds and made indelible the memories of a wonderful experience.

The month after visiting Jackson, we received a thank you letter from Mayor Kane Ditto which contained the following commentary, *"Thank you for the five beautiful magnolia trees that your family planted at the entrance to our city. It is wonderful that you take such pride in your family name and legacy. Thank you for your efforts to beautify our nation."*

Children, whose last names are Jackson, help plant five **Crape Myrtle** trees in front of the Jackson Elementary School.

Jackson, Louisiana

Louisiana

"Back to School"

February 19, 1993

The itinerary allowed us another free day before the next scheduled planting in Jackson, Louisiana, on Friday, February 19, 1993. We lingered around the town of Natchez, MS, until afternoon, soaking up the charm of the old river port with its period mansions and other well-preserved 19th Century artifacts. The highlight was a look at the *"Mississippi Queen,"* a luxury, sternwheeler steamboat that plies the muddy waters of the nation's grandest waterway. It was in port on its way down to New Orleans. Closing your eyes as the steam whistle blew you could picture yourself sitting in the top-side salon of a by-gone era where gentlemen in cutaway finery entertained ladies in billowing hoop skirts while dock hands deftly swung cotton bales onto the decks below.

Louisiana has experienced its share of cultural transition. Initially there were the multiple Indian tribes each carving out their own existence. Then came the Spanish followed by the French, who brought in slaves from Senegal giving rise to the Creole society. The population was further augmented by French Acadians who the British drove out of Nova Scotia and would form the Cajun contingent. Haitians and others migrated to the territory just prior to the Louisiana Purchase which resulted in Louisiana's admittance as a state in 1812. All inhabitants paid the price of secession and occupation after the Civil War and then were unsettled by the repercussions of race discrimination for the next hundred years. Throwing in the effects of assorted natural disasters and the slow pace of political and educational reforms created a gumbo of circumstances that the state struggled to surface from.

But our little trip was headed in a more hopeful direction in a more encouraging time, a quarter century after the enactment of civil rights legislation. The school at which we were invited to plant our trees was a newly-constructed, first-class learning facility open to all people, as were the prevailing political structures that brought it into being. What better place than this to fit our metaphor of planting and nurturing saplings to grow into strong trees for the future.

We knew the planting site was going to be at a school as a result of our contact with Jan Worthy, Secretary of the Feliciana Chamber of Commerce. Through her we discovered that Jackson was originally the seat of justice for Feliciana parish and claims to be the first town named for Andrew Jackson. Reportedly he camped nearby with his troops on the return trip north after defeating the British at the Battle of New Orleans in 1815. The town of Jackson adopted his name shortly afterwards.

Jan suggested Hillside Nursery in Ethel, LA, for the trees even though this nursery had been ravaged by a tornado a few months earlier. We arrived there in late afternoon to find the owner, Truvy Jacobsen, meeting us outside his place of business surrounded by uprooted trees and other clutter. It was the first time that we had ever seen this kind of damage up close. Tornadoes, where we're from in the northeast, are relatively rare and usually only result in some roof damage. But at Truvy's place we saw tree trunks twisted off with their roots still in the ground. It was quite a testimony to nature's power. Truvy, however, seemed to take it in stride saying that something bad happens to him every three years anyway. He shared more of his unique outlook on life as we picked out five crape myrtle trees for the school. He graciously sold them for our budgeted amount and helped us lift the five-foot saplings into the trunk of the car. We really enjoyed meeting and doing business with him.

Returning to Jackson we met Jan in the post office. She said that everyone was eager to see us the next morning at the Jackson Elementary School and gave us directions there. We got the feeling that it was going to be something special. During a dinner of blackened catfish we pondered what we might say if called upon to make a speech and the excitement grew as we checked into the Asphodel Hotel to rest up for what lay ahead.

It was quite a show. All the children in grades one through four, led by teachers Pam Lockwood and Sue Stewart, turned out for the planting ceremony. It was a cold, blustery day with everyone bundled up in hooded sweatshirts and other cold-weather gear. Also in attendance were the Principal, Shirley Cupit, Jerry the school custodian, Jan Worthy, Paul Walters from the newspaper and our nurseryman, Truvy Jacobsen. Six children came forward to help with the planting, just like the group of school children who helped us in Jackson, GA, they were all named Jackson. There was Jaron, Kerrick, Walter, James, Roman and Ricky.

The site was directly in front of the school in a wide grassy area within a circular driveway. Only a little scrub pine and a flag pole already graced this space; as a matter of fact, we didn't notice many other trees on the whole property surrounding the school. Could this be another reason for the excitement? Was someone finally going to do some real landscaping? Actually, we found out later on, that they had already planted over forty trees but only a few had survived.

The ground must have had something to do with that. It was dry and hard. There was no way that our little trenching tools were going to make a dent in this soil. Fortunately, Jerry had brought along a post-hole digger, an idea he probably developed after trying to plant those other forty trees. Even with that tool, the digging went slowly as everyone, including the kids, took their shifts in attacking the *terra extra firma*. That gave us plenty of time to chat with everyone, show the scrapbook and explain proper tree-planting procedures.

Finally the crape myrtles were in the ground with little plastic collars attached to their trunks to keep them protected from mowers and weed whackers. We credit that innovation to Truvy Jacobsen and it was something that we repeated at practically every place we visited after that. Sure enough, they asked us to make a speech. The two of us alternated the talk explaining how we conceived the idea to plant in all fifty states, why we considered it a legacy for our children and their children on and on into the future and how grateful we were for the fine reception by the people of Jackson, Louisiana. The ensuing smiles and claps added to the joy that we experienced to see the trees of our 15th state start out their life and to project how these school children could always look upon them to remember what this day stood for.

Paul Walters wrote a wonderful article in the February 25, 1993, edition of *The Watchman* under the headline *"New Jersey family plants legacy at Jackson school."* The story covered most of the front page, including a picture of Roman Jackson digging away as Joyce, wearing ear muffs, and

John, wearing knee pads, looked on. John was quoted as saying, "*I think now we are a part of this little community of Jackson, LA, and will always be as long as these trees survive.*"

 It was hard to pull ourselves away to begin the long trek back home. Joyce especially loved interacting with the children and the photographs reflected the joy in her face. There was also the realization that another trip was coming to an end. We drove through the woodlands of Louisiana, through areas where their logging industry removes trees even as we are adding our little stand of five trees for a special purpose. We stopped for the night in Natchitoches, LA, not realizing that it was at this town's airport where singer Jim Croce died in a plane crash in 1973. So we had opened this trip near where Buddy Holly had died in a plane crash and closed it in a place where Jim Croce met the same fate. It's just one of those coincidences for which there is no explanation.

With the help of local neighbors, Joyce Jackson plants one of five **White Dogwoods** to beautify Roberts Neighborhood Park.

Roberts, Massachusetts

Massachusetts

"Beautiful Day in the Neighborhood"

May 10, 1993

Originally, we thought there was a good potential for coordinating tree planting trips with John's business travel. As head of sales and marketing for a trucking company, he was often required to visit various parts of the country which could surely offer some opportunity for a planting side trip. That way we could defray some of the travel cost outlays as well as maximize our time. Great plan but it only happened in connection with three states during the whole project. The first occurrence was in May, 1993, when we were able to tie in a tree planting trip in conjunction with attending a trucking convention in Boston, Massachusetts.

At the time we owned a condominium on Cape Cod in Orleans, MA. So it was natural to include that stop in our itinerary especially since there were year-round renters in the condo who needed to be visually checked out every so often. It's about a 300-mile drive from our home in Madison, NJ, to Orleans, MA, and 90 miles between Orleans and Boston.

Before starting out, we visited Cerbo's Nursery to pick up five white dogwoods ranging between five and six feet in height. Tony Cerbo recommended these as great ornamental trees after we told him that the planting site would be in a public park. Joyce had determined the location through contact with Susan Burstein, councilperson for Waltham, MA.

Joyce's research did not discover any places in Massachusetts named Jackson, which meant turning to the first name of a family member. That proved difficult also. The only suitably-named place that we could come up with had some relevance to our oldest son's name of Robert. Joyce discovered that a Roberts neighborhood existed within the City of Waltham, a suburb of Boston. "Neighborhood" is a designated identity for a section within some New England communities and, in this context, Roberts Neighborhood fit our purposes as a bonafide place name. Waltham is the home of Brandeis University and the sign at the MBTA train station near our planting site reads *Brandeis-Roberts*. If we needed any more connectivity to the name of Roberts, it's also the maiden name of John's maternal great-grandmother.

The local application for the name of Roberts appears to come from John Roberts who owned paper mills along the Stony Creek in the early 1800's. The Stony Brook Reservoir is near our planting site, as is Roberts Road.

Susan picked out the planting site with the help of Sandra Place, Director of Parks and Recreation. Arrangements were set for Monday, May 10, 1993, at 9:00 AM, which would allow us to complete the work and then travel to downtown Boston for the start of the convention.

We stayed at a hotel near Waltham on Sunday night where we could air out the trees. Two days of confinement in the trunk of a car can be stressful on saplings of this size even though we did our best to air them out periodically on the journey. We placed them back in the car on Monday morning for the short drive to Roberts Neighborhood Park, following the directions that Susan provided.

There was a fair-sized group waiting when we arrived. Susan and Sandra were there along with Roger O'Connell and Michael Allia from the streets crew, several residents of the area including Joseph Giordano and Dorothy Smith and other unidentified neighbors with their children. It was a perfect warm, sunny day after Mother's Day, with blossoms blooming and everyone wearing short sleeves.

Our planting site was along the side of the park bordering on the appropriately-named Sunnyside Street. We began placing the trees in the lawn between a low chain link fence and the basketball court. Everyone seemed to participate whether it was in digging the holes, removing the trees from the containers, offering advice, simply looking at our scrapbook or just as on-lookers throughout the occasion. We stepped away often to talk with the people while the workers continued toiling away. It didn't take too long to finish the work under those conditions.

Everyone in attendance thanked us for bringing beauty to their little corner of the world and then, one by one, they departed. That's always a moment when we feel connected to a different place and people in a special way. It comes flooding back whenever an area that we've visited appears in the news or we come across old photographs. Whether or not all the trees eventually make it, the realization lives on that we have been enriched by the experience and so have many others.

No media showed up for our ceremony at Roberts Neighborhood Park despite the advance press release we sent out. That's somewhat disappointing but publicity is always an extra-added element to the thrill of doing what we do. Besides, people will be able to get a more expanded, permanent record of our project by reading the book. Be sure to tell your friends and neighbors.

After leaving Waltham, we joined our friends, and employer, Manny and Natalie Rizzuto of Sicomac Carriers. We attended the annual meeting of the National Tank Truck Carriers and then spent time touring Boston together. Later, on the way to Cape Cod, we passed by Plymouth, MA, where the Pilgrims had landed in 1620. It reminded us of the first Thanksgiving with the Wamanpoag Indian Tribe sharing the bounty with the new settlers they had befriended. We weren't aware, until years later, of a ritual that the tribe observes on the remains of their ancestral lands near Martha's Vineyard off Cape Cod. There, they pause each Thanksgiving Day, to mourn the loss of their land.

The Jackson Legacy

Steve Jackson holding a red-topped stake used to mark snowmobile paths by the just planted **White Spruce** tree in Stevens Village, Alaska

Transporting **White Spruce** trees down the Yukon River to Stevens Village, Alaska

Alaska

"Way Up North"

The processes for conducting a project usually improve as actual experience is gained. Pausing in the spring of 1993, to reflect upon the previous plantings, we felt that the lessons learned from actually doing it were being applied constructively. We now had a firm grip on how to promote the concept and reach out to the people involved. That kind of confidence encouraged us to greater heights. We felt ready to tackle the big trip, the one that so many people long to take – way up north to Alaska.

Our growing confidence evidenced itself in other ways early in 1993. When Joyce discovered that two local authors, Helen Bland and Mary Sears, were writing a book on family traditions, we sought them out to tell our story. This led to the mentioning of our project in their book entitled *"Celebrating Family Traditions, An Idea and Keepsake Book,"* published by Little Brown and Co., later in the year. Correspondence with Vice President Al Gore led to a nice return letter and doing the same with Secretary of the Interior, Bruce Babbitt, resulted in being awarded the *"Volunteer Service Award, for stewardship of America's public lands."* The *Star Ledger* of Newark, NJ, heard about the project which resulted in a front-page spread in The Towns Section, complete with photographs of us with nurseryman Tony Cerbo. Even while all this was going on, Joyce was diligently working on plans for the trip to Alaska.

Visiting Alaska is not your ordinary trip and our excursion was to be even more extraordinary due to the location of the only place we could find with a name connected to our project. Lacking any place specifically named Jackson, it was going to have to be an Indian settlement by the name of Stevens Village in honor of our youngest son Steven. Finding it on the map was the easy part.

Stevens Village is inaccessible by road. It sits alongside the Yukon River, 90 air miles north of Fairbanks and sixty miles south of the Arctic Circle. There's only two ways to reach it: by plane or by boat. Our initial inquiries unveiled the fact that no one just drops into an Athabascan Indian village without all the right clearances from the state authorities and from the tribal leaders, themselves.

Joyce discovered this in calling the Stevens Village school and talking with teacher Jon Laughlin. He put us in touch with Chief Randy Mayo who sent us the following hand-written letter in early April:

How are you folks doing? Fine I hope. I am answering your letter about your project. I talked it over with the Village Council. They feel it is a worthwhile thing. Also an honor to be selected as one of the sites chosen. So we would like to invite you to our home for your tree planting. Looking forward to it.

It quickly became apparent that a bush plane wasn't going to be an option due to the number of people that would make up the party. Going on the trip would be ourselves, son Steven, the Indian affairs agent and, of course, the pilot. Adding to this weight and the space requirements would be the five trees and all the gear. That proved to be too much for a bush plane to handle.

That meant the only viable option would be to charter a boat to go up the river to the village. Dave Lacey's company handles such charters on the Yukon for private parties as well as for the *Princess* cruise line tours. He arranged for us to charter a twenty-one foot boat that could accommodate everyone and everything involved with the trip. He also put us in touch with Gena Delucchi, University of Alaska, Fairbanks, Agricultural and Community Development Agent responsible for Indian affairs in the eastern part of Alaska, who took care of the necessary permissions.

With all the approvals gained and the transportation logistics figured out, we set a date of June 15, 1993, for the visit to Stevens Village only to find out that Chief Mayo couldn't make it that day. He was signed up to attend a conference for indigenous people in Vienna, Austria, during that time frame but he advised that Chief Horace Smoke or another dignitary would be appointed to receive us.

Traveling to such a distant land for such a unique purpose would be further enhanced if we could come up with an additional gesture of some kind. We decided to see what our own state could provide us in this regard by calling the office of Jim Florio, Governor of New Jersey. To our pleasant surprise, his secretary arranged for the governor's office to give us a hand-blown glass pitcher made by the artisans of Wheaton Village, NJ, for presentation to the people of Stevens Village as a gesture of friendship from the people of our own state. His letter of May 19, 1993, also complimented us for devoting ourselves *"to the protection and beautification of our environment."*

This was going to be some trip. Just getting there was a challenge to coordinate our departure from Newark airport with a stop in Chicago to pick up our twenty-six year old son Steven and then arranging to arrive at some decent hour in Fairbanks. As it was, we landed at our destination in Alaska at 1:30 AM which was actually 5:30AM as a result of the four-hour difference in time zones. And it was still light out. We hadn't properly recognized that the dates chosen for our trip fell within that time of year when Alaska becomes known as the land of the midnight sun. Luckily we allowed two days to get acclimated before starting the trek north to the Yukon River.

The day before the scheduled planting we drove forty-five miles south of Fairbanks in our rented Ford Explorer SUV to pick up the trees at Woodland Farms in Nenana, AK. Here we discovered that the owner of the nursery, Don Krantzer, had attended West Chester (PA) State University during the same timeframe that Joyce was a student there in the early 1960's. Needless to say he went out of his way to help us, selecting three to four foot white spruces for the plantings and informing us that in the climate near the Arctic Circle they will only grow to a height of eight feet at maturity.

Returning to Fairbanks we were interviewed by Kate Rupprecht, reporter for *The Fairbanks Daily News-Miner* and KATN-TV, Channel 2, reporter Kelly Thomas with a video-camera crew. That night, for the second time that year, we saw ourselves on television.

On the morning of the trip we went to the local office of Yukon River Tours to meet with the owner, Dave Lacey, and Gena Delucchi, from the University of Alaska, Fairbanks. By 9:00AM we were on the road for the long drive north.

Dave and Gena led the way in his four-wheel drive Jeep Trooper. The drive starts out of Fairbanks along seventy-two miles of paved road on the Elliott Highway which leads to the gravel Dalton Highway paralleling the Alyeska Pipeline. There are virtually no conveniences for the next fifty-six miles to the Yukon River crossing and it gets even worse beyond that point to Prudhoe Bay. We were told the state requires stopping to lend assistance to any disabled vehicle on this stretch of highway. Fortunately we never encountered anything like that.

Two hours of flying dust and gravel brought us to the bridge over the Yukon River at a place called Yukon Ventures. The Yukon is the third longest river in North America at 1,975 miles but there are only four bridges over its entire length. Before proceeding further we all had a hearty meal at the nearby outpost at mile marker 56 on the Dalton Highway. After lunch, we piled ourselves and belongings into Dave Lacey's waiting twenty-one foot boat, operated by Captain Ed, and set out on the seventeen mile ride to the village accompanied by Dave Lacey, Gena Delucchi and David Joseph from the village.

Along the way they explained that the river is very deep and is a salmon spawning ground. Only the Indians are allowed to take salmon from the river during the spawning run. This is done mostly with large, wooden fish wheels that operate near the shore where the current turns the wheel scooping up the fish and sliding them down a sluice to the shore where the Indians finish the process of cleaning and smoking the fish. The salmon were about a week away from coming to this point in the river. We passed one of these fishing camps just before turning the bend into Stevens Village.

Our first sight of the village revealed two large towers: a microwave dish for telephone and a satellite dish for television, indicating that technology had come to the tundra. As the boat eased into shore we were met by Robert Joseph who escorted us to the reception committee comprised of Assistant Chief Harold Simon, his children, Sheila and Timothy and some others. They helped put our trees onto a truck for the short ride to the site while we removed the rest of our belongings from the charter boat so it could return to base. It didn't occur to us at the moment that we were now stranded at an Indian village in the middle of Alaska.

The village traces its beginnings to the turn of the 20th Century when three Athabascan Indian brothers first settled there. One of the brothers, Old Steven, was elected chief in 1902 and the village took its name from him. It grew to nearly one hundred people with the establishment of a trading post, the opening of a school in 1907, a post office in 1936 and air service initiated in 1939. The Federal government paid Alaskan Indians $953 million in 1971 to obtain the rights to the North Slope oil fields and pipeline right of way. This money was distributed through community organizations representing all Indians in the state. Each year, every man, woman and child living in Alaska receives a dividend check paid out of oil royalties amounting to over $1,600 per person.

The planting site was outside the Community Center which was under construction. We made a little pre-planting speech to explain our Jackson Legacy program and, in the course of that, presented the glass pitcher donated by the state of New Jersey as a token of appreciation to the people of Stevens Village. Then we set about digging the holes into the rich river-bank soil assisted by Steven, Dave and men from the village, with Gena adding bone meal to the bottom of the holes and Joyce doing the overall supervision. That also allowed her ample time to show the scrapbook to anyone interested and keep up a running dialogue with the Indian children who gathered around us on foot and on their all-terrain vehicles. For protection from such vehicles, we had to install red, day-glow tipped stakes beside each tree to mark their proximity to the snowmobile paths that are in use a good portion of the year.

The afternoon slid by as we worked at a little slower pace than usual. In part we wanted to prolong the enjoyment of being with Steve in an environment that was sure to hold many memories for us in the future. You just don't pick up and go as soon as the tree planting is concluded, especially when there is no way of getting out.

Even before commencing our trip, we knew there was the possibility they would invite us to stay overnight at the fish camp down river, so we decided to bring along sleeping bags just in case of that eventuality. When the chief extended the invitation , Joyce said, "okay let's go for it, we will be here only once," however we hadn't packed any suitable food for the possibility of a sleep over. Robert Joseph appointed his nephew, David Joseph, to be our overnight host. David had spent four years in the Marine Corps, worked on the pipeline and knew how to live in the wilderness. That was quite a contrast to the three Jacksons who were all born outside of Philadelphia and knew from nothing about survival techniques. Our Indian guide shared his macaroni and cheese with us to augment the Slim Jims and other delicacies in our fanny packs. After exchanging our life stories he indicated that it was time to put up the tents and retire for the night, which was still actually daylight. He pointed out the privy to us some yards away and then slung a rifle over his shoulder. In response to our question regarding his last action he said, *"Grizzlies like smoked salmon, too."*

Somehow we got through the night and actually got some sleep amid dreams of grizzlies slashing through the tent walls and accosting us on the way to the bathroom. The putter of Harold Simon's boat coming to pick us up was a reassuring reminder that it was time to return to our brand of civilization knowing that we had collected memories that we would never forget.

Back at the river crossing we grappled with the fact that the Arctic Circle was only sixty miles further north and when would we ever get the chance to see it again. It was a nice day with a lot of sunlight left so we decided to go for it. We probably didn't pass more than twenty other vehicles during the whole drive. The road stretched endlessly over perma-frost and through mountain passes with snow-capped ranges in the distance. One patch of snow was only about twenty yards from the road which gave us the idea of stopping to make some mid-June snowballs. We parked on the shoulder and walked around the back of the SUV and then stopped. There in the soft dirt was the fresh paw print of the only bear species to live this far north – a grizzly bear. Needless to say, we decided to find a safer place to make a snowball.

It was 83 degrees and the car air conditioner was on as we reached the Arctic Circle We knew we were there because the sign said "Arctic Circle --➔". There were five or six other cars there and a crowd gathered around a fellow holding up the first-ever GPS device that we had ever seen and pronouncing "Yep, we are now at the Arctic Circle." In the group was a couple from the Bay area of California, Gordon and Peggy Winlow. We told them about our tree planting project mentioning that Jackson, CA, was the second state we visited. They promised to go to Jackson, since it was relatively close to where they lived, to take photographs of the trees for us, which they did the following year.

Back in Fairbanks that night we picked up a June 15, 1993, edition of *The Daily News-Miner* to see our story on the first page of Section B under the headline "*N.J. family plants itself across country.*" We also obtained a copy of the television video tape. Those made for nice additions to our collection along with another memento picked up on the trip, a "*Certificate for Crossing the Arctic Circle.*"

In a way our second Alaska adventure started north of Fairbanks at the Arctic Circle where the vacation portion of the trip began. Joyce did a fantastic job planning every aspect of the trip. In the remaining five days we went to Denali National Park, visited Santa Claus's village at North Pole, AK, stayed in rustic cabins, took a sternwheeler riverboat ride, saw how sled dogs lived, observed wild life in their natural habitat and had all kinds of other frontier experiences too varied to mention. In all, we put over 1,000 miles on the Ford Explorer. Suffice it to say that Alaska is really worth the trip but we advise you to visit in the summer time and take plenty of mosquito repellant.

Three generations gather for the planting of **Bradford Pear** trees in Jackson, Ohio.
L to R—Rob Jackson, Christine Adams holding eighth month old daughter, Katie, Mike Adams, Joyce, John and Steve Jackson.

Jackson, Ohio

Ohio

"A Family Affair"

The course we set for 1994 included an extended tour in the month of June through five states starting and ending in the states where our children live, Ohio and Indiana, respectively. It would also involve the direct participation of three generations of our family in the actual tree planting for the first time. Rob and Steve signed on for the whole five-state tour while Chris could only join us at the start of the journey in Ohio. Joyce also received permission from The Hermitage to plant a tree at Andrew Jackson's home while we were traveling through Tennessee, on our way between Kentucky and Missouri.

The month preceding the trip, the Borough of Madison, NJ, decided to honor us at their Arbor Day celebration and we were invited to be the keynote speakers at the ceremony on Saturday morning, May 7, 1994. Our prepared speech was made on the steps of the municipal building before local dignitaries and townspeople. In front of the podium we placed a map of the United States with red flags representing each point that we planned to visit in the fifty states. If all went well, we intended to have almost half the states completed by the end of 1994, a goal which we, in fact, attained.

At the conclusion of the speech, Mayor Donald R. Capen presented us with a *"Proclamation Honoring The Jackson Family."* The closing words in the proclamation seemed particularly appropriate as we were about to embark upon the following month's trip: *"(I) do hereby extend sincere compliments and high praise to John and Joyce Jackson and their children, Robert, Christine, and Steven who, as arborists in family unity, are diligently accomplishing a great feat as they bring their message across America."*

Madison's weekly newspaper, *The Eagle*, published our picture and story about the Arbor Day celebration in their May 12, 1994, edition over the caption *"Johnny Appleseeds, of a sort."* It's an appellation that we thought about applying to ourselves from time to time but in the end decided it didn't quite fit what we were doing. It would have needed revision to *"Joyce and Johnny Appleseed,"* anyway.

On June 4th we flew to Columbus, OH, to begin the first leg of the trip. The whole family gathered at the home of our daughter, Christine, her husband, Mike Adams and our first grandchild, their six-month old daughter, Katie. Since the boys, Rob, 29, and Steve, 27, were going to be with us on the whole trip, we rented a Chevrolet Lumina van, with a removal back seat which we left at Chris' home. This was a very practical vehicle for transporting four adults, comfortably, along with their luggage and the five trees that we usually had to haul from the nurseries to each planting site.

The next morning, Sunday, June 5, 1994, the whole family of seven people started out for Jackson, OH, in two cars. For four of us, it was to be the beginning of a week-long, 1,400 mile trek involving five states and six planting sites. As always, Joyce had everything arranged in advance. All we had to do was get there, purchase the trees and make contact with the people who were waiting for our arrival.

In the case of Jackson, Ohio, the contact was Mike Stroth, representing the local parks and recreational department. Joyce had been directed to Mike as a result of her contact with Mayor Tom Evans' office and the Chamber of Commerce. They graciously accepted our request to plant on a Sunday so that the Adams' family could participate and also enable us to get a head start on the week's ambitious schedule, which called for a planting on every day of the week.

Our trees were to be part of the revitalization project at Manpower Park. Kenny and Roxie Mercer of Green Leaf Florist made available four Bradford pear trees and one Serviceberry, which Mr. Mercer transported to the park in his pickup truck. Once there, Mike Stroth showed us where he had staked out the five planting sites close by a creek from which we could draw water. Then we all started digging holes for the six-foot trees placing them about thirty feet apart from each other. It was a perfect day to be out doing something with the family; warm, sunny, with a light breeze blowing and the chirping birds waiting to test out the new roosting places.

Mike Stroth had departed by then leaving us alone to plant at our own pace. The family members joined in with a mixture of excitement and devilry. Two or three of us would work on one hole while others would carry the equipment from site to site, help to prepare the soil with nutrients and transport water when it came time for that. All throughout there was plenty of laughing, posing for pictures and admiring each tree as it stood straight in the ground beginning its life in this place.

When they were all in the ground, son-in-law Mike Adams took a picture of all five trees with each of us wearing our special tee-shirts standing beside the one designated for us. First in line was Chris holding Katie, then John, Joyce, Rob and Steve, way out back, near the creek and the school buses. Throughout our time there, birds kept landing near us and circling overhead. Joyce took them as harbingers indicating that we were meant to be here at this time for some greater purpose whether it was providing habitat for God's winged creatures or beauty to be enjoyed by the people who would visit this site in the future. We worked hard to create this scene for our own reasons since Jackson is within sixty miles of Columbus which made it easy for us to visit again on future trips to see Chris and Mike.

Before Mike Stroth left we showed him our scrapbook and gave him a copy of the press release which he promised to forward to the town newspaper, *The Jackson Journal Herald*. We don't know if the story every appeared in the newspaper because no one ever sent us a copy of an article.

We did establish that the town was named after Andrew Jackson. Like so many other places, its early days as a community corresponded to the time of the War of 1812 and the emergence of new communities throughout the eastern half of the country. Jackson County, Ohio, was formed in 1816, and the town of Jackson appointed as its county seat the following year. Both are named in honor of war hero Andrew Jackson.

In May, 1995 we went through Jackson, OH, returning from plantings in neighboring states. All five trees were dead. That prompted us to visit City Hall in an attempt to find out what happened and what could be done about the situation. Mayor Evans explained that there had been some mix-up regarding the School Board's assumption of responsibility for caring of the park. Consequently, the trees were neglected and didn't survive. Then and later, the city has made some indications to us that they would replace at least one of the trees but nothing has happened to date.

In 2005, we relocated to Delaware, OH, just north of Columbus. That means that Jackson, OH, is now the closest to us of any place where we planted our trees. It's the place where we would take our grandchildren to show them a living example of our project. We cannot let our adopted home state exist without physical evidence of all that the Jackson Legacy was meant to signify. Sometime, soon, we will take measures to once again establish our gift of living trees in the city of Jackson, OH.

Mayor Frank Noble lends a hand planting one of five **different species** of trees. Steve and John Jackson also joins the mayor

Jackson, Kentucky

Kentucky

"Terra Extra Firma"

June 6, 1994

Late on the Sunday afternoon of June 5, 1994, our daughter's little family headed back to Columbus while the rest of us set out on the 160-mile drive to Jackson, Kentucky. The route runs alongside the Ohio River which eventually assumes a northeasterly direction at Huntington, WV. We were on the Kentucky side of the river approaching Huntington when something appeared to be happening ahead of us. Many cars had pulled off the highway on both sides and everyone seemed to be looking up. Finally suspense got the best of us, so we stopped to find out what was going on. Just as we got out of the car a squadron of Blue Angels in F/A-18 Hornet fighter jets came roaring over us, low enough to see the numbers on the fuselages. We had stumbled onto an air show which had us transfixed for the remainder of their performance.

Then it was back on the road to southeastern Kentucky on a circuitous route dictated by the hills and hollers in this part of the country. Kentucky comes from the Iroquois Indian word "*kentake*" which means "*meadow land,*" which applies more to the bluegrass areas of the state. The natives who inhabited the hills of Southeastern Kentucky were mostly Cherokee and Shawnee, all of whom were displaced to Oklahoma during the Indian Removal Act. Today, the Federal government doesn't recognize that there are any Indian tribes still living within the state of Kentucky.

Most of the Europeans who settled in this area were Scots and Irish which may account for them identifying the region as the central highlands of Eastern Kentucky. Breathitt County was formed here in 1843 and the town of Jackson appointed as its county seat, named in honor of, you guessed it, Andrew Jackson.

Jackson has a population of over 2,000 people which makes it one of the larger communities in the region. It certainly fit our profile for a preferred place to visit because it had all the aspects required, such as a municipal structure, a newspaper, a post office and a place to purchase the trees. Mayor Frank Noble made sure that we knew where to go, even to the point of arranging our stay at the *Jackson Inn.* He also put us in touch with Martin Douthitt who made the trees available from the nursery section of his True Value hardware store.

The day of our planting, June 6, 1994, was also the 50th anniversary of D-Day in World War II. Before going for the trees we visited with Marge, the city clerk, who gave us directions to the City's mini-park and told us that the Mayor would meet us there. That left us time to swing by the True Value to pick up the trees, only Mr. Douthitt wasn't there. He showed up a few minutes later with apologies for arriving late saying he had been up until 3:00 AM in the morning watching the D-Day anniversary ceremonies on television. Even this little encounter in Kentucky, on this particular day, reminds us how much we owe those who fought for our freedom and pause to remember those who would never survive to enjoy that freedom on earth.

Mr. Douthitt set out a variety of tree species for us, all of them around six feet tall. He explained that the after-effects of a hurricane had wreaked havoc on the trees in town which made them wonder what varieties could withstand such punishment in the future. They decided that it would be better to plant several different species with that thought in mind. I guess you could say, in a way, we became part of a horticultural experiment. But then, that might be said about our whole project.

Our hosts provided a pick-up truck to transport the trees the short distance to the park. A five-man crew from the city, lead by Ozzie, was already there with tools in their hands, ready to go to work. That was always a beautiful sight for us to see. Everyone was putting their heads together to pick out the best place for each tree when a two- car convoy lead by a police escort heralded the arrival of Mayor Frank Noble. Actually the nature of his arrival on the scene shouldn't be misconstrued in any way; the Mayor turned out to be a very down-to-earth type of individual, sincerely interested in our program.

With his influence *The Jackson Times* had published an article in advance of our arrival incorporating our press release verbatim. The headline over the four-column story proclaimed, *"New Jersey family to plant trees here as a living legacy to their family."* Too bad it didn't mention the name of the park which might have attracted some more attendees and would have allowed us to provide the name of the park in this book.

Now it was time to get down to business in the hot, humid weather. We could have assigned two men per hole with the work crew, the Mayor, the police officer and the three male Jacksons all taking up shovels and picks. We didn't think to ask what the pick was for until the first swing bounced off the ground with a loud "CLINK." That was followed by repetitive jabs at the hard-packed earth which did its best to repulse the intrusions. Never before had we encountered such uncooperative soil, not even in the granite state of New Hampshire or its neighbor in Vermont. Somehow they chipped away deep enough and wide enough to make a suitable space for the trees. The dirt in the root balls together with the top soil and peat moss that we added collectively amounted to a proper planting base. One thing seemed for sure, no windstorm was going to have an easy time toppling over these babies.

Mayor Frank stayed for the whole time, alternately looking through the scrapbook with Joyce and leaning on a shovel. Joyce did her usual supervising of the digging, the placement, the watering and tamping down the soil at the base of the tree with her dainty little foot. The sweaty men, shirtless Rob and cool Steven faithfully executed her instructions and everyone could say that they had a direct hand in the proceedings.

When everything was done, the Mayor went to his car and returned with something in his hand. It was an official certificate that commissioned Joyce Jackson as an "Honorary Citizen of Jackson, Kentucky, *with all the rights, privileges and responsibilities thereunto appertaining."* As a consequence, Joyce is not quite a Kentucky Colonel but she now has the right to consider herself as a kernel of Kentucky.

The people of Jackson, KY, gave us an honest, down-home welcome for which we are very grateful. They identified with our project in a way that characterizes most of the places we visited throughout the country. Their reception showed pride in their own community, a willingness to help outsiders and an acceptance of us into a special place where we shall always reside.

Overleaf
Inset photo- Joyce and Steve Jackson plant a **Tulip Poplar** under the supervision of Mark Provost, Horticulturist at the Hermitage, June 7,1994
Main photo - September 2008, the **Tulip Poplar** had grown to forty feet or more....

Hermitage, TN

The Hermitage

"Old Hickory's Place"

June 7, 1994

Getting to Nashville was a drive of over 300 miles from the previous stop in Jackson, Kentucky. Most of the travel was through the state of Kentucky. It started out passing through the Daniel Boone National Forest, continued along I-64 past Lexington and then I-65 south to the Volunteer State. This nickname for the state of Tennessee is derived from the militiamen who signed up with General Andrew Jackson to go fight the British and the Indians between 1812 and 1818. His troops named him "Old Hickory" relating his toughness to the hardwood tree of that name.

The sites chosen for our 1994 tour were along a circular route passing through five contiguous states. In addition to their proximity to one another, each point we were to visit had a connection to the name of Andrew Jackson. In fact, that could be said about practically all of the places we visited up to that time, something which can be confirmed in the contents of the previous chapters. Since we would be passing through Nashville, Tennessee, it seemed only natural that we pay a visit to the nearby homestead of the man known as Old Hickory – The Hermitage.

The formation of the museum occurred in 1889, in an era when Tennessee could still be considered an out-of-the way destination for the average person. It was only forty-four years after Jackson's death. Some indication of the high esteem in which he was held can be drawn when contrasting the date of The Hermitage's acquisition, in 1889, to the years in which similar actions were taken to preserve other famous landmarks such as George Washington's Mount Vernon in 1859 and Thomas Jefferson's Monticello in 1923.

We considered it truly an honor when the Board of The Hermitage accepted our request to plant a tree on the grounds as part of our Jackson Legacy project. Joyce arranged this through the sponsorship of Sharon MacPherson, Deputy Director for Research. Sharon in collaboration with Mark Provost, horticulturist, chose a site near the Visitors Center and also approved the placement of a plaque. This was all pre-arranged well in advance of our visit which enabled us to include the details in an advance press release sent to Nashville's leading newspaper *The Tennessean*.

We arrived in Nashville late in the afternoon and after checking into the hotel headed straight for Opryland. There we enjoyed a live performance by country and western singer Tanya Tucker in addition to touring the amusement park until closing time. The next morning John had to return to New Jersey to attend a trucking show at the insistence of his boss who paid the round-trip airfare. As a consequence, the visit to The Hermitage was left in the very capable hands of Joyce, Rob and Steve.

Tuesday, June 7, 1994, began as a hot, humid day with the threat of a storm. Our family arrived at The Hermitage shortly after nine o'clock where they were met by Mark Provost, who had a copy of our article in that day's edition of *The Tennessean* in his hands. He had arranged for a seven-foot Tulip Poplar tree to be delivered to the site and already had it standing alongside the hole in the ground. The Tulip Poplar is the state tree of Tennessee. It is also one of our favorite trees that we had planted at former homes in Pennsylvania and Ohio. Now, through the efforts of ourselves, The Hermitage and Moss's Florist of Mt. Juliet, TN, one of them would be growing in this place as a symbol of our family name.

The group was joined by Sharon MacPherson and Margaret Ann Lane of The Hermitage staff. They looked through our scrapbook of previous plantings as Joyce commented on each one. Meanwhile, Mark, Rob and Steve attended to the tree planting on the rise of the hill just outside of the Visitors Center. The site is well separated from nearby trees which creates a prominent view for our tree. We had no trouble locating it on future visits to The Hermitage. Of course it also helped that they placed a plaque inscribed as follows:

TULIP POPLAR
PLANTED AS A LEGACY
FOR THE JACKSON FAM ILY
JOHN ROBERT STEVEN
JOYCE   CHRISTINE
HERMITAGE, TN
JUNE 7, 1994

At the conclusion of the planting ceremony, Margaret Ann gave us free passes to tour the grounds. The mansion and other buildings were very well presented but the gardens impressed us the most. At the entrance is a plaque which states: *"In 1819 General Jackson engaged an Englishman, William Frost, a noted gardener of Philadelphia, to design and plant this garden for Mrs. Jackson."* It goes on to state *"Her memory will remain fresh there as long as life lasts."* His wife, Rachel, never got to live in the White House, dying just after her husband was elected to be the seventh President of the United States. He had her tomb placed in the Hermitage's garden and every evening, when he was there, he went to sit beside it. One hundred and seventy five years later, another family born outside of Philadelphia came to this site to leave behind a single Tulip Poplar tree as a testimony to its branch of the Jackson clan.

However, the research staff of The Hermitage assured us that we are not related directly to Andrew Jackson because he and Rachel had no natural-born children. That's not to say that somewhere way back our family lines don't converge but it was never our intention to dwell on that possibility. It's enough for us to start our own family tradition, something that hopefully will endure for generations to come.

We have been back to The Hermitage occasionally in the ensuing years each time to find the tree growing strongly. Rob made the initial check-up on his own. John saw it for the first time when he was driving through the area on the way to relocating to Kingwood, TX, in 1997. Then in October, 2007, we arranged a more formal visit where a member of the staff actually took us out to the site for a close-up examination. We estimated the tree to be nearly twenty-five feet high at the time. The plaque has been removed subject to restoration. But the tree stands as a lasting symbol in ways that Andrew Jackson may have said *"will remain fresh there as long as life lasts."*

The Jackson Legacy

Jackson, Tennessee Chamber of Commerce (red jackets)
Center, L to R—Rob and Steve (kneeling), Joyce and John Jackson.
Far right—Mayor of the county of Madison, J. Alex Leech stands behind one of five **Willow Oak**
planted in Highland Park

Jackson, Tennessee

Tennessee

"The Red Coats"

June 8, 1994

Joyce, Rob and Steve spent the rest of the day touring the city of Nashville, after the morning's planting at The Hermitage. They saw the Ryman Auditorium, site of the Grand Ole Opry, the state capitol building and other sites before departing on the 130-mile drive to the important city of Jackson, Tennessee.

As with other places we visited, Jackson, Tennessee started out under a different name. Originally named Alexandria, it was renamed in 1822 through the influence of its founder, William Edward Butler, whose wife was a niece of Rachel Jackson. Her husband wasn't yet in the White House but he was already nationally known for his other exploits. The Tennessee Supreme Court is still required to conduct its proceedings in the city of Jackson having been established there in 1834 when Memphis was considered a secondary city in the region. It was also the hometown of legendary guitarist Carl Perkins.

While the rest of the family was having fun, John was entertaining customers at the Bulk Carriers Day tank truck show in Edison, NJ. This event lasted well into the night causing him to get up early the next morning for a flight to Memphis to rejoin the planting tour. The original plan was to rent a car for the drive over to Jackson but upon arrival John noticed a commuter flight about to depart for Jackson and he talked the gate attendant into letting him hop aboard at no extra cost. Actually it was to cost him a good deal in the way of anxiety. As the plane lifted off the ground the pilots sensed something was wrong and decided to put it back down on the remaining portion of runway. That didn't pose much of a problem for them but some of the passengers let out strange sounds as it dropped back down to the ground. The pilots taxied off the runway to check their gauges and collect their thoughts and then announced that they were going to try another take-off. (*Note to Northwest Airlines – please tell your pilots never to use the word "try."*). Thankfully, the second ascent was uneventful and the plane covered the 80 miles to Jackson without further incident.

The airport was so small that the man who directed the plane's arrival to the gate also gave John a ride to the hotel where the rest of the family was staying. The people of Jackson were already going out of their way to help us and that degree of kindness would typify the whole visit.

We spent the morning at the Casey Jones Museum, dedicated to the famous railroad engineer, and then went to see Don Bailey of Four Seasons Nursery and Garden Center to pay for the trees. Don said that he would deliver the Willow Oaks to the planting site in his pick-up truck. His was the third straight nursery on this trip to deliver the five trees to the site. His thoughtfulness was appreciated.

After lunch we leisurely made our way downtown to City Hall for a 2:30PM appointment. Meeting us was the Mayor of Jackson, Charles Farmer, along with Linda Butler, Director of the Convention and Visitors Bureau, Kathleen Singleton, City Beautification Director and Gene Browl. Joyce had communicated with them many times and they were completely prepared for our visit. They eagerly examined the scrapbook accounts of previous plantings. This time Joyce had brought along the big scrapbook since we had two strapping sons to heft it around.

The Mayor couldn't attend the planting ceremony but he did sign a Proclamation, along with J. Alex Leech, Mayor of the County of Madison commemorating June 8, 1994, as *'Jackson Family Day."* Mayor Leech presented us with the Proclamation at the planting site in Highland Park, the oldest park in this city of 60,000 people.

Kathleen led us out to the park where a group of people were waiting for us, many of them wearing red blazers. The six-foot trees were in the care of Gary LeForgee, Superintendent of Groundskeeping and Landscaping, whose crew had already excavated the holes. He pointed out that three of them would be placed along the main path through the park while the other two would be along the perimeter road. The willow oak that Don Bailey had chosen is a shade tree, native to the south, which will grow to over sixty feet in height. Its leaves are long like a willow while the branches and trunk are more like the typical oak tree even to the extent of its acorns. It was the only time that we used this type of tree on our project and it was perfect for placement in this park.

Gary motioned for us to go down the path towards the adjoining school grounds to begin the actual planting, as the whole entourage began to follow along. There was Mayor Leech, Kathleen, the four Jacksons and some interested park visitors but the most conspicuous were the twenty members of the Chamber of Commerce decked out in their red blazers. The gathering can only be described as festive. Everyone had big smiles on their faces and truly treated us as visiting dignitaries. They cheered after prevailing upon John and Joyce to make speeches explaining our project and again after the Mayor gave us the proclamation. They lingered even after the planting was done, asking more questions and making sure that we received the warmest of welcomes. All of this occurred in the middle of a workday afternoon involving people prominent in their large city. We consider it as one of the best receptions accorded us during the entire ten-year project.

The Jackson Sun sent reporter Delores Ballard and photographer Larry Atherton to cover the event for the newspaper. Their article appeared on the front page of the June 9, 1994, edition extending over five columns of the lower half of the page. The headline read *"Adventuresome pair gives new meaning to 'family tree."* The newspaper even ran a separate box on page 5A detailing the name of every location named Jackson in all fifty states, some of which we weren't even aware of ourselves.

With all the pageantry, the planting went at a slower pace than usual. Rob and Steve did their best to remain focused on the placement of the trees but dropped off occasionally to join in the festivities and photo shoots. Joyce and John also joined in, moving dirt around with their trusty, collapsible shovels and generally trying to live up to everyone's expectations of being expert tree planters. It all came to a peak with the last tree which happened to be the 100th tree that we had planted in the project. When we announced that, the cheering started all over again and a lady came over to give Joyce one of the pins off her blazer.

We had a wonderful time in Jackson, TN. The people couldn't have been nicer to us. It was like leaving old friends when we finally drove out the gate of the park, looking back as long as we could at a place that was to hold special memories of smiles and red coats.

The people of Jackson were on our minds in January, 1999, and May, 2003, when major tornadoes hit the city taking nineteen lives. Seeing the television and newspaper reports struck us even more profoundly than when we had observed the aftermath of such storms at the nursery outside of Jackson, LA. Mayor Farmer was still the mayor during these times which personalized the tragedies even more for us thinking about him and all the other people whose lives had crossed with ours a few years earlier. We prayed for the folks of Jackson, TN, and sent a donation to their recovery fund.

John, Steve (standing on the ball of the tree) and Rob Jackson are waiting to plant the large **Red Oak** in Jackson City Park. This was one of five trees planted that day.

Jackson, Missouri

Missouri

"Oldest community named Jackson"

June 9, 1994

The Mississippi River takes its name from the Ojibwe Indian word *misi-ziibi* meaning "Great River." Crossing it is always something special for those of us who don't get that experience very often. We encountered it at the Caruthersville Bridge on I-155, about half-way into our three-hour drive from Jackson, TN. The width of the river is imposing and can be even more so at certain times of the year when the levees do all they can to contain the flow. It's hard to span that mighty river without thinking about its significance in our history, of the French explorers Joliet, Marquette and LaSalle, of Huckleberry Finn and Mark Twain, of its role in the Civil War, especially at places like Vicksburg, of sternwheeler steamboats from a by-gone era and the modern-day barge commerce of today.

Our crossing took place between Tennessee and the boot-heel portion of Missouri on which it borders. We continued up the western bank opposite the border with Kentucky eventually passing across from the area of the famous river town of Cairo, on the Illinois bank where the Ohio River surrenders its flow into the Mississippi.

Jackson, Missouri, is seven miles inland from Cape Girardeau, MO, where we paused at the downtown riverfront to get a closer look at Old Man River. There's no greater testimony to its power than the concrete flood wall that separates the town from the river. The wall was completed in 1964 after eight years of construction. Before the wall was built, stores and homes were inundated by the overflowing river every several years or so. The flood wall contains markers depicting record high water marks. The record was recorded on August 8, 1993, less than a year before our visit, when the river crested at 48.49 feet, nearly seventeen feet above flood stage.

On the way to the hotel in Jackson we passed by another landmark in Cape Girardeau -- the law offices of Limbaugh, Russell, Payne and Howard. This is the firm started by the grandfather of Rush Limbaugh, the noted conservative radio commentator.

About 12,000 people live in Jackson. Its civic pride is evidenced in tidy neighborhoods and in its slogan, *"What America is meant to be."* The city claims to be the oldest place in the country named after Andrew Jackson. They date that occurrence to 1814 which demonstrates some degree of prescience on the part of the city's founding fathers since Andrew Jackson didn't become really famous to the rest of the U.S. until after the Battle of New Orleans in January, 1815. Before then he was mostly engaged in fighting the Creek Indians in the southeastern United States. His leadership in defeating the Indians resulted in promotion to the rank of Major General in 1814 and assignment to lead U.S. forces against the British in Louisiana. The earliest other date that we uncovered for naming a community in his honor occurred in Jackson, Louisiana in 1815.

On the morning of June 9, 1994, we stopped for breakfast before going to City Hall for our pre-arranged meeting with the mayor. As we entered the restaurant parking lot a lady pulled up alongside our van and shouted across to us: *"You must be the Jacksons. I'm Theresa Popp."* She happened to be the wife of Steven Popp (pronounced Pope), the Park Board President with whom the mayor had consulted regarding our project. So the word was spreading around town that the Jacksons had arrived. Even when we stopped at the post office to have them hand-postmark a post card for us, the attendant said *"You must be the Jacksons."* We were getting off to a pretty good start.

At City Hall we met Mary Lawry who had been the first person Joyce talked with in setting up our visit. She led us into Mayor Paul W. Sander's office for introductions and then escorted us out to Jackson City Park for the tree planting. We were met there by Mayor Sander, Max Prill, Jackson Park Board Chairman, and city employees Mark Statler and Jerry Morton. Through prior discussions we were aware that the city was going to obtain the trees from Franke's Nursery, at no cost to us, but when we actually saw them our jaws dropped. In the collection of red oak and pin oak was one tree over twenty feet in height. This far surpassed our expectations and also had the distinction of being the largest tree ever planted during our whole project.

The workmen had to transport the tree to the site with a front-end loader. One of our pictures shows Steven standing up on the ball of the tree before it was put into the ground. The holes were already excavated at the site near the band shell but we only noticed three of them. The officials explained that they weren't sure where to plant the other two but gave us assurances that those would also be somewhere in the park. While Mark and Jerry were dealing with the big tree, Mayor Sander took us back to his office for a ceremony. He gave us some mementoes of Jackson and we showed our scrapbook to him and David Bloom, newspaper reporter from *The Cash-Book Journal*. By the time that we returned to the site, the workmen had just finished up with the big tree and were starting in on the other two. The other trees weren't any slouches as far as height either, at about eight or nine feet tall.

The four members of our family joined in with the planting chores wherever we could, offering advice to the workmen how to position each tree, backfilling the holes with our trenching tools and lugging water in five-gallon pails from the nearby pavilion. The activities attracted some other park visitors who may have heard that the Jacksons were in town. Everyone stayed around until the last tree was in the ground and all the tools packed away. The work of planting three trees took about an hour to complete, with all the assistance provided by the town work crew. One by one we thanked everyone who had made this day possible. The newspaper took photographs, the townspeople departed and we were left with the thoughts of a very successful visit to the City of Jackson, Missouri.

The newspaper article appeared on the front page of the June 15, 1994, edition of *The Cash-Book Journal,* over most of the bottom of the page, accompanied with a photograph taken at the conclusion of the planting. It's one of our favorite pictures because it shows us with our sons, Steve and Rob, leaning on a shovel, along with the two city officials and the two workmen. That sort of represents all of the types of people connected to the Jackson Legacy tree project.

We've always avoided singling out any community over another one. Without exception, every place we visited in all fifty states had its own particular memories for us. It's only natural that some will stand out above the others in some respect or another. By that measure, we consider Jackson, Missouri, as one of the best with regard to the quality of the overall reception accorded us. We'll remember the big tree, the warmness of the town officials and the atmosphere that emanated from the town, best described by Joyce as an All-American City.

We'll also remember these other sites around Jackson:

- Theresa Popp's Whistle Stop Café – a converted Railway Express Depot where she served us a lunch of corn chowder with kielbasa in a "50's" décor complete with a life-size cutout of James Dean.

- Brookside Veterans Memorial – a striking tribute to servicemen who fought and died in all of our wars from the Revolution to Desert Storm. The words of "Taps" are engraved in stone and they echo over the years

- Trail of Tears State Park – located at the site where nine of thirteen groups of Cherokee Indians crossed the Mississippi River in the harsh winter conditions of 1838-39, resulting in numerous deaths from exposure. Their sad trek was part of the forced displacement of eastern Indian tribes resulting from the administrative policies of President Andrew Jackson, whose other exploits are so often immortalized in the naming of communities in his honor.

Steve, John and Rob Jackson along with the reception committee pause for a strategic meeting on planting ideas for the new **Tulip Poplar** to be planted on the court house lawn in the county seat. Four other trees were planted around the corner.

Brownstown, Jackson County, Indiana

Indiana

"Land of Indians"

June 10, 1994

The final stop on the five-state tour for 1994 was in Jackson County, Indiana, at the county seat of Brownstown. This choice of site resulted from the application of our selection criteria in the following order of preference: 1) community named Jackson; 2) county seat in a county named Jackson; 3) community name containing some derivative of Jackson, such as Jacksonville, Mt. Jackson, etc.; or, 4) place name matching one of the first names of the five family members. Indiana marked the first time that we opted for a county named Jackson after failing to uncover any community named Jackson within the state.

It was a six-hour drive from the previous planting site in Missouri making for a lot of void to fill along the way. The four of us passed the time by alternately driving, listening to the Walkman, reading and conversing. But the most endearing memory of the drive that stays with us is the singing of *"Happy Birthday"* to Joyce. It wasn't the usual version of the song that everyone knows. Somewhere in the recesses of John's mind loomed a version from the Happy Days era that was probably a composite of Pat Boone crooning with a subtle dose of doo-wop. It's impossible to re-create the musical effect on paper but this is the best we can do: the verse was based around the words "Happy, Happy Birthday Baba" repeated five times with varying inflections and flourishes and concluding with a four-bar hold on the final syllable, administered by three baritone voices ranging in timbre from monotone to apoplexy. Anyway, we liked it.

Discoveries occurred to us in the writing of this book that were never a part of our planning or experiences at the time of doing the actual project. The principal discovery of this nature is the emergence of Native-American themes within the scope of our travels. During the course of the adventures our minds were focused on the name Jackson and everything involved with getting to and from the places connected to our family name. Not until writing the chronicle of these pursuits did other aspects come into view such as the impact that a powerful man named Jackson had on the welfare of the Indian people. That raised our sensitivity and awareness in ways that we hadn't contemplated before. We decided to include some of these references in recognition of the inescapable fact that each one of the fifty states has some history connected to native peoples. Oftentimes the past is unpleasant with respect to our government's conduct but it is not our intention to enter into any controversies. But neither do we want to ignore relevant connections as we encounter them in the telling of our story. Each of the fifty states we visited has a unique history behind their existence and we wanted to include a little associated background regarding each place. In the process we discovered that half of all states derived the name of their state from a word of Indian origin. In the case of Indiana, it was literally derived from the phrase *"land of Indians."*

The Indiana Territory was part of the Northwest Territory until it was separated out by Congress in 1800. The government had evicted most eastern tribes to the fringes of the frontier where the indigenous people already in those areas had to allow the assimilation or contest it in battle. Our government didn't stop there in keeping the Indians on the move. General William Henry Harrison was a typical example. As first governor of the Indiana Territory, he negotiated treaties during 1803 and 1804 with the Wabash, Kaskaskia, Sauk and Fox tribes which appropriated over 60 million acres of their land. Similar arrangements were worked out with the Miamis, Delaware and Shawnee people living in adjacent areas. All of them were promised hunting, fishing and other rights which were largely ignored by the ever-encroaching white settlers and the government. Through the Indian Removal Act of 1830 , all Indians were basically expelled to lands west of the Mississippi River by 1840, leaving the Americans to their peaceful enjoyment of the eastern half of the United States. Of course, the story doesn't end there, either, but we'll refer to those episodes later in the book.

Jackson County, Indiana, was created on January 1, 1816, as the fourteenth county in the Indiana Territory. It was named in honor of Andrew Jackson. Brownstown was appointed as the county seat in April, 1816, and remains so today. The land for the Jackson County Courthouse, which rests in the heart of Brownstown, was donated by Col. John Ketcham for this specific function. It was on these grounds that we would plant a tree on June 10, 1994. Also on the grounds is a plaque dedicated to Col. Ketcham which describes him as a fearless pioneer, Ranger, surveyor and public servant. The state of Indiana was admitted to the Union on December 11, 1816, as the nineteenth state.

Brownstown is in the south central part of the state about 60 miles north of Louisville, KY. We passed through some hilly, forested land on the way there. Many people picture all Midwestern states as flat prairie land but there are portions like southern Indiana that rival any place for scenic beauty. As tree people, we like to bring that form of beauty to every place we visit, whatever the existing nature of their surrounding countryside, based on the theory that you can never have enough trees.

Our contact in Brownstown, Robert Bane, President of the Chamber of Commerce, was very enthusiastic about our tree planting visit. One of the trees would replace a tree blown over in a tornado on the grounds of the Courthouse while the other four were destined to grace the grounds of the County juvenile detention center a few blocks away. Joyce had been directed to the Chamber of Commerce as a result of her original contact with City Clerk, Pat Forgey, who forwarded our request to Bob Millman, President of Town Council. It was Chamber of Commerce member Judy Gilbert who met us on the morning of June 10, 1994, to escort us to the Courthouse.

Judy said we should be very thankful to Margie Strange of the Schneider Nursery for providing us with such large trees at our budgeted price of $50. The tulip poplar selected for the Courthouse grounds was eleven feet in height while the two red oaks and two Indian Summer crab apples were between six and seven feet tall. The trees were waiting for us at the sites. That kept our record perfect -- we never had to use the rental van to transport any trees on the entire trip.

A small reception committee turned out at the Courthouse led by Bob Bane, his wife Melissa and their infant toddler. There was also local horticulturist Bob Meyers, reporter Marcia Walker from *The Jackson County Banner*, some interested townspeople and an 86-year old gentleman named Junior who provided us with all the mulch, free of charge.

Our boys, Steve and Rob, did most of the digging at both sites. Bob Meyers informed us about the particulars of the local soil and exchanged planting tips with Joyce who, by this stage of the project, had established her own approach on that subject. We all contributed to the work of digging into the fairly-hard soil, putting a mixture of mulch and nutrients into the holes and then inserting the tree. As usual Joyce and John took it from there. Our participation at this stage gave us that care-giving feeling as we made sure that the tree was straight, tamped the earth around its base to remove air bubbles, formed a dike by molding the dirt with our hands and trenching tool and then carrying life-sustaining water to our little creation. We wanted to invest as much of ourselves as we could in helping to provide this living gift with a good start in life.

Someone from the town had placed markers where they wanted the trees to be planted at the Juvenile detention site. They were placed in a straight line about twenty-five feet apart. These four trees represented our three children and one of their parents. We're not sure which parent's tree got to symbolically stand guard at the Courthouse but a likely candidate would be Joyce in recognition of her pioneering effort in devising the whole project.

The Jackson County Banner published a photograph of the four of us at the top of page 8 in the June 16, 1994 edition with the caption "*A Tree For All Jacksons.*" It showed us planting the tulip poplar at the Jackson County courthouse, supplied by Schneider's Nursery, and mentioned some of the background behind our venture using the word "*legacy*" which we always feel is the best way to characterize what we've done.

After leaving Jackson County we drove to Indianapolis to do something which we've always wanted to do – drive around the track of the Indianapolis Speedway. Someone else did the driving in a mini-tour bus but the thrill of the brickyard was still there. The Memorial Day 500 mile race has always been a part of our lives, especially when it was actually held on May 30th holding the attention of all who attended our traditional Memorial Day family picnic.

Then it was time to return to Columbus, OH, say goodbye to the family and return home. It was a wonderful trip, beginning with the whole family at the first planting site in Ohio and continuing with the two boys for the rest of the 1,400 mile journey. We hope you enjoyed hearing about it as much as we enjoyed the company of each other during the quality time we spent together.

The firemen at this firehouse were instrumental in helping us locate our planting site and gave a great rendition of the Hope-Jackson area.

The five **Bradford Pears** trees stand out among the beautiful landscape of the New England fall season.

Jackson, Rhode Island

Rhode Island

"Autumn in New England"

The next time out to do our planting was timed to occur during the fall foliage season. What better time to be traipsing around New England than when the trees are adorned in their magical mantles of red, yellow, orange and other hues. It was also a recommended season of the year for planting according to those who know such things, like our nurseryman Tony Cerbo.

Tony chose five Bradford pears and five white pines for us. Joyce had already been told by her Rhode Island contact that they didn't want pine trees, so we packed them along to plant in Connecticut. Tony had also suggested sweet gum trees but they were eleven feet tall and not a good fit for our Mercury Grand Marquis. The ten trees we took were all six to seven feet in height and it was enough of a challenge to coax them into the trunk.

We cleared our calendars for the first part of the week by Joyce taking Sunday and Tuesday off from her country club job, in addition to Monday when the club was closed anyway, and by John using two vacation days. That was enough time to circumnavigate the states involved in the round trip of 450 miles from our home in Madison, even with a couple of side trips thrown in.

On the way to Rhode Island we enjoyed the changing leaves along with a stop at Mystic Seaport, CT. We also stopped to visit our niece, Carrie Cummins, who was a student at the Johnson and Wales culinary school in Providence, RI. That night's dinner consisted of dishes prepared by fledgling chefs. We were happy to act as guinea pigs in the interest of advancing their education.

That night at the hotel outside of Providence, we called Richard Iverson of the Scituate, Rhode Island Department of Public Works who had been working with Joyce on the arrangements. He gave us directions to the site at the Hope Memorial Park and we went out to locate it after letting the trees out of the car to breathe. Even with the directions provided, it still took stopping at the Hope-Jackson Fire House to get things clear in our minds. The firemen listened intently as we explained our reason for being in the area. Then they gave us some shoulder patches and directed us to the bell that had been taken from the Old Jackson Mill when it closed in 1938 after 118 years of operation.

Similar to our experience in the other New England states, the intended planting site in Jackson was considered a part of the larger Town of Scituate. In our view, the town structures in New England are similar to the township structures that prevail in other parts of the U.S. The Town of Scituate is comprised of Scituate and many other villages including Jackson and the surrounding villages of Fiskville, Hope, Arkwright and North Scituate. Joyce discovered this in the course of making calls to the Town of West Warwick because in looking on the map it appeared that Jackson was closer to their town than Scituate. They redirected us to Scituate municipal authorities who assigned Richard Iverson and John Winward of the Highway Department to our project.

The village of Jackson takes its name from a cotton mill owned by Charles Jackson which operated along the Pawtuxet River at the start of the 19th Century. As evidenced by the bell near the fire house, the mill is no longer there but the surrounding area is still known by the name of Jackson.

Monday, October 17, 1994, was a typical fall day with the varied-colored leaves reflecting the bright sunshine and a cool crispness in the air as we arrived for our early-morning planting. Richard Iverson was waiting for us. He pointed out the area alongside the basketball courts where they wanted the trees placed in a straight line about twenty feet apart. One look at the hard-packed soil indicated that it wasn't going to be easy digging. However, Richard began helping us and was shortly joined by John Winward. The press was also there in the person of reporter, Joe Hutnak, and photographer, Tim O'Hara of *The Daily Times of West Warwick.* They didn't have time to look through our scrapbook but had a copy of our press release with them and took some pictures before they had to hurry off.

The rest of us continued with the work of chipping out the holes and putting the Bradford Pear trees into them. The main challenge to their survival would be water. The ground was very dry and it didn't look like any water sources were nearby but John Winward promised to look after the trees after we were gone. It was a source of concern for us wherever we went. The trees always looked so sturdy when we had them planted and the people in attendance always vowed to keep them that way but it would be unrealistic to think that everyone fulfilled those promises without fail. All we could do was give them the best possible start in life. For that reason, we were careful to mix in some fertilizer, build little earthen dams around the base and fill them to overflowing with water as much to impress the observers as to thoroughly soak the roots at the outset. As a final step, we encased the trunks with plastic sleeves to protect them from weed whackers and gnawing critters.

The Bradford Pear blossoms would be the first touch of color in the spring, if all went well. That prospect contrasted with the vivid fall colors that existed throughout the park at this particular time of year. The town must have wanted to add more color to the surroundings as they were very insistent that we not offer them pine trees for planting.

The men had other duties to get to so they thanked us for coming and packed their tools away at the conclusion of the planting. The two of us waved goodbye then turned to make our own dedication in private. Each tree was named for one of our family members and we gave thanks to God for giving us such a wonderful family, for inspiring us to do this project and for keeping us safe as we made our way over the highways and byways to this and all other destinations. Then we got in the car after saying a few words of encouragement to the pine trees in the trunk.

The article in *The Daily Times* appeared in the next day's edition. It was our standard approach to ask the reporter to mail us a copy of the newspaper and offer to pay the costs involved. Most publications honored our request but there are a few that didn't which is one reason why we don't have a newspaper account for each placed visited.

In this case, *The Daily Times* of West Warwick, RI came up with one of our favorite headlines describing the essence of what we were doing: "*Jacksons put down roots – everywhere."* The lead sentence stated *"Ask Joyce and John Jackson what's in a name, and they'll likely tell you about 30,000 miles."* At that point we were approaching the half-way point of the Jackson Legacy with no real way to calculate what the total project miles would eventually turn out to be. We'll have that final tally for you by the end of the book.

The hundred acre site donated by the Late Charles H. Arnold is to be used as a park, picnic areas and hiking trails and will be home to our donated five **White Pines** trees.

Robertsville, Connecticut

Connecticut

"The Lure of Litchfield Hills"

The one hundred mile drive to the next destination of Robertsville, Connecticut, was almost entirely over two-lane roads traversing dense forests. The scenery was postcard-perfect causing us to stop many times to capture the fall foliage in photos. We were headed for the northwestern corner of the state near the Massachusetts border. One piece of local literature described our destination as follows: *"In the Litchfield Hills, foothills of the Berkshires; a gentle landscape of rolling fields and woods, lakes and streams, picturesque villages with white-steepled churches and hilltop farms."*

It's understandable if that description puts one in mind of a Currier & Ives print or a Norman Rockwell painting. In fact, Rockwell's studio in Stockbridge, Massachusetts, was only thirty-eight miles away from our planting site in Robertsville, Connecticut.

Connecticut is one of those ten states where there's no community connected to the name of Jackson. Neither did it have any other place that fit our site-selection naming criteria. The closest that we could find was the village of Robertsville, which is part of the Town of Colebrook. As with Massachusetts, we had to do some massaging to fit the name Roberts into our protocol. Think of it as the possessive case of our son Robert's name or consider that John's maternal great-grandmother's name was Roberts. The important thing was that we had found a suitable place where we could continue the quest.

By four o'clock in the afternoon we were in Winsted, CT, only a few miles from Robertsville and Colebrook. We decided to look up John Fitts who is the local correspondent for *The Register Citizen,* serving Litchfield County. John couldn't locate the press release that we sent in advance but he did interview us for a half hour and promised to come out to the site the next morning. Apparently he had been in contact with the town officials to determine that the planting site was going to be at the Charles Arnold Recreation Area. He was also able to give us directions to the place.

We stayed overnight at the Old Riverton Inn, removing the five white pine trees from their confinement in the trunk of the car. Joyce called Selectman George Wilbur who assured us that all was in readiness for the planting event and he would meet us at the hotel the following morning to lead us over.

George met us at the hotel on the morning of October 18, 1994. He explained that our plantings would be the first new entries onto a 100-acre site donated by Charles H. Arnold, a prominent citizen who had bequeathed the property to the town fifteen years earlier. That caused us a little unexpressed concern in wondering why it had taken them that long to start developing the property. These concerns elevated a little more when we drove up to the place where a lot of people had gathered. There was nothing else there except a granite monument with Mr. Arnold's name

119

on it. We had to visualize the hiking trails, picnic areas and other park accommodations that were planned for the future. As it turned out, those worries proved to be unfounded.

Selectman Wilbur and fellow Selectman Ralph Hazen were very pleasant and interested in what we were doing. They had enlisted some other gentlemen to help with the planting, including Bud Tice and Robert Rice from Eno Hill. Also in attendance was John Fitts from the newspaper. One person who was not there was Joyce Nelson, Colebrook Town Clerk, with whom Joyce had made the initial contact. She had referred us to the Selectman.

Before proceeding with the planting they provided some history of the area. Robertsville had been a separate town with its own post office from the 1840's to 1915 at which time it was included within the Town of Colebrook. The Roberts family, for which Robertsville was named, was part of the chair-making industry notable to this section of New England. Another member of the family, Clark Roberts, had been the postmaster. This region of Connecticut was the last to be settled, in 1765, and has largely remained at the same population level since the early 19th century. They remarked that the population of Colebrook in 1980 was identical to what it was in 1820, and implications were made that they like it that way.

The ground was very rich and pliable, not requiring any of the peat moss that we had purchased at the start of the drive over. The planting site was in a large open space where they arranged the white pines in a wide circle. We began to think that they had planned all of this in advance. Mr. Hazen stated *"I thought perhaps this recreation area was the best. This is one of the finest pieces of property here in Robertsville."* Mr. Wilbur also remarked *"It should help make this area a little more pleasant."* Some of these qualities started to emerge in our minds as we took more notice of the woods bordering the site and the vista that presented itself out over the valley we had overlooked initially. There we saw a large body of water with mist rising in front of the multi-colored trees lining the shore. This was going to be a nice spot after all.

Within the customary one-hour's time the work was done and everyone standing around to admire what they had wrought. The two of us had played an active part in digging the holes and all the other aspects of planting. The scrapbook remained handy for viewing by everyone with Joyce answering all of their questions. Joyce's quote appeared in the article published the following day, *"It's a great feeling after you've planted the trees to know you're in every state."* And it was a great feeling to know that we were almost at the half-way point of our project.

The last half of 1994 brought some more national recognition our way. The National Arbor Day Foundation in Lincoln, NE, became aware of the Jackson Legacy, perhaps as a result of the Arbor Day award we received from the Borough of Madison, NJ, in May. They ran an article on us entitled *"Move Over Johnny Appleseed."* in the July / August edition of their *Arbor Day* publication. The opening line of the story stated that *"The legendary tree planter now has competition from a New Jersey family with a most unusual – and beneficial – hobby, (they've) found a great way to commemorate their family, make friends nationwide, and have a lot of fun traveling for a good cause."* Then, on November 30, 1994, the Arbor Day Foundation awarded us a *"Certificate of Merit"* in recognition of your efforts on behalf of trees and environmental stewardship."* The words used in their two acknowledgements aptly sum up the purposes that we had outlined for the Legacy from the start. It was very gratifying to receive this kind of feedback from a nationally-recognized organization.

A feature story put together by free-lance author Cheryl Baisden appeared in the November / December, 1994, issue of *American Forests* magazine. She accurately summarized the reasons behind the project and our planting activities through 1993, ending with the trip to Alaska. A few years after the completion of the project in 2000, the magazine ran another story to update readers on all the adventures that had transpired since the original article.

By the end of 1994, the sites visited totaled 25 and the number of trees planted was 121. We looked forward to spending the winter researching the next year's activities because we had discovered, by this time, that a good deal of the fun was actually in the planning.

John and Joyce Jackson stand by one of five **Flowering Crabapple** trees that they planted on the grounds of the Jackson County Junior Fair grounds.

Cottageville, Jackson County, WV

West Virginia

"Country Roads"

Sometimes the process for selecting states was similar to completing a giant jig-saw puzzle. Each year it was a matter of matching up states into sequences that connected to the other places already visited while also trying to visualize the combinations that would be compatible for future annual trips. With twenty-four states visited in four years, we were ahead of the five-states-per year pace, giving us a little comfort zone in the event of something unexpected happening. Planning five more states for the year of 1995 extended this reasoned approach. The journey for that year would be comprised of one four-state junket through the heart of Civil War territory with one state added as part of the trip to attend our son Steven's wedding.

The best possible itineraries were those where we could combine the tree planting with other reasons for traveling, such as visiting family or friends, sight-seeing, business or other purposes. Once again this year, a starting point of Columbus, OH, would allow us to see our daughter's family and also to attend the wedding of our friends' daughter. From there it was only a drive of 150 miles through the Appalachian foothills to a location in the state of West Virginia that fit into our program.

No singular place named Jackson was available in the state but there is a Jackson County. The County was established on March 1, 1831, as part of the Commonwealth of Virginia. It was named in honor of Andrew Jackson who was serving as President of the United States at the time.

 The area in and around Jackson County has connections to both the Revolutionary and Civil Wars. The battle at nearby Point Pleasant, occurring in October, 1774, was recognized by the U.S. Congress in 1908 and a monument erected at the site. Some believe, inaccurately, that it was the first engagement of the Revolutionary War. This was during the time when the Indians supported the British with the expectation that their eventual triumph would lead to permanent recognition of territorial rights. The Shawnees were then the predominant tribe residing in the region. Their famous Chief Cornstalk was elected to head the Algonquin Confederation of seven tribes including the Shawnee, Delaware and Mingo. Unfortunately for them, the Americans prevailed in the battle. Three years later, Chief Cornstalk was murdered by soldiers at the fort where he had been detained for peace negotiations. Subsequent military operations, such as Fallen Timbers, OH, in 1794, accelerated the spread of frontier settlement that was never again curtailed. The Shawnee were later dispersed to the Oklahoma Indian Territory. Today, there are no Indian tribes recognized by the Federal government as living in the state of West Virginia.

Jackson County borders on the Ohio River. Confederate General John Hunt Morgan and his raiders were repulsed at the Battle of Buffington Island in July, 1863, across the river from Ravenswood, WV. It was the only significant campaign of the Civil War occurring within the state of

Ohio. West Virginia had just been established as a state the previous month having been separated out of the state of Virginia. Fifteen Civil War battles would be fought in what is now West Virginia, including the Battle of Harper's Ferry where Colonel Thomas Jonathan "Stonewall" Jackson first gained his reputation. As a result of the creation of West Virginia out of Virginia, both Harper's Ferry and Jackson's birthplace of Clarksburg became part of West Virginia. However, it never fully assimilated into the Union sphere of influence during the War.

Joyce wrote to Mayor Willa McGinley at the county seat of Ripley on March 29, 1995, describing our project and asking permission to plant locally. She referred our request to County Commissioner, Donald G. Stephens, who accepted the request. With his help, a number of people were enlisted including Mayor McGinley, Mayor John Alderson of nearby Ravenswood, representatives from the West Virginia University – Jackson County Extension Office and others. The visit was set for Monday, May 8, 1995, at the Jackson County Fairgrounds in Cottageville, eight miles from Ripley.

Before going out to the site on Monday morning, we had to stop at the Ripley Florist & Garden Center to complete arrangements for the trees. Theresa McComas, owner of the garden center, had kindly agreed to provide us with trees that were worth much more than our $50 budget. But those trees were still in the ground when we got there. Her father, James Kelly, scrambled to come up with five other trees ready for immediate transportation which turned out to be Flowering Crabapples, each about seven feet in height. We stuffed them into the trunk of our son-in-law's borrowed Ford Taurus and hurried out to the Fairgrounds.

The reception committee was waiting for us in force. There were Mayors McGinley and Alderson, Patty Morrison, Jackson County Extension Agent, Linda and Richard Waybright from the University, Suzy McGinley, Reference Librarian, Brian Murrey, Maintenance, Pat Stapleton, reporter from *The Jackson Star News* and Lois McCann reporter from *The Jackson Herald*, an affiliated publication. Commissioner Donald Stephens had to leave just before we arrived. James Kelly had also come over to the Fairgrounds where he and Brian Murrey started digging the holes.

There weren't many other trees in the surrounding area. They wanted to place three of the trees in the Recreational Vehicle parking lot and two on the bank near the parking lot. The facilities are used for many events, most frequently by a gospel group who, we were told, would be very pleased with our plantings. The soil in the parking lot was fairly workable but the bank was hard-packed, as if all of the rocks graded off the road surface had been piled there. The men were able to get one tree planted on the bank but then decided to add the remaining one to the others in the parking lot. With all of the digging, accompanied by Brian Murrey's running dialogue, it took us nearly two hours to finish the work. John did most of the heavy work contributed by the Jacksons, reshaping the roughed-out holes and making sure everyone followed Joyce's directions. Mrs. Jackson was also able to handle some of the final planting work, like smoothing off the topsoil around the trunks, when not showing off the scrapbook and talking about the project to the group.

There was plenty of time to show the scrapbook and for the reporters to ask their questions. This resulted in a nice story published in *The Jackson Star News* in the May 17, 1995, edition on page

B4. It contained a photograph of us accompanied by the mayors and the extension representatives together with an account summarizing the day's activities. Exactly five years later, the same newspaper reported on the conclusion of the 50-state project in their May 17, 2000 edition; this time it appeared on the front page above the fold.

It was a very nice turnout by our new friends in Jackson County, WV. Commissioner Stephens sent us a letter the following month thanking us for the trees and wishing us success in the remainder of the venture. He was our most important supporter in this community and, unfortunately, we never got to meet him in person.

After everything had been taken care of, we drove back to Columbus, OH, to return the car and prepare for the next morning's flight to Richmond, VA, to attend to the next state's planting.

Overleaf: A montage of signs identifying places named Jackson and the first names of the Jackson family members (5) represents all fifty states where the trees were planted.

JACKSON M.T.

Jackson
COUNTY LINE

ENTERING
JACKSONVILLE
POPULATION
2190
HISTORIC DISTRICT

Jackson Junction

JACKSONPORT
POP. 264

VILLAGE OF
JACKSON

JACKSON ST

JACKSON PL
KRUKOWSKI

Welcome to
MT. JACKSON
THE HEART OF THE
SHENANDOAH VALLEY

WELCOME
JACKSON
CITY LIMITS
OBSERVE SPEED LIMIT AS POSTED
TREE CITY USA
A
Public
Power
Community

126

With the town's people looking on including Dixie Harrell and Jim Gossip, John and Joyce Jackson supervise the last part of planting the **Crape Myrtle** tree on the Northampton Memorial Library's front lawn. Four other trees were planted elsewhere on the grounds.

Jackson, North Carolina.

North Carolina

"Southern Hospitality"

Perhaps we've been overly influenced by tales like *"Gone With The* Wind" but they have left many of us with mental images of a certain style of life unique to the old South: of sophisticated, genteel people living in towns stretching from Virginia through the Carolinas and into Georgia, holding on to their heritage, proud to be who they are; of demure ladies with lilting accents and gentlemen of honor beyond reproach. Joyce's contact in Jackson, North Carolina, Dixie Harrell, was the living embodiment of these impressions. Her reaction to our request to visit her town was so effusive and her interest in meeting us so genuine that we looked forward to our visit with heightened anticipation. And we were not disappointed.

Before going there, we spent a day touring Richmond, Virginia. That certainly did a lot to immerse us in the regional culture, especially at the Museum of the Confederacy and the Confederate White House. You don't have to be a Civil War buff to be impressed by the knowledge gained at these places. It's an emotional experience that adds to your perspective in ways that only seeing it can do. You also don't have to be a moralist to understand the people's point of view and to sense some appreciation for their pain. If it wasn't all so tragic it would be an epic tale worthy of the ages.

The people of the south no longer cling to these times but there is plenty evidence left around to make their own statements. There are statues of generals, street names, preserved mansions with beautiful English gardens, like Agecroft Hall, the capitol building and the understated elegance of a place so important in our history. A place from which sprang many of our founding fathers and first Presidents, whose contributions continue to benefit us all as Americans. We came away from Richmond much richer for the experience.

Jackson is in the Coastal Plain section of northeastern North Carolina, an easy ninety-mile drive south of Richmond, with only a few miles on roads other than Interstate I-95. We rented one of our favorite cars, a Pontiac Bonneville, which we would use for the rest of the week and then turn in at Newark airport in New Jersey. The car is big enough to carry five trees but, as it turned out, we never had to pack any saplings into it because all three of the communities provided the trees for our visit.

Detailed plans regarding the nature of each reception were seldom known to us in advance. We always felt some uncertainty on the way to a site but this time it was magnified by the fact that this was our fourth day away from home and we had only planted five trees. It made us feel like we weren't making much progress.

Joyce called Dixie Harrell as soon as we settled into The Hampton Inn in Roanoke Rapids, NC. As the town's Revitalization Committee Chairman, Dixie seemed very excited that the Jacksons had finally arrived after months of anticipation. Her attitude buoyed our spirits for what lay ahead. Following her directions, we went into Jackson to inspect the planting site at the North-ampton Memorial Library. It's on the main street of the town not far from the stately County Courthouse. Jackson only has a population near seven hundred but it's the county seat of North-ampton County with enough air of importance to convey that image. The holes for the trees had already been dug – three of them were placed prominently in the front of the building and two of them on the side. Normally, we would have liked to keep the five trees grouped together as sym-bolic of our family unity. However we quickly devised an alternative naming convention that identified with each of the planting locations. After examining other parts of town, we headed back to the hotel, pausing to buy some peat moss at the Bi-Lo Store.

Wednesday, May 10, 1995, had the air of a local holiday in Jackson, NC, or so you would have thought. Even the early morning rain had stopped, though leaving behind its heavy humidity. Dixie Harrell had invited us to a breakfast in our honor at the upscale Sir Archie's Restaurant. Walking into the building we casually said hello to the uniformed police officer who held the door only to have him join us along with about twenty other people at a long table set up near the fireplace. Besides the police chief, there was the mayor, a magistrate, an attorney or two, a whole bunch of Harrells, kids and many other people with smiling faces. Mr. Gossett, head of the local bank, made a speech formally welcoming us to the community with John and Joyce taking the floor to express their appreciation, followed by rounds of applause. The talk during the meal was filled with questions addressed to us concerning aspects of the project as well as some of our questions about the history of the area. Naturally we had to ask who Sir Archie was? In response they pointed to several framed horse sketches on the wall near the fireplace and explained that the celebrated stallion, Sir Archie, was the foundation sire for most American thoroughbred race horses, including Man O'War. He established Northampton County, NC, in the early 1800's, as the country's pre-eminent region for the raising of thoroughbred horses.

Practically the whole entourage went across the street to the Library for the planting ceremonies. If anything, the crowd swelled a bit more with the County Commissioners joining in along with library attendants and other townsfolk. We couldn't copy down all of the names but those in at-tendance included Dixie, Ken, Geneva and Steve Harrell, Jim and Judy Gossip, John McKellers, Judy Harrison, City Clerk, Margaret Barns, of the Northampton County Museum and Keith Hog-gard, News Editor for the *Northampton News*. Alongside each hole stood a seven-foot crape myrtle provided by the town from Creekside Nursery.

After waiting until the first tree was planted on the front lawn of the library, Mayor Bill Cooley stepped forward with a plaque in his hands. He read the words out loud which marked the honor of the occasion concluding with *"Their contributions to help protect, beautify, cleanse and pro-vide habitat for nature is hereby recognized."* In addition, they gave us a basket of goodies con-taining local agricultural products, tee shirts and literature about Northampton County.

The literature documented that Northampton County was established in 1741. Jackson became the name of the county seat in 1826 and was named in honor of Andrew Jackson. A new-Greek revival courthouse building was constructed in 1856 which is still in use today.

The conclusion of the Mayor's presentation seemed to convey to everyone that the festivities were over because the crowd of people quickly started to melt away. Many of them came by to shake our hands and wish us well for the future. The museum curator invited us over for a tour. Jim and Judy Gossip invited us to stay at their home the next time we visited Jackson. In no time, we were standing alone in front of the library with four more trees to plant. The breakfast reception, the speeches, and the presentation left us appreciative but also thoroughly drained as we tried to respond in kind to the intensity of the well-wishers. Joyce was a little less mobile after twisting her back in planting the first tree. With our remaining energy ,we finished off the rest of the plantings. Lucky for us that our work didn't include any digging of the holes. We were very appreciative to the townspeople's effort to making our short stay comfortable.

With all the work completed, we did our little meditation ritual assigning names to all of the trees and spiritually expressing thanks for our good fortune, especially in getting to meet such wonderful people. We walked ourselves over to the museum for a brief look and then quietly hit the road after spending a total of four and one-half hours, from breakfast to lunchtime, in this town. It was with exhausted but pleasant feelings that we pointed the Bonneville towards Mount Jackson, VA, only 227 miles away.

The *Northampton News* published an extensive report of our visit in the May 17, 1995 edition. The story covered the whole bottom of the front page with two photographs and was continued over to the next page. Keith Hoggard did a fine job in reporting on the event in words like "*They were given a warm welcome in Jackson, North Carolina last week ...their trip will not be forgotten.*" Yet nothing could have truly captured the emotions that we have towards the people we met there. The treatment they accorded us expressed everything that we could possibly expect from a community who caught the essence of what we were trying to do, to an extent that few others have.

Joyce said it best in writing a follow-up letter to the Gossips: "*We've always loved the closeness of a small town and we could feel the camaraderie filtering through the people at breakfast.*" She also captured the right phrase to describe our experience in her letter to the Harrell family when she thanked them and all the others for their "*southern hospitality.*"

John Jackson and a town employee, Randy plant one of five **Flowering Plum** trees in Mt. Jackson, VA

THERE STANDS JACKSON LIKE A STONE WALL

Lt. General Thomas Jonathan "Stonewall" Jackson. Statue at Manassas, VA

Virginia

"The Heart of the Shenandoah Valley"

May 11, 1995

Over two hundred miles of our drive to Mount Jackson were within the Commonwealth of Virginia. The most direct route for the journey was back through Richmond and then northwest towards the extreme upper corner of the state. Along the way there was ample time to notice evidence of the state's prominent involvement in the Civil War. The U.S. National Park Service recognizes 123 significant military engagements as having occurred in Virginia, far more than any other state. By comparison with the states we visited on this trip, North Carolina recorded twenty battles, West Virginia, fifteen and Maryland, seven.

Consequently, the greatest number of battlefield deaths during the War happened in Virginia. Every one of those lost lives is significant but one death, in particular, resonates above all others, both in the context of impact on the Confederacy and relevance to our family name; it was the death of the second-most famous American who bore the surname Jackson – Lt. General Thomas Jonathan "Stonewall" Jackson.

Thomas J. Jackson was born in Clarksville, VA. He was a graduate of West Point and a professor at the Virginia Military Institute in Lexington for ten years. Some of his greatest military achievements occurred in Virginia, at Harpers Ferry, in the Shenandoah Valley and at Manassas, where a fellow general spoke the words that launched his legend, *"There stands Jackson like a stone wall."* His end came at Chancellorsville, VA, mistakenly struck down by friendly fire, at a time when he was commander of Lee's Army of Northern Virginia. Many historians rank this as one of the greatest setbacks incurred by either side in the War Between the States.

Shenandoah is a mythic word in the American vernacular. Literature, music and motion pictures have imparted the vision of a verdant Appalachian valley stretching between the majestic Blue Ridge Mountains to the east and the highlands to the west. Three great rivers also define its make-up: the Shenandoah running through it, with the Potomac bounding it in the north and the James in the south. Through this valley ran The Great Warriors Trail of the Delaware and the Catawba Indians, the latter of whom, annihilated the Shendo Tribe in the late 17th Century, the tribe whose identity most attribute to the origin of the name Shenandoah.

The place now known as Mount Jackson has existed in Shenandoah County since the middle of the 18th Century. It was called Mount Pleasant until January 28, 1826, when the General Assembly of Virginia changed the name of the village in honor of General Andrew "Old Hickory" Jackson. It is believed that President Jackson stayed at the Rude House, outside of Mt. Jackson, on his way to and from his home in Tennessee. During the Valley Campaign of General "Stonewall" Jackson in 1862, which largely took place in Shenandoah County, he also used the Rude House as his headquarters. The two famous Jacksons were not related but share this one connection in their lives.

As famous as both Jacksons are, we could not locate a place or a county in Virginia by that name. It seems ironic, especially in the case of native-son Stonewall Jackson, that he has not been so-honored. We had to go to our third name-selecting criteria, which uses some derivative of the name Jackson, before deciding on Mount Jackson, a town of about 1,700 in population.

Regardless of how they got chosen, the people of Mount Jackson seemed very pleased that we selected them. That was very evident when Joyce called Judy, the City Clerk, to ask to talk to the mayor. At the time, he was tied up with a loquacious constituent but Judy said several times that it would be over in a minute or two. Finally, she passed the call along to Mayor Dewey Jordan. The mayor was very taken with the idea even to the point of enlisting his wife, Midge, to spearhead the project. There was a piece of property in need of development just across the way from the town hall and the mayor cleared all the municipal approvals relative to our visit. They even appropriated funds from the town budget for the purchase of the trees. Mayor Jordan later told us how he pitched the idea to town council in words to the effect: *"These folks are doing a great thing for the environment…maybe we can help them a little."*

Needless to say, we were excited. The excellent reception in North Carolina was still ringing in our ears and it appeared that our next stop was going to roll out the red carpet, too. Mayor Jordan reinforced that impression when he called us at the hotel to assure that everything was in order for the next day, May 11, 1995. Reporter, Jane Edder, also called from *The Shenandoah Valley-Herald* to go over our press release and to advise that she would be attending the next morning's ceremony. As is our custom, we drove into the town to scout the planting site, based upon how the mayor described it to us – on the other side of the main street, two blocks down from Town Hall, in a newly-landscaped area near the Town Pump and, along the shoulder of the street across from the Super-Save and just before the entrance to the recycling center. It wasn't too hard to figure it out because all the holes had already been dug. Things were really looking good.

 The next morning we all gathered at the Town Office / Council Chambers for the final preparations. Mayor and Mrs. Jordan were there, along with Randy, the town employee who dug the holes, Judy, the Town Clerk, another couple that the Jordans had invited, the reporter, Jane, and photographer, Steve. All of us walked to the planting site with the mayor keeping up a running dialogue that would continue for the entire time that we were together. He made sure that we had seen the sign outside of town proclaiming Mt. Jackson as *"The Heart of the Shenandoah Valley."* he told us about the many connections that the area had with the Civil War: the Valley was known as the Breadbasket of the Confederacy; the Battle of New Market was fought only seven miles away; the town was a major hospital center ministering to the wounded and how many of them are buried in the Confederate Cemetery, which is still tended with reverence, today, and, of course, about everyone's pride and joy, Stonewall Jackson.

The size of the trees was consistent with what we had come to believe was the best chance for survival – around seven feet tall. They were all standing next to the holes, courtesy of Stoney Creek Garden Center and the town council. Randy made it very clear that he would be taking care of the tree placements but we had to do our part in keeping up with the tradition of always participating in some aspect of the planting work. The only annoying part was the barrage of gnats that kept buzzing around our faces. Randy told us to hold our hats above our heads because the gnats gravitate to the highest place; Joyce was a little skeptical about that advice. A weeping cherry was planted in the newly-landscaped public park area near the town pump. The other four trees were Flowering Plums which we placed in a small stretch of land running parallel to the train tracks. Some other trees already occupied part of this area, interspersed with utility poles, which caused the plums to be strung out over a distance of about two hundred feet.

Dirt from the holes was piled up alongside each excavation which we used to backfill around the tree trunks and build the earthen dams to hold back the water. Joyce made the ceremonial display of doing this with the folding trenching tool but Randy had provided enough suitable tools to take care of the job. Being near the town pump and within proximity to the mayor's office window, appeared to us as a good formula for the prospect of long-term survival.

Everyone who accompanied us from the mayor's office stayed for the duration of the planting activities. Mayor Jordan was very engaged the whole time. Combining his attention with Joyce's natural supervisory abilities made for an expeditious conclusion to the planting process. That left plenty of time for more conversations, interviews, scrapbook looking and, eventually, pleasant good-byes. The people we met in Mt. Jackson went out of their way to accommodate us and they were very enthused about participating in our project.

The newspaper article appeared in the May 17, 1995, edition of *The Shenandoah Valley-Herald* on the front page of the second section, under the headline *"Family legacy means trees for Mount Jackson."* John was quoted as saying, *"Trees will almost always outlive us all and that's what a legacy is all about."*

We weren't done with Stonewall, yet. On our way north to Maryland, we stopped at the Manassas, VA, battlefield, also known as Bull Run. This is where Stonewall Jackson got his name and sealed his reputation. But in all the places named Jackson that we visited during the whole project, only one was named after him; that was Jackson County, Oklahoma. It's not a case of *"Sic transit gloria"* because his fame is still celebrated today, but just not when it comes to naming places in his honor.

The fourth grade students from the Jacksonville Elementary School help plant one of five **various species** of trees.

Jacksonville, Maryland

Maryland

"The Children's Hour"

May 12, 1995

We skirted the Washington, DC area on the 90-mile drive to Jacksonville, Maryland, from Manassas, VA. Living most of our lives within three hours of the nation's capital had afforded us plenty of opportunities to visit there on pleasure trips, business purposes and other kinds of reasons so we saw no reason to stop in DC on this trip. Plus, we were reserving that visit for the climax of the Jackson Legacy project which called for planting a tree near the Capitol building in the year 2000.

The drive is relatively unexceptional, unless for some reason you like continuous heavy traffic, or endless vistas of office buildings, town houses and shopping complexes, but there is one notable exception. At the intersection of the Capital Beltway with Connecticut Avenue stands the imposing Mormon Temple. It's the only temple the Church of Jesus Christ of Latter-Day Saints has constructed east of the Mississippi River. The building's architecture is inspirational, regardless of one's faith, especially to see it fully illuminated at night.

Jacksonville is in Baltimore County, MD. Finding it on a map is no problem but it seems to have somewhat of an identity conflict. Many listings refer to it as a part of Phoenix, MD, even though the two places are geographically separated by a few miles. They both have the same ZIP code of 21131 and many of the buildings retain a reference to Jacksonville, such as the place where we were going to plant the trees, Jacksonville Elementary School, and the Jacksonville Volunteer Fire Co. Even the sign on the local bank referred to it as the Jacksonville Office.

Joyce decided to contact Mayor Kurt Schmoke's office in Baltimore to commence the effort towards obtaining permission to plant our trees. They made her aware that the City of Baltimore became independent of the County in 1851, but kindly redirected her to a contact at the Baltimore County Department of Recreation and Parks in the county seat of Towson. Bob McClelland, Community Supervisor for the Carroll Manor Recreational Council, was assigned to co-ordinate with us since their organization was linked to the Jacksonville Elementary School recreation site. That gives some idea of the amount of effort it often took for Joyce to locate the proper person to work with. She labored doggedly through any bureaucratic channels that existed to find that right person in each state.

Bob told us that he would take care of all the arrangements, including the trees. All we had to do was show up at the school at 9:30AM on the morning of May 12, 1995. He reaffirmed those directions when we spoke with him from the hotel the night before our visit. After talking with him we headed for the night-time pre-inspection of the site but couldn't find any evidence of holes being dug at the school. As it turned out, our field of vision had been too small. There was a lot more to the property than we could see in the fading light of a spring night.

As instructed by Bob McClelland we appeared in the office of the Principal, Michael Citro, just after nine o'clock in the morning. By that time the children had been settled into their classes although the word was around that something special was about to happen. A few minutes later Bob McClelland joined us. He's one of those people whose good nature immediately puts you at ease. The two of them explained that certain children from the fourth grade had been selected to spend an hour helping us plant the trees. They and their teachers would meet us out at the back of the school property where the holes had already been dug and the trees placed alongside them. After waiting for Pat Van Den Beemt, reporter, and Paul Cory, photographer, from the local newspaper to arrive, we all went out to the site.

It was quite a distance. The depth of the property became apparent as we began to observe baseball fields, tennis courts and other sporting and recreational venues over the wide expanse of acreage. Our previous night's examination had only centered on the property immediately adjacent to the school building. Now we could see how far the whole place extended.

At the first site we were greeted by Scott Walker of Sweet Air Nursery, whose family's business had provided the trees. There was a variety of healthy stock including Norway spruce, Douglas fir, magnolia, dogwood and cherry, all of suitable planting height. Scott was very enthused with the opportunity of having his business identified with our project.

Then five selected fourth-graders arrived with their teachers to help us out. The students included Carolyn Der, Matthew Jacen, Jeffrey Borowitz, Russell Skeberds and Blair Barber. The teachers who attended were Ms. Chapman, Mr. Thurlow, John Brown, S. Delgado and Moore. Including the others who had accompanied us from the Principal's office, there were now a total of fifteen people gathered around. This number grew as other teachers walked their classes out to observe what was going on and then were replaced by the next class until the whole school had experienced some part of the celebration.

Our five kids wanted to get right to work but the grown-ups had remarks to make to each other and instructions to pass out to the smaller workers. Scott Walker was very careful to explain the proper tree planting procedures for the benefit of the five student-helpers who were probably doing it for the first time. In the process, he added a tip or two to our own knowledge bank just by listening to him talk with the children. As soon as those formalities were taken care of the kids jumped right in. Since the holes had already been dug into the rich earth, their help consisted mainly of numerous little fingers grasping the tree trunks as they were lowered into the ground and then the same fingers and hands pushing the dirt around the base of each tree. Naturally all of this was interspersed with youthful squeals and a variety of questions as only young minds can dream up. But it was a pure pleasure for us to interact with a bunch of ten-year olds since we, as wise old parents, knew that ten was one of the best ages for a kid / parent or grandparent relationship.

The trees were spaced all over the place, sometimes far apart from each other. There was one near the ball field, one on the crest of a hill, one at the bottom of a hill. The trees, themselves, were splayed out akin to children frolicking over the hills and dales on the manicured expanse of green grass.

That part of it was over in about an hour. Unlike other attendees the children couldn't linger around looking at scrapbooks or asking more questions. They had to return to their lessons but it's probable that the teachers had somewhat of a problem getting them to focus on class work the rest of the day. Maybe they should have scheduled the planting for 2:30PM, instead.

Children really add a lot of flavor to such activities. This was the third time we planted at a school and always derived a special feeling from the kids each time we did it. They're the ones who will return to these sites in forty years and remember the day that a great big tree started its life in a place with special memories for them. That's exactly the kind of legacy we had in mind in creating our project.

The newspaper article appeared in the May 18, 1995, edition of *The Jeffersonian.* Pat Van Den Beemt's words contrasted us to the more famous Jackson Five singing group *"that disbanded after squabbles, (but) this Jackson 5 represents harmony and the promise of a growing future."* She also quoted Principal Citro in saying, *"The whole community uses these fields. These trees will eventually provide some much-needed shade for everybody."*

Another successful venture was in the books. We left Jacksonville thinking what a great four-state trip this had been. Each one had been distinctive in its own way. Every place we approached welcomed our visit, the people actually participated in the effort and the nurture from each experience helped us to carry on with The Jackson Legacy..

The Forestry Division truck transported five trees of **various species** to the rest area near the U.S. Postal Building and the Amtrak Train Station, to beautify the small space.

Jackson, Michigan

Michigan

"After the Wedding"

September 18, 1995

The most important happening in the Jackson family during 1995, was the September marriage of our youngest son, Steven, to Deborah Crist, daughter of Rev. Wesley and Marilyn Crist. They had met while working together at a Christian bookstore in Elkhart, Indiana, a place where we had lived before moving to New Jersey.

It was a memorable event; everything that a wedding should be: the bride was resplendent, the groom dashing, the witnesses wet-eyed, etc. We could go on and on about the nuptials but, in the end, there is a connection between this blessed occasion and the Jackson Tree Legacy that needs to be mentioned – Jackson, Michigan is only a 130-mile drive from Elkhart. That afforded us the opportunity to prolong our stay in the area for one more day in order to add this planting site to our "completed" list. By that time, Steve and Debbie had received a grand send-off on their honeymoon trip to Bar Harbor, Maine, which was our wedding gift to them. While they were walking the beach alongside the Atlantic Ocean on Monday morning, we were planting trees in Jackson, Michigan.

That was where we needed to be. Michigan was sticking out there all by itself with all the other states near it having been already covered. It was a natural fit to add onto the trip that we were taking to attend the wedding.

Maybe the wedding was so foremost in our minds that we didn't give enough attention to promoting the tree planting arrangements. Joyce gained approval from the city but no one there organized any kind of special program. The local newspaper, *Jackson Citizen Patriot,* was likewise unresponsive, despite the ample elaboration contained in our press release. We had to keep reminding ourselves of the reason for visiting each place named Jackson and take satisfaction in that purpose, rather than expecting too much of a clamor at each and every site. And that's what we did.

There were more than a few positives to take away from the experience. The city had assigned Brian McKenzie, Superintendent, Forestry and Grounds, to co-ordinate with us. He had selected a location within the city that could use some beautification and put us in touch with a city-approved nursery who gave us a discount on the trees. Brian told us that he would be coming to the site on the morning of September 18, 1995, to help with the planting.

Before going out for the 9:30AM meeting, we stopped at Applewood Landscaping to pick out five trees of varying species and heights. They included a serviceberry (*Amelanchier Allegany*), Thunderchild crabapple, Red Splendor Crabapple, double-flowering plum (*Prunus Triloba*) and a flowering cherry. The trees ranged between four feet to six feet in height. We left them there for pickup by the Forestry Division dump truck for transportation per prior agreement with Brian.

The site was described as a rest area, although it's situated inside the city near heavily-traveled streets. The location is in the vicinity of the Amtrak train station and the Grand River near where Louis Glick Highway and South Cooper Street intersect. A piece of Liberty Street also runs behind the small plot which has a sign noting

"REST AREA – PROVIDED BY – CITY ENGINEERING DEPT"

Brian brought a helper, Kevin, with him. The two of them removed the trees from the bed of the truck and placed three of them at the front corner of the property near the street intersection. The other two were installed along the sidewalk in a straight line towards the river bank. All of us helped to dig the holes without much conversation. The soil really wasn't the best but we had bought mulch at the nursery to mix into the dirt. Watering the trees was going to be a problem at this site since we didn't notice any water supply within reach. However, we took comfort in the fact that the crew was from the Forestry Division which indicated to us that they would take proper care of our babies.

Nobody else stopped by during the planting. When their work was done, Brian thanked us for coming and then jumped into the truck with Kevin. It was all over in less than an hour. The two of us did our thing when we were alone. It was like leaving your child on the first day of school – you gave them a good start in life, you dressed them properly and put something to eat in their knapsack and now it was time to leave them alone to the world. But before leaving, we went back to each tree to check on its condition one last time.

There was still plenty of time left to the morning. It gave us a chance to look around the city, stopping at historical markers and reading the stack of pamphlets from the Convention and Tourist Bureau. From all of this we learned that the city was originated by Horace Blackman simply by registering a land claim of 160 acres at two dollars per acre, as permitted by the territorial government. Previously the land was inhabited principally by the Potawatomi Indian tribe, although Shawnee, Sac and Fox also lived in the area. It's unlikely that they were consulted regarding the sale. The town was named after Andrew Jackson at its founding in 1829; it is also recognized as the birthplace of the Republican Party tracing that origin to July 6, 1854, when Abraham Lincoln and others met under the Oaks to form a new political party. It is the birthplace of some notable people, including Supreme Court Justice Potter Stewart, television talk-show host, Jack Paar, actor James Earl Jones and NFL football coach, Tony Dungy.

This concluded our planting activities for the year 1995. With a total of 29 states visited in five years, we were running ahead of a time-line that called for completion in 2000. Michigan had put us one step closer to that goal and our visit there occurred coincident with one of our fondest memories – the wedding of our son. However, we never did ask Steve and Debbie to go over there to water the trees.

The Jackson Legacy

Doug Tibbetts helps John Jackson dig the holes to plant five **White Pine** trees.

Jackson, Maine

Maine

"The Maine Event"

May 6, 1996

After five years of doing the project we had covered all of the states in the eastern part of the country except for Maine. We always knew it was one of those states that could be combined with a business trip anytime that we needed to avail ourselves of that approach. That time arrived in May, 1996, when John arranged to make a sales call to a paper mill in Bucksport, Maine, less than thirty miles from a town named Jackson.

We never knew at the conclusion of one year's planting what state would lead off the program for the next year. Usually there was time to contemplate this over the late fall and early-winter months as personal and business appointments for the year ahead came into view. It was always beneficial to line up the planting trips with our other activities, whenever possible, for no other reason than to hold down travel costs.

However, there was no premonition involved when we planned Steve and Debbie's honeymoon trip to Maine in September, 1995, only to have us travel to Maine, ourselves, in May, 1996, to plant trees. Ironically, Jackson is only thirty miles from Bangor which was the airport they used to travel to Bar Harbor. Not only could they have watered the trees in Jackson, Michigan, they could have helped us plant the trees in Jackson, Maine, theoretically.

It was a drive of over 460 miles from our home in New Jersey to the sales call in Bucksport, ME, but it was made even longer by the decision to visit our condominium on Cape Cod, at Orleans, MA. That gave us a chance to see how well our year-round renters were taking care of the property, which is something we liked to do at least once a year. It also qualified part of our trip expenses as a tax write-off against the rental property income.

This would be the final time that Cerbo's Nursery in Parsippany, NJ, provided the trees for our project. All of the states from here on were located in far-off places where we had to use other suppliers. Tony Cerbo provided us with five white pines, approximately two feet in height, which fit nicely into the trunk of our Lincoln Town Car with plenty of room to spare.

Early May is still iffy when it comes to weather in New England. The temperature was definitely in the nippy range as we pulled into the Hiram Alden Inn in Belfast, ME, late Sunday night. It was too late to say more than the essentials to our hosts, the Lovejoys, but one of the pleasures of a Bed and Breakfast is the fact that you can expect to get more fully acquainted at the breakfast table the next morning. We were surprised to find out that Jim Lovejoy was President of the Belfast Chamber of Commerce. When he heard the reason for our trip to the area, he immediately called both local newspapers and invited them to come right over to interview us. Within no time, two reporters were looking at the scrapbook and our press release while taking down notes.

The arrangements for the planting site were somewhat unique. Jackson is rather small with a population of only around five hundred souls and without many suitable places to hold our trees. Consequently, the Town Clerk, Eleanor Tibbetts, thought that it would be a good idea to plant them on the corner of her property, which happens to be at one of the major intersections in the town, where everyone could see them. She said that the state highway department had removed trees from that location in anticipation of widening the road. That had been fifteen years ago which made it unlikely that those plans would still be in effect. She also explained that pine trees had been the particular favorite of her husband, who passed away three years earlier, which would give our trees the added significance of serving as a sort of memorial to her late, dearly beloved. It all sounded good to us, especially when she sealed the deal by assigning her son, Doug, to help with the plantings.

They led us to the corner of the property just in back of an enormous stack of chopped wood that must have held a hundred cord. Beyond the wood pile was a mound slanting down to the highway which they pointed out would be where the trees took up residence. The pines were set out on this diagonal course about twenty feet apart. Our first spade-full of dirt revealed a wet, heavily-texture soil that offered promise of a speedy completion to our tasks. Actually it took us nearly two hours before we could wrap things up. Doug stayed right with us the whole time, lending a hand with the digging and keeping us verbally supported as we went about the planting processes. He kept up a constant, friendly banter about his mother's spread, the volunteer fire company, the horse and pony club, the church on the opposite corner and most everything else there was to tell about Jackson.

As we worked people driving by would blow their horns and wave. We waved back as earnestly as a native Yankee with big smiles on our faces and a warm glow in our hearts. For this was rural America relatively unspoiled and probably as close to the original New England life style as it's possible to get.

The original Maine settlers didn't have to run off the native people; European diseases wiped out nearly 75% of them before the end of the 17th century. Today there are a few federally-recognized tribes in the state including the Penobscot and the Passamaquoddy but others, like the Abenaki, had to survive by blending in with other bands and have lost their identity.

The community of Jackson was named after local Revolutionary War General Henry Jackson. It was settled in 1800 and incorporated as a town in 1818. The area could be described as the upper reaches of the Appalachians with neighboring peaks rising towards 1,200 feet. The economy is largely based on forestry and livestock farming. However some parts are comprised of primeval forest and bogs which have never been managed.

At the completion of the planting, we returned to provide more information to the reporters in Belfast. This resulted in stories appearing in the May 9, 1996, editions of the two newspapers. *The Waldo Independent* article, written by Toni Malloux, appeared in the form of a story and accompanying photograph on page 2, under the headline *"The Jackson tree legacy comes to Maine." The Republican Journal,* (Maine's Oldest Weekly Newspaper – Established 1829) contained a captioned photograph by Jennifer Thornburn, taken of us at the Hiram Alden Inn before departing for Jackson on Monday morning, May 6, 1996.

The inclusion of Maine brought our count of states to thirty. Now all of the states east of the Mississippi River were completed, except for Wisconsin and Illinois.

John and Joyce Jackson standing by one of five planted Northwood **Red Maples** in Sunset Park. The water trucks are there ready to irrigate the trees.

Jackson, Minnesota

Minnesota

"A Hearty People"

The states remaining to be covered were west of the Mississippi River and the two states bordering on the west of Lake Michigan. That meant we had twenty sites left to visit in the vast reaches of the American Plains, Rocky Mountains and other western lands. The greater distances involved would present challenges when it came to designing itineraries but by careful planning we still held to the routine of planting in four states during the course of each week's vacation.

According to the experts, the best times for planting trees in most of these locations is in the late spring or early fall. We may have hedged a little bit on that timetable. For whatever reason, the best times for us to take our vacations turned out to be the months of June and September. This was to be our *modus operandi* in three of the next four years.

As with the pioneers of another time, we confronted the Plains states on our march westward. Like those hearty people, we had never really experienced this type of topography before, except through the imagery from *Little House on the Prairie* and other examples of media portrayals. Flatlands were not our idea of scenic. Where we came from, cornfields did not roll on endlessly to the horizon. We were also accustomed to the shade of large deciduous trees, the cascade of waterfalls and the salty exhilaration of an ocean wave. It was going to be a real education to observe how people lived in an environment so different from what we were accustomed to.

The Interior Plains stretch east for a thousand miles from the Rocky Mountains. A common phrase used to describe this region is "America's Heartland" but, for some, that seems as presumptuous as calling the Dallas Cowboys "America's Team". All of us live in our own little heartland. The single greatest impression that we took away from our whole project was the reality that nearly everyone is proud of where they're from and wouldn't want to live anywhere else.

Most of the true prairie lands in the eastern Plains have disappeared due to farming. At one time Illinois was known as "The Prairie State" but, today, only a fraction of prairie land still exists here and in the adjoining states of Iowa and Wisconsin that we visited in 1996. The Minnesota prairie starts in the western part of the state where one can still encounter the typical vision of a landscape filled with tall grasses, herbaceous plants, wild flowers and other shrubs, mainly without any sizeable stands of trees.

The City of Jackson sits on the prairie in southwestern Minnesota. There is no better way to convey an image of this place than to tell you that its location is only sixty miles away from Walnut Grove, Minnesota, where the Ingalls family lived.

Any discussion involving the settlement of the Plains has to include mentioning of the Indian tribes who lived there when the pioneers arrived. Jackson, Minnesota's experience serves as a striking example of what the settlers encountered. A trading post was established, in what was then called Springfield, in 1856, consisting of thirteen families of European extraction. The Indians attacked them in March, 1857, killing seven of them and wounding three. The remaining people abandoned the site for safer conditions in Iowa. Two months later, the Minnesota legislature established a county in the surrounding area naming it for an influential merchant in the state capital whose last name was Jackson. The county seat also took this name despite the fact that no one was living there at the time. Apparently the state's actions emboldened some citizens to take another stab at establishing a life in this part of the frontier. Gradually people started moving back into the area. The Sioux Indians waited until August, 1862, to once more attack the town of Jackson, this time killing thirteen and wounding three. Once again the remaining people deserted the county seat leaving it totally unpopulated. During the time of the Civil War over eight hundred white people were killed by the Sioux Indians on the frontier. Finally, in 1864, the government established Fort Belmont outside of present-day Jackson for protection against the Indians. Even then, the inhabitants, mostly Norwegians, cowered inside the fort for three years until the Army had driven the Sioux Nation west into the Dakotas. This show of force made the difference in sustaining the third reincarnation of settlement along the banks of the Des Moines River at what is now known as Jackson, Minnesota.

As a point of reference, Charles Ingalls moved his family to nearby Walnut Grove in 1874, by which time the Indian troubles had somewhat subsided. Laura Ingalls was seven years old at the time. The family lived in a hovel dug into the creek bank until the father could construct them what passed for a house. From such similar beginnings sprung the hearty stock of people who inhabit this part of Minnesota today.

The names of all four states on our 1996 circuit have some connection to Indian origins. These four states also have something else in common – all of the trees we planted came from the Bailey Nurseries in St. Paul, MN, recommended to us by Tony Cerbo. Without knowing it, many of the trees that we've planted in other states may have also come from this source because Bailey's is the wholesale nursery which supplied Cerbo's with much of its tree stock. With Tony's help, Bailey's shipped twenty trees for us to the Stubbe Flower Market in Jackson, MN, where they awaited our arrival on June 10, 1996.

We arrived the night before to discover that our hotel room was underground, shades of Laura Ingalls' first shelter in Maple Grove. It's one of the few underground motels in the country and is unique for several reasons. For one, we could have planted a tree on top of our room. After unpacking, we set out to find the nursery, noticing the welcoming banners mounted on utility poles along the way containing the stylized image of a tree incorporated into the name "Jackson." No one was at Stubbe's nursery but we found the trees and watered them because they appeared to be very dry. Then we gathered up some dinner and returned to our burrow for a good night's rest.

First thing in the morning, we went to Dave Stubbe's place to pick up the trees. Bailey had shipped us twenty maple and oak trees despite the fact that we knew the mayor at our next stop in Iowa didn't want any large-growing trees. Joyce and Dave worked out some kind of arrangement involving another nursery where we switched a few of the maples for pines, to everyone's satisfaction. Then we stuffed the twenty trees, some over seven feet in height, into every corner of our rented Pontiac Bonneville. The back seat was removed to make room for as many trees as possible inside the rear sitting area. It was a hot day which required protecting the tips of the trees with burlap where they came in contact with the rear window. The remaining trees went into the trunk along with the two shovels we purchased at the local hardware store and bags of peat moss. With unspoken apologies to General Motors and National Car Rental, the vehicle was now prepared for hauling ourselves and our wares over the next eight hundred miles.

Next we headed for City Hall, by prior arrangement with Mayor Ray Hansen who was Joyce's original contact. Jackson is a city of about 3,500 in population whose people radiate a lot of pride in their community. This was exemplified in the warm greeting we received at the administrative offices by Mary, the receptionist, George Tower and David Anderson, along with Mayor Hansen. They explained that the City Planner, Dean Albrecht, had approved the necessary permit for planting trees at Sunset Park, a two-year old facility located on the west side of Jackson along Louis Avenue. The Mayor asked us to follow the Council Secretary, Steve Walker, out to the site, apologizing that Mr. Albrecht couldn't join us due to a prior commitment at his favorite fishing hole.

The tree locations were all marked out with green flags in a straight line between the street and the picnic pavilion. It was a perfect location for the Northwood Red Maples which would grow to over fifty feet in height and provide much-welcomed shade during those hot days of summer on the prairie. George Tower had assigned a couple of city workers to help with the work along with a city water truck. Everyone assisted with one aspect or another, whether it was unloading the trees, carrying them to each spot, digging the dirt, straightening up the trees in the holes or whatever else was required. Those in attendance included Mayor Ray Hansen, George Tower, Steve Walker, Dave Anderson and some neighbors from across the street. There were plenty of hands, including our own, to put to the tasks and the trees quickly took up their positions in little more than one hour.

Jarrod Igou from the *Jackson County Pilot* stayed the whole time taking photos and interviewing us. His article was featured on the front page of the June 13, 1996, edition with a large photograph showing the two of us standing next to the unplanted tree while Mayor Hansen tossed dirt out of the hole and City Clerk, Steve Walker, looked on.

After the planting was over Mayor Hansen invited us back to City Hall. There he presented us with tokens of appreciation on behalf of the citizens of Jackson. Mr. Tower surprised Joyce by remembering that it was her birthday and everyone joined in to wish her Happy Birthday. The Mayor said that he would personally assure that the trees were well taken care of in the future. Late the following year we received a letter from Council Secretary, Steve Walker, stating that the city had added more maple trees to extend the tree line to the southern border of the park. He attached photographs showing our trees as indications that they had survived their first two Minnesota seasons in good shape. The Jackson Legacy lives on in Minnesota.

Everything about our visit to Jackson, Minnesota was exceptional. The people we met there were interested in our project as confirmed by the spirit they showed throughout the entire visit. We were impressed with the vitality the people exuded in their conversations with us and the written material we examined which expounded upon not only the history but the structures they had put in place to enhance the lives of their citizens. One of the brochures captured it this way: "*The City of Jackson is the present day outgrowth of Springfield, a trading post established by thirteen white families in 1856. The perseverance and determination of those early settlers is still reflected in the enterprise and stability of Jackson's current citizenry, which – through proficient, professional people, progressive business leaders, and steady, agriculturally-oriented citizens— continues to strive to provide itself with a high quality of life."*

The Jackson Legacy

Leonard Chipera, John Jackson, Mayor R.M.(Rudy) Pitzenberger and Chipera's children are taking a rest from planting five 2 foot **Scotch Pine** trees on the Jackson Junction City Hall and Community Centers front lawn.

Jackson Junction, Iowa

Iowa

"Gopher It"

June 11, 1996

The 200-mile trek to Jackson Junction, Iowa was mostly straight-line travel over land with a sameness of topographical features. In early June the crops aren't high enough to alter vistas that are therefore only broken by farm buildings, fence lines and the occasional tree. The largest city along this route is Mason City, IA, which we had visited three years earlier when our son Rob was working at the Winnebago plant in Forest City. It was in Mason City that Buddy Holly, the Big Bopper and Richie Valens died in a plane crash, a tragic event which inspired Don McLean's famous lyrics *"The day the music died"* in the song *"American Pie."* Mason City is noted for its Prairie Architecture construction which includes buildings designed by Frank Lloyd Wright. It was also the home of composer Meredith Wilson who drew on his boyhood memories in creating the River City portrayed in the hit musical *"The Music Man."*

Jackson Junction is in Winneshiek County. The county takes its name from a chief of the Winnebago Tribe which is related to the Sioux Nation. The adjoining county of Choctaw and the nearby county of Delaware are other testimonies to the prior presence of eastern Indians displaced beyond the Mississippi River in the early 1800's. Today, most Winnebagos are located in Nebraska and Wisconsin. Many people relate the name of Winnebago to the ubiquitous motor homes which are manufactured at a plant in Forest City, Iowa, county seat of Winnebago County.

A highway sign confirms your arrival into Jackson Junction. A few vintage buildings drew our attention as places to initiate contact with the locals and to inquire the directions to City Hall. The one we picked out to enter was the general store but no one was on duty inside. Coming back out, we noticed some people standing around across the street in a fashion that seemed likely to be our reception committee. And it was.

They were gathered outside a one-room former schoolhouse that now served as the "Jackson Junction City Hall and Community Center". The first one to greet us was Mayor R.M (Rudy) Pitzenberger. He was dressed in the work clothes of a farmer as was his brother-in-law Leonard Chipera. There were Chipera's two children and newspaper reporter Lisa Brainard, from *The Decorah Journal*. They probably had no problem identifying us as the Jacksons even before we introduced ourselves.

Rudy was the one who had told Joyce not to bring any large-growing trees when City Hall employee Mae Schmitt had forwarded her call to him a few weeks prior to our trip. He was pleased to see that we had brought along Scotch pine trees that were only two feet in height. There were some deciduous trees around the grounds of the building but he must have figured that a little year-round green would look nice on the property.

Things were very informal. We showed everyone the scrapbook contents, covering previous planting trips, while inviting their questions. The Mayor talked some politics and gave us a little history of the place, noting that the town's namesake was an early settler also by the name of John Jackson. At one time the railroad stopped here bringing people to do business at the grain elevator or at one of the stores in town. However, the area had been in a gradual decline throughout the 20th Century and its population was down to only sixty folks. Rudy wasn't too happy about a story that Jackson Junction was about to lose its status as a town, along with its post office, that the reporter had written and relayed his displeasure to her before helping us with the trees.

The little group moved with us to each planting location. We did most of the work while hearing how the men specialized in growing popcorn. Rudy had his own marketing company, Interstate Popcorn Sales, which used the slogan *"Original Super-Pop Tenderized Popcorn."* All the while we continued to make holes into the turf, uncovering the rich dirt below in preparation for receiving the five little trees. The work proceeded at a slow pace until interrupted by the Mayor's scamper to his pick-up truck.

While we were digging into the turf, one little creature was digging up from the other direction. With experienced eyes the Mayor recognized the signs of a pocket gopher about to break ground from underneath the grass and rushed to the truck for his shotgun, steadying it across the hood of the truck. Sure enough, a little brown head tentatively popped through the grass, quickly glanced around and then submerged. It did this a couple of times while the Mayor was gauging the time between appearances. Scratch one gopher. If that wasn't bad enough for us city slickers, the Mayor then reached down into the hole to retrieve the poor little fellow and display it to us as some kind of trophy. We had to keep on smiling because the planting work wasn't done yet but it really tugged at our heartstrings to witness the demise of one of God's creatures.

The trees were placed in two separate lines running perpendicular to the road with plenty of space in between for easy mowing when they were full-grown. Leonard brought water from the house next door and placed it inside the earthen dams that we built up at the base of each pine tree. We took a lot of photographs to record the various stages of planting, always looking for that one outstanding shot that would eventually wind up in the book.

They left the building open for us to inspect after they left. It was somewhat modernized but still had a blackboard harkening back to its days as a schoolhouse and an indoor privy without plumbing. Joyce wrote on the board: *"The Jacksons thank JJ (Jackson Junction) for allowing us to plant 5 trees."*

One of our aims was to obtain a hand-cancelled postmark showing the name of each place we visited. This required a trip to the post office to ask the postal person to hand-stamp a post card in our presence. In our brief trip to the general store, before the planting started, we noticed that it also served as the post office. When we returned, the owner of the store and postmistress, Rose Jirak, invited us into her house to hear more about our adventures. She showed us pictures of the town as it had appeared at the turn of the 20th century, just about the time that she was born. It was a very congenial visit after which she postmarked our cards. We left town soon afterwards.

In September, 1997, we received a letter from Mrs. Clementine Kinkor, of Calmar, IA, who explained that she had been the caretaker for Mrs. Jirak and she remembered our visit to Jackson Junction to plant the trees. She informed us that the government was shutting down the post office on October 10, 1997, after 114 years in operation. Mrs. Kinkor arranged for us to obtain last-day cancellations using postcards made from the old photographs that Mrs. Jirak had shown us. Much to the mayor's chagrin, the predictions in the newspaper turned out to be true. Jackson Junction may have taken a step backward in this regard but they still had acquired our trees and a place in the story that goes along with that.

Clementine wrote us again on May 19, 2000, enclosing two copies of an article that she compiled and submitted to *The Decorah Journal,* which was published the previous day. Her material was turned into an article by Lisa Brainard who had also been in attendance at our planting in Jackson Junction which resulted in the original publication of our story in the June 19, 1996 edition on page A7. The updated article recounted the completion of our entire project and mentioned that a story would be appearing in the June 2, 2000 edition of *Family Circle* magazine. Clementine said that she was praying for our success in publishing a book about the Jackson Legacy and asked us to notify her family when it was available. She also sent us a souvenir cup with a note saying "*Thank you for all you've done to save America's trees.*"

Donna Spaeth, President of the Village of Jackson, John and Joyce Jackson and Paul Lohmiller, Director of Public Works are preparing to plant a **Northwood Maple** along side of the Jackson Fire Station.

Jackson, Wisconsin

Wisconsin

"It Takes a Village"

There was more Iowa prairie land stretching ahead of us on the 250-mile journey to Jackson, Wisconsin, near Lake Michigan. After going the first fifty miles we came upon the riverboat, Miss Marquette, moored on the Mississippi River just across from Prairie du Chien, Wisconsin. It looked interesting with the large statue of an elephant out front, the festooned smokestacks of the sternwheeler boat and the long enclosed entranceway extending out from the bluff to the waterborne casino. We're $20 per-day-limit gamblers who like to occasionally enjoy the unique atmosphere of a gambling house. The riverboat was a scenario we had not experienced before and we wanted to add this type of operation to a list of places we've visited that includes Monte Carlo, Las Vegas, Atlantic City and Nassau. We also had never been to an Indian-run casino and thought this might be our first one.

Miss Marquette Casino, which has since been renamed the Isle of Capri Casino, was not established by Native Americans but it claims the distinction of being the first state-licensed gambling casino on the Mississippi. The first Indian casino is further north on the river near Red Wing, Minnesota, which began operation in 1984. It was in Minnesota that a legal precedent was set in 1976 when the U.S. Supreme Court ruled that states do not have the authority to regulate Indian activities conducted by Indians on their tribal lands. Other decisions followed culminating in The Indian Gaming Regulatory Act of 1988. In a 1981 decision leading up to the act, the U.S. Circuit of Appeals reaffirmed that part of Chief Justice John Marshall's 1832 ruling which states that Indian tribes have sovereignty rights under federal law that states cannot infringe upon. This was the decision that Andrew Jackson ignored in his drive to expel all Indians from the east to beyond the Mississippi River. After more than 150 years, the U.S. legal system finally did something to rectify the injustices done to Native Americans.

Like the other four states on this tour, Wisconsin long ago lost its prairies to the agricultural pursuits of its industrious farmers. All that remains today are isolated prairie preserves and other protected artifacts in the safe possession of historical societies. But even without the free-blowing wild grasses, the tilt of the land still evokes visions of the plains life to the travelers along Interstate 94. Our own journey along this route brought us close to the Village of Jackson.

In the mid-1800's, the Village of Jackson was one of three small unincorporated hamlets situated within the Towns of Jackson and Polk. When Joyce did her research in the winter of 1995-96, the Village of Jackson was nearing a population of 5,000, while the Town of Jackson had a smaller population of around 3,500. She first tried contacting the Town but they referred her to Donna Spaeth, President of the Village of Jackson.

Many of the initial settlers came to the area from Germany in the 1840's. They bought the land from the United States Government for ten shillings an acre, most of the tracts being 40 acres in size. The native Indians had largely been dispossessed by 1836, but stragglers still roamed the

159

countryside, occasionally making trouble enough to be a cause of concern to the new land owners. Numerous nearby place names survive as a testimony to Indians having lived there, like Oconomowoc, Menomonee and Milwaukee. The Winnebago Tribe also lived in the area.

In anticipation of our visit, Donna Spaeth sent us a book on the history of the village, named in honor of Andrew Jackson around 1846, and a pin on which was printed *"I Love Jackson."* Evidently, she was energizing other Village officials as seen in a letter we received from her Administrative Assistant stating how excited and delighted they were about our visit. *The Milwaukee Sentinel* published a long article in their June 10, 1996 edition based on our advance press release and including quotes from an interview they did with the Village President. Donna is quoted as saying, *"The whole situation is certainly unique...I'm real excited to meet them."* The *Daily News* of West Bend, WI, also published a preview article on June 3rd. Donna mentioned to Joyce that Jackson enjoyed the distinction of being *"A Tree City, USA"* and included a form which they hand out to residents specifying the ten types of trees suggested for planting in the village. Maples were numbers one and two on the list which was one of the reasons why we chose Northwood Maples for planting here.

We let the seven-foot trees out of the car the night before for watering and airing. The next morning, June 12, 1996, we put them back in the car along with the bags of bark mulch and humus peat moss which we bought at the garden center behind the American Hotel. Then we headed off for the Village Hall wearing the *"I Love Jackson"* pins. There we met Paul Lohmiller, Director of Public Works, who escorted us to the tree-planting site at the nearby fire station where the others were waiting for us.

At the fire station, Donna Spaeth welcomed us like old friends. She introduced us to Cliff Holmes, a Parks and Recreation Committee member, Del Beaver, administrator, and Russ Kreiger, the town employee who had already dug the holes for us. A few other friends and neighborhood people were there in addition to newspaper reporter Barry Gantenbein. That made for a lot of conversation as we responded to the numerous questions coming from all quarters. Everyone was glad to have us in their community to do something which connected all of us through the name of Jackson. With thirty-two states already completed, they undoubtedly felt part of something noteworthy which is certainly the impression we got from associating with them.

The trees were spread out along the walkway leading to Jackson Drive. In addition to the holes, Russ had also placed three stakes to which guide wires would later be attached to keep the trees growing straight. We took it the rest of the way using the shovels purchased in Jackson, MN, the ceremonial trenching tools that went with us to every site, the bags of soil conditioner that we purchased and the plastic sleeves to protect the trunks from weed whackers. By then, everyone had returned to their normal job activities, leaving us alone to finish off the plantings. The preparatory efforts performed by Russ Kreiger allowed us to complete all the remaining work in an hour with half the morning still ahead of us.

That enabled us to visit the Village Hall once again to express our appreciation and to soak up a little more local atmosphere. Then we returned to the planting site to be alone with our thoughts one final time. This was the time when we reflected upon what we had done, why each place was always as important to us as any other place and to re-enjoy the people-to-people aspect of the encounter. The visit to Jackson, Wisconsin fulfilled all of our expectations.

On the way out of town we paused to take a picture of an impressive sign serving to welcome the traveler to Jackson. Like everybody and everything else we witnessed in this village it conveyed an expression of community pride, in this case with the banner "Jackson – *The Village With A Future.*"

The Daily News of West Bend, in a June 13, 1996 article, informed their readers of our completed visit to Jackson. Reporter Barry Gantenbein's headline pronounced "*Jacksons spread their Jackson roots.*" He quoted Cliff Holmes as saying, "*They talk about living memorials. I can't think of anything nicer than trees.*" Neither can we.

A few years later, our friend FayAnn Hannon of Houston, TX, stopped in Jackson, WI to see our trees. Four of them were growing nicely but one had not survived. We talked about the situation with Village President Spaeth and Del Beaver on July 8, 1999. They assured us that a replacement tree would soon take its place alongside the others. Sometimes, it takes a village to raise a tree.

Joyce Jackson centering the **Pin Oak** tree that was planted at the Community Park on Flag Day, June 14,1996.

Jacksonville, Illinois

"Big Eli"
City of Jacksonville, IL Landmark

162

Illinois

"Flags of Our Fathers"

June 14, 1996

Thursday of the week we toured the prairie states was reserved for a little business and sight-seeing. We normally scheduled an off-day to give us a breather, especially when there was something in particular that caught our attention in the areas we were going through. In the case of this trip, John wanted to visit with a potential employer in Hinsdale, Illinois, outside Chicago, while both of us wanted to check out the Lincoln sites in Springfield, IL, which is less than 40 miles from Jacksonville.

The business part was quickly concluded in the early morning allowing us to arrive in Springfield with most of the afternoon available to do some touring. The first site we headed for was Lincoln's Home at the corner of 8th and Jackson Sts. The street name gave us another connection to our favorite President that we weren't aware of before. In addition to touring his home, we went to his law office, the old state capitol building and his tomb. Every venue evoked indescribable feelings that our attempts at describing could not adequately convey. Volumes have been written about Abraham Lincoln in words that are *"far above our poor power to add or detract."* Suffice it to say that it was a moving experience, one that every American should contemplate at some point in their lives.

Lincoln was no stranger to the people of Jacksonville, IL. He represented clients in the county court house there many times as well as making speeches during campaigns for the U.S. House of Representatives and the Presidency. His archrival, Stephen A. Douglas became Morgan County's prosecuting attorney in 1835 and took up residency in the county seat of Jacksonville. It is from here that he would have traveled around Illinois to engage Lincoln in their famous debates.

Traveling around Illinois in the mid 1800's would have meant traversing a lot of prairie land. As far back as 1842 it was known as *"The Prairie State"* a nickname that was not superseded until 1955 when the official state slogan was changed to *"The Land of Lincoln."* Even today, the state still designates the third full week in September as *"Illinois Prairie Week."* despite the fact that only a fraction of the land in the state can still qualify as prairie land.

As the prairie has gone, so have the Indians. Today, there is no tribe in Illinois officially recognized by the Federal government. The last encounters between Indians and the settlers can be traced back to the "Winnebago War" in 1827 and the "Black Hawk War" in 1832, and even those were hardly more than skirmishes around the local area.

Jacksonville was formed in 1825 and named for Andrew Jackson. It has been an important state contributor in the fields of health, law, business and the military, notably during the Civil War. In addition to its connections to Lincoln and Douglas, it has also been the home of William Jennings Bryan, famous politician, orator and lawyer.

We arrived at Jacksonville City Hall just before the offices closed on Thursday afternoon. Sue Large, the City Clerk, was still there. She was the person whom Joyce had initially contacted at the start of our planning for this visit. Sue told us that Mayor Ron Tendick had arranged everything with Bruce Surratt, City Parks and Lakes Department Superintendent. All we had to do was show up at the Chamber of Commerce offices the following morning, which happened to be at the entrance to the Community Park where the trees would be planted.

There were a few things that we needed to take care of before calling it a night. That included buying items to complete the plantings, such as the plastic protector sleeves and peat moss. We always like to go to the planting site to get some idea of the location that had been assigned to us. The park was large and well-maintained with plenty of mature trees. In the front stood a city landmark, the recently-preserved "Big Eli" Ferris wheel, near the paved road that circled through the whole property. After touring the park, we fulfilled a promise that Joyce made to one of the New Jersey country club members, by visiting with a friend who had moved to Jacksonville.

The day of the planting was picture-perfect, sunny, warm and ideal for being outdoors. Friday, June 14, 1996, was Flag Day and the city had lined the park roadway with U.S. flags every twenty feet or so. A light wind stirred all of them into a continuous dance of color. We went to the Chamber of Commerce at the head of the park to meet with the President, Jean Cummins, along with newspaper photographer Zuzana Jackevicius, from *The State Journal-Courier* of Springfield. Jean gave us some information on Jacksonville along with two travel mugs displaying the name of the city. We spent some time discussing our project and showing them the scrapbook then followed them out to the site.

Our little entourage proceeded along the flag-draped roadway to the back of the park. It stopped across from an impressive memorial that itself was surrounded with more flags. The stone tableaus on the memorial contained the names of servicemen from the area who had lost their lives in the Korean War. Park benches were placed around the memorial offering people a chance to sit and reflect upon what these men, and all other servicemen and servicewomen, sacrificed for the rest of us. To have our trees encompassed within this site was an honor that touched us deeply.

Bruce Surratt was waiting there for us. He had placed stakes at the point where each pin oak was to be planted. There were no other trees nearby, which meant that our trees would be the first to look back upon the memorial. The five-foot trees that we planted could grow to over sixty feet tall and live for more than a hundred years. Bruce's stakes were about fifteen paces from the road and twenty-five feet apart from each other. Even in as short a span as ten years these trees should be over twenty-five feet tall with a full canopy of green in the summer and bronze in the fall.

No one helped us with the actual digging work. They did stay around talking with us as we scooped out the dirt, removed the trees from the containers, positioned them into the holes laying the handle of the shovel across the hole to measure the depth of the ball relative to the ground around it, backfilling the dirt, tamping it down, building the dams around the base to hold in the water and then securing it for straight growth by tying twine between the trunk and the upright stakes.

We enjoyed the total experience right down to the significance of using our collapsible trenching shovels. It made us connect the military purpose of these tools to the scene nearby. These two shovels went with us to each planting site. As a result, their blades retained some residue of dirt from other locations, which means we were mingling soil from one state into that of another state. The full-sized shovels which we had bought for this trip in Minnesota were another matter. Those became our donation to the City of Jacksonville when the planting was completed, which Bruce Surratt graciously accepted.

After everything was completed, we received an invitation to recite our story on radio station WLDS. They sent a reporter with a microphone to interview us. While waiting to go on the air we listened to a sound bite from Mayor Tendick about some local activity. That may be the reason why he couldn't come out to our planting. Anyway, we did our little piece which lasted about three minutes. It was the second time during our project that we were on live radio; the other time being in Jackson, Mississippi.

Two newspapers ran stories on us in advance of our visit. In fact, *The State Journal-Register* published articles by Correspondent Carole Hack on May 31 and June 12, 1996. The content was taken mostly from our press releases but she added her own reference to us being like *"modern-day Johnny Appleseeds."* The *Jacksonville Area Showcase* published a preview article on May 22, 1996, alerting their readers to our impending visit. The only post-planting publication was a fine photograph taken by Zuzana Jackevicius that appeared in the June 15, 1996 edition under the caption *"Recreational Rooting"*.

After leaving Jacksonville we headed for Hannibal, Missouri to visit Mark Twain landmarks and then spent the next day touring the sites in St. Louis before flying home to New Jersey.

The Illinois visit concluded our planting activities for the year of 1996, even though there was still half a year remaining. It was never our intention to accelerate the project timetable. We were still on schedule for completion in the year 2000 and there didn't seem to be any need to hurry things along. Both of us had full-time jobs to contend with and John's involved a good deal of traveling in his capacity as Sales Director of a trucking company. We also had other interests in the New Jersey area that had accumulated over our ten years of living there. What could change?

Joyce and John posing by two of five **Silver Trumpet** trees planted on Tripler Army Medical Center grounds.

Honolulu, Hawaii

Hawaii

"Aloha Oe"

Even before starting The Jackson Legacy project, we had been to forty-four states during our first twenty-seven years of marriage. Travel has always been our number one family hobby. Doing it was helped by the fact that employers kept sending John all over the United States which gave us lots of opportunities to tie trips into equal parts business and pleasure. But one of the few states that we had never seen was Hawaii.

Visiting Hawaii became inevitable when we created the fifty-state project but the first six years slid by before we could come up with the right itinerary. It would have made sense to include Hawaii while traveling to west coast states but we had already done Washington and California in the first year of the project which only left Oregon. There were only sixteen states remaining to be covered when Joyce began plotting the next year's schedule in the late fall of 1996. However there was something else going on which would have a decided impact on these plans.

In December, 1996, an executive recruiter contacted John regarding a position with a major trucking company in Houston, Texas. The prospects for a job change came at a propitious time. John's original employer in New Jersey had sold the company in 1995 and then that company was acquired by a larger concern in 1996. These successive acquisitions allowed us to stay in New Jersey but at a lesser organizational level. The Houston job offered more stature and income but it also meant relocating to a place that we had sworn never to consider living in. With all of this soul-searching going on, it was not the best time to be planning an extensive schedule of tree planting for the coming year.

We figured out that it would take a couple of months to go through the job interview process especially as it would be happening over the Christmas and New Year's holidays. If we decided to take the job, the amount of vacation time allowed in the first year by a new employer was an unknown factor which limited how much advance planning we could do regarding the tree project. The month of February seemed like a safe prospect and we looked at combining visits to Oregon and Hawaii. However, the month of February proved to be too early in the year for successful tree planting in Oregon, so we dropped that possibility. In the end we decided that a trip to Hawaii was enough justification all by itself. It got us out of the New Jersey winter, we could combine it with a side-trip to see our friends in San Francisco and Carmel, California and we had enough frequent flyer miles to pay for one of our airfares. What better way to spend these free miles than on a 10,000 mile round-trip from Newark, NJ to Honolulu.

It became quickly apparent that the name Jackson was not common in a region whose place names were mostly in a Polynesian language containing only half as many alphabetic letters as English. The native language in Hawaii does not have a "J" or a "C" or an "S". Spelling Jackson using only their alphabet would come out "_a_k_on." Translating our first names also didn't offer much potential: John translates to "Keoni" and Joyce to "Ioke." How could we effectively explain this usage to people who might wonder what Keoni Ioke had to do with the Jackson tree project?

The research did uncover a location named Jackson Place on the grounds of the Tripler Army Medical Center in Honolulu. We discovered, later, that the streets in this famous facility were named in honor of medical specialists, mostly from the Second World War and Korean War era. Corporal Levi A. Jackson was a medical corpsman who heroically attended to wounded soldiers under heavy enemy fire on a hill in Korea in 1950 until cut down by machine gun fire. For his brave actions he was posthumously awarded the Distinguished Service Cross, the nation's second highest decoration for valor. Cpl. Jackson had been a U.S. Army heavyweight boxing champion and his regiment was the last in Army history to see combat as a segregated black unit.

Joyce contacted the medical facility which led her towards Rodney Chong who managed the military office of public works which takes in Schofield Barracks, Fort Shafter and Tripler Medical, not far from Pearl Harbor. All of this had promise of connecting our project to some of the famous place names of the Second World War, which John's father had seen while serving on a Navy ship in the Pacific Theater.

Mr. Chong arranged for Patrick Ching, an agronomist for the Department of Public Works, to work with us on the project. Patrick sent us a letter the month before our visit suggesting the type of tree, where to purchase it and stating that their shop people would dig the holes at the intersection of Jackson Place and Krukowski Road. He also notified the base newspaper of our arrival plans. They agreed to cover the event, in fact, their reporter was designated to handle our initial reception when we arrived at the Medical Center the day of the planting.

Originally, Patrick had suggested planting Gold trees but we wound up getting Silver Trumpet from Takano – Nakamura Landscaping. The Silver Trumpet only grows in Hawaii; it's somewhat smaller than the Gold tree and has yellow blossoms in the spring. The trees would be waiting for us at the site along with the rest of the reception / work detail.

We departed from Newark, NJ airport on February 15th heading for our first stop in San Francisco to see our high school classmate Father Larry Finegan. The tree story was old news to him, having hosted us after we planted in Jackson, CA, in 1991. Nevertheless we regaled him with tales of the thirty-two other states we had planted since last seeing him. After a brief stay with Larry, we headed down to Monterey Bay. Carmel is our favorite spot in the whole world, although we wondered if that would still be the case once we had seen Hawaii. In a few more days we would be able to make that comparison.

The plane touched down on Oahu around dinner time on February 18, 1997. The trip to the hotel quickly established that we were in a different place than we had ever been before. That impression was sealed when we discovered there was no front door to the hotel. It was completely open to the outside as if you were entering one of the amusements at Disney World. They also didn't have a room for us but that worked out alright. Instead of staying outside of the city they upgraded us to a large room at another property in downtown Honolulu with a view overlooking Waikiki Beach. We strolled around downtown that night and then returned to the room, threw open the patio door and let the trade winds lull us to sleep. Not a bad start in paradise.

168

Joyce's advance planning was always meticulous. It gave us confidence that everything conceivable had been programmed and all we had to do was follow the script. Hawaii was no exception. Specialist Gamble of the Hawaiian Army newspaper was waiting for us at the entrance to Tripler Army Medical Center when we arrived at nine o'clock the next morning. She added a little touch of military courtesy with her "*Yes, Sir, Yes, Ma'am*" responses and total attentiveness to our needs. She drove us over to the site on a hill which we noticed had a view of the Pacific off in the distance. Waiting for us were Rodney Chong, Patrick Ching, Clarence Wilhelm, representing Major R. F. Martinsen, and a two-man work crew.

For a moment our eyes took in all of this while many happy feelings washed over us. Here we were in a beautiful place with people that had come together to help us do something special. Even though we would only be here for a relatively short time, the memories of this day would live with us forever. But then it was time to shake hands, talk about the reasons for our project and get along with the work of planting five trees.

The holes for three of the trees were dug near the "tot lot" across the street from where Jackson Place meets Krukowski Road. The other two were on the other side of the street next to Quarters 324 and 325. The trees were about four feet tall with broad, glossy green leaves loosely spaced out on the branches. The soil was deep red in color with the consistency of clay but the proper description would probably have more to do with some volcanic origin. The trees would stand in a well-kept lawn which elevated slightly up from the roadway towards an area of wildly-growing bushes and grasses. On the downslope of the road stood the Fisher House, the military's equivalent of the Ronald McDonald House, with its red-tiled roof and beyond that the misty blue of the Pacific Ocean.

The crew did most of the work but we finished back-filling the holes with our trusty collapsible shovels. The rich soil from Hawaii would cling to their blades until rubbed off into the dirt of other states to come. Mr. Wilhelm draped flower leis around our necks and read from the framed Army Commendation saluting us for:

YOUR GENEROUS GIFT OF FIVE SILVER (TABEBUIA ARGENTEA) TREES PLANTED AT JACKSON PLACE, TRIPLER ARMY MEDICAL CENTER, OAHU, HAWAII ON 19 FEBRUARY 1997. YOUR LIVING LEGACY WILL BEAUTIFY THIS MEDICAL CENTER IN THE YEARS AHEAD. IT WILL ALSO BE A TESTAMENT TO THE LOVE AND DEDICATION IN PRESERVING THIS BEAUTIFUL LANDSCAPE OF THE UNITED STATES ARMY. YOUR FAMILY'S CONTRIBUTION WILL ALLOW FUTURE FELLOW AMERICANS TO ENJOY THE BENEFITS OF YOUR GENEROSITY

The reference to "fellow Americans" is what resonates with us. Our project brought us more in touch with people from all over the country, people just like us – proud of our country and grateful for the sacrifices that so many have made in our behalf. What better place to realize that than looking over a body of water that encompasses Pearl Harbor. The next day we would visit the USS Arizona Memorial and Punchbowl National Cemetery and feel those emotions resound even more.

Patrick Ching took us on a tour of the military bases after the planting was done. They appeared to look much as they did in old movies taken during the War. You can still envision military vehicles going down palm-tree-lined streets and olive drab sedans with blackened headlights awaiting their commanders outside of austere white buildings. Later, we would have dinner with Patrick and his wife Amanda. They went out of their way to make our visit successful and we enjoyed being in their company.

The next three days were spent sampling a lot of the attractions on the island of Oahu. It is truly a unique place and one which fulfilled all of our expectations. Being on vacation involves a light and carefree perspective and there are plenty of chances to fully apply that attitude. But we also dealt with the somber. At the USS Arizona Memorial we talked with Dick Fiske, a Pearl Harbor survivor from the USS West Virginia, who appeared in many documentaries regarding December 7, 1941, notably on *The History Channel*. He was very accommodating of his time, as he had been with tourists since taking up his volunteer work as a docent at the Memorial in 1982. His final tour of duty came to an end in 2004 and he is greatly missed. The *Arizona Memorial* is striking on so many levels. There are few places you can go to that radiate so much reverence. Only in Hawaii, of all the fifty states, can you have access to an actual battleground of the Second World War, what many believe to be the most cataclysmic and far-reaching conflict in the history of mankind. It touched us profoundly to see the Arizona's anchor on display with the note that it was cast at the Sun Shipyard in Chester, PA, where Joyce's father Raymond Crooks had spent the war years in making his contribution to our nation's defense.

At the National Memorial Cemetery of the Pacific we visited the grave of Ernie Pyle, the most famous reporter of World War II, who lost his life on Ie Shima in April, 1945. He had transferred to the Pacific Theater after chronicling G.I. Joes in Europe until V-E Day only to meet his fate from a Japanese machine gunner. There are more than 49,000 other souls in what is affectionately called Punchbowl Cemetery and elsewhere over the wide expanse of the Pacific there are thousands of others *"whose earthly resting place is known only to God."*

After paying proper respect and acknowledgment to the vestiges of war, we proceeded out in the rental car to take advantage of all the island had to offer. This included experiencing everything we could possibly cram into our remaining stay. Being seasoned travelers we could map our own course without relying upon packaged touring programs. Joyce had always been very adept at identifying sites of greatest interest and placing them into a travel sequence that included maximum consideration of the geography involved. Consequently, we enjoyed the luau at Germaines, hiking inside the crater at Diamondhead, swimming in the lagoon in front of the Royal Hawaiian Hotel on Waikiki Beach, watching surfers at Waimea Park (the day after a shark-bite attack on Sunset Beach), walking on Kalama Beach in Kailua, touring Iolani Palace and the State House, the cliff views from Kaohikapu Point, the Dole pineapple plantation and Wahiawa Botanical Gardens. These were all great but it would be hard to top the buffet and fantastic show at The Polynesian Cultural Center at the northern end of Oahu.

The PCC brings together all of the diverse cultures of Polynesia through the representations of more than one hundred performers. There are separate entertainment segments performed by native people from Hawaii, Samoa, Tonga, Fiji, Tahiti, Easter Island, New Zealand and other is-

170

lands. Each helps to provide a deeper understanding of their culture, customs, spirit and, especially, their music. It's a must-see extravaganza for anyone visiting Honolulu, Oahu, Hawaii.

As if tree planting in an exotic land while taking in the other enticements of a paradise-like setting weren't enough, something of a life-changing event also occurred on this trip. Remember the part about the job interview for the company in Houston that was going on at the time we started the trip? Well, John had provided the company with our contact information at the Waikiki Banyan Hotel in case they needed to reach us for any important matter. On our last night, the front desk called to tell us that an express package had arrived which they delivered up to the room. With much excitement we took the unopened package out to the high-rise patio and sat down to discover its contents. Inside was a letter from Philip Abraira, President of DSI Transports, Inc. of Houston, Texas, extending an invitation to join the company as Vice President of Pricing and Methods accompanied by an impressive offer of salary and benefits. There, as the sun set its course into the Pacific, with tradewinds lightly wafting through our hair, two doves nestling on our railing and tropical atmosphere filling our senses, we decided to embark upon the great unknown – life outside the East Coast. We hadn't factored in that Hawaii could be the last state we were to cover while living in New Jersey, that the remaining fifteen states would be easier to cover from the Lone Star State and that henceforth we would be known in the newspaper accounts of our tree plantings as the couple from Texas.

One last thing – that part about Carmel, California being our favorite spot in the world. Now we have to refer to it as our favorite spot on the mainland.

Jacksonport Court House—oldest surviving building in Jackson County was the setting for planting five **Purple Leaf Plum** trees. The fire hydrant will provide needed water for the trees survival.

Jacksonport, Arkansas

Arkansas

"White River Monster"

As expected, the start of a new job put a serious dent into the tree-planting activities for 1997. It takes John around six months to reach maximum effectiveness in handling a new position the size of the one in Houston. During that time frame we weren't about to go off on a lengthy refor-estation project. Consequently, the tally for the year was only going to be two states and it was only that many because we tied the adjoining state of Arkansas into a business trip.

The opportunity came about through attendance at a company picnic on a Saturday in Marshall, TX. The company had more than eighty truck terminals throughout the U.S. It was customary for one or more corporate officers to visit each location at least once a year, usually in connection with some other event such as a picnic, safety awards banquet or similar activity. Marshall was within driving distance of Houston, so we volunteered to accompany the President and his wife, Philip Abraira and FayAnn Hannon, to this location which just also happened to be almost half-way to Jacksonport, Arkansas. We went in separate cars and he authorized a vacation day for Monday so we could take care of our planting visit.

The plan occurred to us less than thirty days prior to the picnic date. Therefore Joyce had her hands full making all the arrangements on such short notice. It helped that she was no longer a part of the labor force and therefore could devote more time during the day to our project. That was one of her requirements for agreeing to move to Texas – she wanted to stop working in order to explore other aspects of life.

Jacksonport was our choice in Arkansas because it was also located in Jackson County. The dou-ble application of our last name gave us two reasons for planting there. We learned later that the area originally came to be known as Jacks Port after trappers established a camp on the banks of Jacks Creek in the 1820's. It was then part of the Arkansas Territory which had morphed out of the Louisiana Purchase and the Missouri Territory in 1819. Jackson County was formed in 1829 and named for Andrew Jackson who was then President of the United States. The name of Jacks Port evolved into Jacksonport after the county seat was established there in 1853. The Jackson-port Court House was finished in 1872 and is the oldest surviving building in Jackson County. Jacksonport was a leading commercial river port on the White River, which flows into the Mis-sissippi River, until the railroad became the main mode of transportation in the region. Thereafter the town began a gradual decline in importance and eventually the county seat was moved to nearby Newport in 1892. Newport is famous as the site of Sam Walton's first retail venture, a Ben Franklin five and dime store, which he operated before starting Wal-Mart Stores in 1962. Today there is a post office in Jacksonport to serve barely more than 250 residents.

Because of its strategic prominence at the time of the Civil War, the Jacksonport area was a hot-bed of military activity throughout the war with five different generals, Union and Confederate, maintaining their headquarters there at various stages of the battles. On June 5, 1865, two months after the Confederate surrender at Appomattox Court House in Virginia, southern General Jeff Thompson, "Swampfox of the Confederacy" surrendered his 6,000 troops to the Union commander at the Jacksonport Landing.

The name "Arkansas" is derived from the Quapaw Indians who were called the "Arkansea" tribe by other natives. The Quapaws lived in what is now called Jackson County before being joined by tribes such as the Cherokee, Choctaw and Delaware who were forced out of the eastern U.S. The route, taken by the eastern Cherokees which became known as "The Trail of Tears," crosses through northern Arkansas on its way from Missouri to Oklahoma. There have been no Indian reservations or enclaves in Arkansas since the Quapaws were removed in 1834.

Our primary contacts in setting up the visit were Mayor William Smart and his wife, Pat. They welcomed our tree plantings as a way to replace trees lost in a major tornado that struck the town six months earlier. Mark Ballard, Jacksonport State Park Superintendent, also joined the group at the invitation of the mayor. The date was set for Monday, September 15, 1997.

Our first introduction to the town was a sign on the outskirts which read: "*Welcome to Jacksonport – Home of the White River Monster.*" This refers to a well-known tale regarding past sightings of a Loch Ness-type creature which is said to inhabit the river. As with Nessie," no one has actually been able to capture "Whitey" or produce irrefutable proof of its existence. However, the more serious occurrence of a White River monster was the tornado that swept through on March 1, 1997. It took the lives of two townspeople, rendered the 125 year old City Hall building unusable and destroyed the post office and other structures, in addition to uprooting 85 trees. Mark Ballard survived the tornado in his crushed pickup truck. Phil Grendale was at the levee when he saw the tornado coming; he gathered up two girls at City Hall and all three escaped into the vault as the storm ripped up the building. For the third time in our venture we had witnessed the after-effects of a tornado but this one was the worst we had ever seen.

It lent a different tone to the occasion. Here were people who had actually come face to face with the worst that nature can deal out and they survived. Here was a town that still carried the scars evidenced by damaged buildings and the stumps of what had been towering trees. We always looked for special relevance in our tree plantings and it was movingly expressed by Mark Ballard when he said that our plantings "*came at the most opportune time with our recovery from the March 1st tornado.*"

Present at the plantings were Pat Smart, Mark Ballard, two of his staff, Doug Humphries and Phil Grendale, and reporter Verneal Hodge from *The Newport Daily Independent*. They had run a preview story on September 11th and followed with a picture of us planting the trees which appeared in the September 18, 1997 edition.

The Pruitt Nursery in Newport, AR had suggested Purple Leaf Plum, a flowering tree. They were six to seven feet in height which barely fit into the trunk of our Mercury Grand Marquis for the short drive over to Jacksonport. The area had not seen rain in over a month. It was our first-time introduction to the soil-baking summers of the Deep South. All of our previous plantings in the south had occurred during the early half of the year before the heat and constant sun reduces the ground to hard pan. It took a lot of effort to make a dent in this kind of soil and we were fortunate to have all the help that the park service men provided.

Three of the trees were placed at wide intervals across the front lawn of the Court House where it was bereft of other plantings or shrubbery. Two of the trees were placed on neighboring Park land. Peat Moss helped to enrich the soil but despite its use we could barely scrape up enough earth to make the dams at the base of the trees for holding in the water. The men tapped into a nearby fire hydrant in order to run a hose line for watering the trees. This gave us hope that someone would continue to apply this method over the next few months to give the new trees as much of a chance as possible to survive the rest of the summer.

Everyone present was thankful for our coming to their town. Mark Ballard also expressed that in ending his September 26, 1997, letter to us with "*Your legacy is truly one that inspires people to serve others, which is so important in our country today. Once again we thank you for your generosity and service to our community.*"

Everything came together nicely on this trip. We were able to cover one last state by driving from our home after we had thought that the state of Maine would be our last drive-to state. We experienced the first-time charm of being considered a Texas couple doing their thing for a southern neighbor. But most importantly, we were able to join our project with the needs of a community that was still hurting from a natural disaster. That human element added so much more to this particular stop on our journey.

Mayor Kyle Fliniau planting a clump of **Aspen trees** in the Vic and Sigrid Hanson Memorial Park
Walden, Jackson County, Colorado.

Colorado

"Rocky Mountain High"

May 26, 1998

It took almost a year of living in Texas before we thought the time was right to resume our project. In the process we fell behind the ten-year timeline which necessitated that we accelerate the planting itinerary at some point in the remaining three years. The resolution was reached to postpone that surge period until 1999 when we would feel more acclimated to our personal and business surroundings. At the same time, any further delays in 1998 would make the succeeding year more difficult, so we ultimately came up with the plan to do five states in 1998 and eight states in 1999.

Except for a few remaining plains states, all of the other places were spread out along the mountains of the Continental Divide. It seemed like a daunting task to come up with enough four-state combinations to fit within the usual one-week vacation period assigned to each trip. But, much to our surprise, the geography allowed just that. We were able to construct travel programs which traversed reasonable distances within pods of four adjoining states. The only state that didn't fit this pattern was Colorado and our children's involvement resulted in a viable plan to take care of that one.

In celebration of our thirty-fifth wedding anniversary, Rob, Chris and Steve went together to give us a four-day trip to Colorado. It started at Estes Park, gateway to the Rocky Mountain National Park, which offers an unmatched taste of life in the high mountains. Rob had been there before. His enthusiasm for the place resonated with our own desire for such an adventure. The Rocky Mountains appear on the to-do list of most Americans and we were no exception. The fact that it also held the potential for including one of our tree-planting stops was just an additional benefit to what would be a great trip.

We stayed in our own cabin in the woods the first two nights. Each day we monitored the opening of US Highway #34 which travels sixty miles through the park. Usually it opens for the season on the last weekend of May but it was still closed due to snow the first day we were there. We spent the time touring all around Estes Park. One of the places we visited was The Stanley Hotel, a famous luxury hotel opened in 1909 by the inventor of the Stanley Steamer automobile. The building is constructed entirely of wood and has hosted world-famous dignitaries and celebrities throughout its history. It was used by Stephen King as the basis for the Overlook Hotel featured in the book and movie called *"The Shining."*

Finally the road opened on Monday, May 25th, which happened to be the day on which Memorial Day was celebrated that year and also our actual wedding anniversary date. Our plan was to travel the sixty miles through the park to the town of Granby from where we would drive to our planting site in Walden, Jackson County, another eighty miles or so away.

What a drive! The snow was piled up eight to ten feet high along both sides of the road the whole way through the park; in some places it was still laying on the road surface. The walls of snow proved to be a good thing because they mostly hid views of the precipitous drop-offs that always seemed to be on Joyce's side of the car. This route is not for the squeamish. At one point the road reaches an altitude of 12,183 feet which has to be one of the highest, if not the highest, public highway in the U.S. The road stays above the tree line for most of its distance as it passes through mountain tundra and alpine landscapes. It truly is breath-taking whenever you can pry open your eyes to look at it.

Beautiful as it was, we were glad to get down to a somewhat lower elevation in the town of Granby. This was the picture of a typical western town, perhaps a little of it constructed for the benefit of the tourist, but enjoyable just the same. We did some shopping, had lunch and then started out for Walden comforted by the fact that no more high-mountain passes lurked over the next eighty miles.

Walden is the county seat of Jackson County, named after Andrew Jackson, and the only incorporated municipality in a county of 1,621 square miles. The total population of 1,700 makes for a density of one person per square mile with just under a thousand of them living in Walden. The county was created in 1909, after years of litigation between two other counties who laid claim to the North Park area but were fearful of the Ute and Arapaho Indians defense of their ancestral hunting grounds. The discovery of minerals helped overcome the fear of incursion into these lands and the town of Walden, originally founded in 1889, became the center for processing land claims and other legal matters when it was appointed as the county seat in 1909. Most of its mineral wealth slowly ran out over the next one hundred years but ranching, hunting and other activities remain. Today, 64% of Jackson County is owned by Federal and State agencies and Walden calls itself *"The Moose Viewing Capital of Colorado."*

Our visit was arranged in discussions with Mayor Kyle Fliniau and his mother Sandra. They were extremely hospitable in setting up the plantings and assisted us in many other ways. Upon our arrival in Walden, we went to the Mayor's office for introductions and orientation. Kyle, one of two lawyers in town, gave us some local history then took us out to the "Vic and Sigrid Hanson Memorial Park" a few blocks from City Hall. His mother, Sandy, and her lady-friend joined us there. The park was mostly grass-covered with a gazebo, some small lodgepole pine trees and children's playground equipment. Off in the distance were snow-capped mountains rising another 4,000 feet above Walden's elevation of 8,099 feet. This would be the highest elevation at which we ever planted our trees.

Joyce mostly showed our scrapbooks to the ladies while the Mayor helped John dig the holes. We had brought along aspen trees purchased at Taiga Trees in Wellington, CO. They were about six to seven feet in height and we arranged them into two clumps with three in one and two in the other. The soil seemed rich enough but we later discovered that watering was a problem due to the semi-arid climate in the summertime. In one of her later letters, Sandy reported that she often had to carry water to the trees in buckets.

It was a fun event. The weather was perfectly clear and crisp as befitting a town near the top of the world. During most of the time we were able to wear the special short-sleeved tee shirt with the pictures of twenty-five different species on the front. Occasionally we would take a break at the picnic table but that was mostly for purposes of explaining something in the scrapbook rather than to cope with any shortness of breath. It didn't seem like we were affected by the altitude even though the place where we were was over 8,000 feet higher than the thirty-foot elevation where we lived outside of Houston, TX.

After the plantings we went to the newspaper office for an interview with Jim Dustin of *The Jackson County Star.* The newspaper had featured us in two preview articles on May 7 and 14, 1998, and followed these with a picture in the June 11, 1998, edition under the caption *"The Jackson Family Tree."* Then it was back to the mayor's office where he presented us with a Proclamation declaring May 26, 1998, as "John and Joyce Jackson Day" in Walden, Colorado.

Sandy Fliniau asked us to stop by her home before beginning the four-hour drive back to the Denver airport. There she served us refreshments as we each talked about the tree planting project and other aspects of our lives. She promised to stay in touch and she has. In a later note she described her efforts to obtain *"Tree City USA"* status for the town with the Arbor Day Foundation, something which we are very familiar with. In May, 2001, she authored an article in *The Jackson County Star* remembering our visit three years earlier and tying that into their on-going mission to continue planting trees in the community. She wrote *"So as you see, it's not hard to plant a tree. You can start with one and expand, maybe build a dream or a forest of your own. The Jacksons did it...How privileged we are to be part of their dream. We thank them for trusting us with their legacy."*

Randy Marple, Director of Parks and Recreation, Mayor T.L. Gramling and John and Joyce Jackson receiving a plaque inscribed "Certificate of Appreciation" from the City of Altus, Jackson County, Oklahoma for planting five **Fruitless Mulberry** trees.

The impressive bronze statue called "The Vision Seeker" sits in the East City Park, Altus, OK

H.Holden—Sculptor

Oklahoma

"Indian Territory"

September 7, 1998

The four states we selected for September, 1998, were stacked atop each other from Oklahoma to the Dakotas. All of them were characterized by open plains through which roads mostly ran on a straight line. Even the cities we were to visit almost lined up vertically on a map, with the exception of Altus, county seat of Jackson County, Oklahoma.

Oklahoma became a state in 1907 by combining the Oklahoma Territory and the Indian Territory. The latter was the termination point of the "Trail of Tears," while the former would be one of the stops on our "Trail of Trees."

The state of Texas claimed the 1.5 million acres around the Red River where Altus sits today. The Supreme Court of the United States decided in 1896 that it was part of the Oklahoma Territory which constituted the western portion of the modern-day state. Jackson County was formed out of this area upon statehood in 1907, named in honor of Thomas Jonathan (Stonewall) Jackson. It's the only place in our project named after the Confederate legend.

Oklahoma was the 46th state admitted to the Union; only New Mexico and Arizona, in 1912, succeeded it in statehood admission among the contiguous U.S. states. Other neighboring states were taken into the union much earlier: Texas (1845), Kansas (1861), Arkansas (1836), Colorado (1876), Missouri (1821). It's not unreasonable to suspect that its late admission to statehood was due, in part, to the Indian question.

For the majority of the 19th Century, the Indian Territory was the major resettlement point for Native Americans displaced by the U.S. government. We talked about some of those movements earlier in this book. By reliable accounts, 67 tribes are represented in the state today. Oklahoma has the greatest number of tribal headquarters, 39 federally-recognized nations and the second largest population of Native Americans in the country. A list of county names conveys a little of that flavor which includes tribal names like: Cherokee, Choctaw, Creek, Delaware, Ottawa, Potawatomie and Seminole. The history of the Delaware tribe provides another point of irony – the tribe originally known as the Lenni Lenape in their homelands along the Delaware River in Pennsylvania and Delaware, who were successively forced into Ohio, then Indiana, then Missouri and Kansas and, finally, the Indian Territory, the people who signed the first treaty with the newly-formed United States in 1778, now requires for admission to their tribal rolls proof that your blood ancestor was living in the Indian Territory in 1906. At long last, the tribe apparently has a place that they can call home. A place that eerily resounds with the Choctaw words that formed the state's name, *"okla homma."*

The ultimate break-up of the Indian Nations was accomplished by The Dawes Act of 1887. It was promulgated by a well-meaning Senator from Massachusetts who felt that giving each Indian 160 acres of land in Oklahoma would serve as reparations for any harm they experienced.

Unfortunately, this broke apart the tribal communal culture and, since the land was re-saleable, a good deal of it wound up in the hands of unscrupulous American speculators who often duped the Indians into giving up their property.

The Indians also chose the wrong side in two national wars for which they paid a dear price. Generally they supported the British in the Revolutionary War and suffered the consequences, especially those living in and around the eastern Great Lakes whose lands were confiscated and doled out to former colonial soldiers. In the Civil War, the Oklahoma Territories tended to side with the South. In fact, Brigadier General Stand Watie, a leader of the Cherokee nation, became the last Confederate general to surrender his troops on June 23, 1865. As punishment, this led the government to allocate more Indian lands as available for white settlement, eventually resulting in such events as the Oklahoma Land Rush of 1889, from which the term "Sooners" was derived.

No sooner than a few miles after leaving the Dallas-Fort Worth airport did we discover that the Pontiac Bonneville rental car had out-of-round tires. We should have gone back for a replacement but that would have meant adding more time to the four-hour trip that already lay ahead of us to Altus. So instead of returning it, we had to endure thumping sounds and vibrations over the next 1,500 miles of driving. It didn't dampen our enthusiasm for the trip but we sure were glad to end the annoyance by turning in that vehicle in Minneapolis on September 11th.

Crossing the Red River between Texas and Oklahoma, immortalized in the song "*The Red River Valley,*" we couldn't help but notice that it was dry, not a drop of water, nada. That's not what tree planters like to see but we continued on in the summer heat arriving in Altus in the late afternoon. We were able to find the park that Mayor T. L. Gramling had described to us. The search was aided by the sight of an imposing ballistic missile positioned upright on the property, hence the name Cole Heights Missile Park. That was an additional indication that helped us to realize that a major Air Force base is located here. It's a training base for the largest cargo planes and tankers in the service. The rest of the town is a very nice home to over 20,000 people.

We went right out to the park early the next morning. It was already 84 degrees with an overcast that hinted at rain. At the entrance stood a man who greeted us with "*You must be the Jacksons,*" it was Mayor Gramling. With him were Randy Marple, Director of Parks and Recreation and Carol Cole from *The Altus Times*. These people had given up part of their Labor Day holiday to attend our tree planting. They proved to be the only townspeople to do that despite a very nice preview story that ran in *The Altus Times* on September 6, 1998, which included a photograph of our greeting card that depicts each of our plantings on a map of the United States.

Randy had selected planting sites behind the backstops of baseball fields, number one and two, that were part of a four-diamond layout fanning out from each other. The holes were already dug and beside each one stood a large Fruitless Mulberry tree. They were eight to nine feet in height, sitting in twenty-five gallon containers. He had obtained the trees from the Southwest Garden Center & Dempsey Nursery in Blair, OK. They agreed to provide them under a special cost-sharing arrangement between us, the city and themselves that fit within our budget.

Randy was very genial and a hard worker. He labored on the trees while we showed the mayor through the scrapbook and told tales of our various travels. Actually we didn't let him do all the work by himself. We all joined in with us doing some of the backfilling of the holes and the mayor watering the trees with a garden hose. They also told us that a drip line would be installed to keep the trees watered during those hot, dry summer days. That discovery did a lot to resolve our concerns.

Mayor Gramling conducted a little ceremony at the conclusion of the plantings presenting us with a plaque inscribed *"Certificate of Appreciation from the City of Altus, OK."* He said that this would be one of his last official acts as he was retiring as mayor. Then he invited us back to his office which we did after conducting our own private meditation at the planting site. We said our prayers behind Field #1 where three trees represented our children and Field #2 where the other two represented their parents.

It was a very pleasant visit and we were thankful for meeting new friends like T.L. and Randy. Their warmness and enthusiasm for our mission to their town was apparent. It was a real comfort to know that they would be taking a continuing interest to provide our trees with the best care possible and to spread the story of our visit.

After visiting with the mayor we went on to the newspaper office. There Sandy Grimm took us back to the press room to give us a copy of their *Newcomer* magazine. Later, they sent us a copy of the September 8, 1998 edition with an article and photograph by Carol Cole under the head-line of *"A living legacy."*

We lingered a bit longer in the city to take in the courthouse and its Remington-like sculpture of a mounted cowboy herding cattle across the Red River. Then at East City Park we saw "The Vision Seeker," the impressive bronze statue of a war-bonneted Indian, sitting atop a flat rock with his hand on his chin in Rodin-like contemplation as he gazed across the plains towards some far-off vision.

Brad Mears, City Manager, Dianna Wilson, Chamber of Commerce Administrator and Mayor Richard J. Mulroy look over the Jackson's tree scrapbook while John and Joyce Jackson are out planting five **different species** of trees in Rafters Park.

Holton, Jackson County, Kansas

Kansas

"On the Edge of the Flint Hills"

September 8, 1998

The next stop after Altus was the home of our friends, Alton and Jo Ann Shexnayder, in Wichita, Kansas. We left around noon for the three-hundred mile drive north to visit with them overnight. The trip carried us into the Flint Hills of Kansas, considered to be the country's largest remaining tract of tall-grass prairie land.

The Charles Ingalls family briefly made their home in this area during which time daughter Carrie was born. Laura recollected that it was located near Independence, KS. Actually the parents of television personality, Bill Kurtis, owned the land on which the Ingalls family lived in 1870. He still owns a ranch in the vicinity. He and his sister, state Senator Jean Schodorf of Wichita, own the Little House site on which has been constructed a replica of the Ingalls' family cabin.

The Ingalls lived on Indian Territory in Kansas which, like Oklahoma, was originally designated to hold Native Americans displaced from east of the Mississippi. Many Kansas Indians, including the six resident tribes of Arapaho, Comanche, Kansa, Kiowa, Osage and Pawnee, had to undergo a further removal to Oklahoma. Today, the federally-recognized tribes living in Kansas are the Kickapoo, Iowa, Prairie Band, Sac and Fox.

After a pleasant visit with the Shexnayders, we drove three and a half hours northeast to Holton, county seat of Jackson County, KS, for our early-afternoon tree planting ceremony. The county traces its history to 1859 when the Territorial Legislature changed the one-year old county's name from Calhoun to Jackson. Apparently, John C. Calhoun, Senator from South Carolina and former Secretary of War, was pro-slavery and no longer considered suitable for recognition in a state where most citizens wanted to avoid taking a stand on this issue prior to statehood being granted in 1861. Andrew Jackson was considered a safer choice for the renaming of the county. The State Legislature reconfigured the boundaries for surrounding counties in 1868 with the county seat of Jackson County being retained at Holton.

Joyce held good expectations from her prior talks with City Manager Brad Mears and Rex Cameron, Parks and Lakes Committee member. We arrived early enough to look around the town. First we located Marianne Jarboe of Jarboe's Nursery who was ready for us with two Red Sunset Maples, two Shumard Oaks and one London Planetree. Not only did she arrange the costs inside of our budget but she also included fertilizer and mulch at no extra charge. We still had time for lunch so we headed into the city. It impressed us as a typical All-American town, with brick streets, a court house in the middle of the town square and well-kept establishments surrounding it. We had lunch at *New York on the Square* which was a little incongruous for us since we had recently moved to Texas from Northern New Jersey where we often took advantage of opportunities to explore the actual New York City.

We then went to City Hall to meet with Brad Mears. He was very enthusiastic about the gathering that awaited us at Rafters Park, the area's most-used facility. Brad led us over to the park and, sure enough, there were a lot of people assembled to greet us. Joining him and Rex were Mayor Richard Mulroy, Dianna Wilson, Chamber of Commerce Administrator, Sandra Siebert, reporter from *The Holton Recorder*, Kerwin McKee and Chuck Hill, city employees, and Marianne Jarboe.

Mayor Mulroy welcomed us to the city with a proclamation declaring September 8, 1998 as *"Jackson Day"* in Holton. As he spoke the work crew was maneuvering a dump truck and a water truck into position near the children's playground. Kerwin and Chuck proceeded to toil over the holes as we showed our hosts the scrapbook of previous plantings encouraging them to take all the time they wanted. Sandra Siebert of *The Holton Recorder* used a lot of this information for the front-page story which ran in the September 10, 1998 edition along with two photographs taken at the planting site.

After wrapping up with the newspaper reporter, we headed over to help the city employees who had been joined by Rex Cameron. The four of us men made short work of the excavations and tree positioning under Joyce's careful supervision.

While backfilling the dirt around the holes someone noticed the different shades of soil on the blades of our trenching tools. These two collapsible shovels had accompanied us to each planting. In Hawaii we picked up some extra-sticky volcanic residue that was really hard to dislodge. That got added to soil specimens from the three subsequent places we visited. Each time we used the shovels at a new site a little more of the combined soils rubbed off into the ground. Who knows – maybe some seeds were mixed in along with the dirt and now there's a pineapple tree growing in Kansas.

The trees were between three and seven feet in height. They were placed in a horseshoe formation with Joyce providing the following symbolism: the points of the horseshoe represented herself and daughter Christine, while the three men in the family were somewhere around the bend. The trees were placed well apart as some of them will grow to a height of 70 to 100 feet with a spread of 65 to 80 feet. They were also selected for their hardiness within a city environment. Rafters Park is well patronized by the residents who can enjoy fishing in the adjacent Elkhorn Lake, swimming in one of the largest WPA-sponsored swimming pools ever constructed, playing baseball, softball and sand volleyball or picnicking in the shelter houses.

The whole affair proceeded at a leisurely pace with people taking the time to talk with each other. Conversations and work stretched out over two hours, which is twice the amount of time that we usually spent at a planting site. It indicated how much everyone was interested in our project but it also revealed some of the "just folks" charm for which prairie people are famous.

After everyone departed, we attended to those last details that occur at each site. We checked to make sure that the earthen dams around the base of each tree would hold water; slipped the plastic protectors around the tree trunks to prevent damage from the weed whackers and took off the tree labels used at the nursery. It was a pleasing feeling to realize that we had left the community with five young trees that should eventually be of a size to provide much-needed shade in that part of the park.

Our last act in Holton was to return the unused mulch and root stimulator that Marianne Jarboe had given to us at no charge. We figured she could always use that stuff around the nursery and, besides, we just thought it would be the neighborly thing to do.

It's amazing how much this project has affected us in a positive way.

Father Michael G. Printy , Pastor of St.Patrick's Catholic Church (circa 1880) recited "Trees" by Joyce Kilmer and blessed the five **Mayday** trees planted at the Community Park.

Jackson, Nebraska

Mayor Brian O'Neil helps John Jackson plant a **Mayday** tree at the Community park.

Children from the local Elementary School help Mr. Jackson plant another **Mayday** tree.

188

Nebraska

"God Bless These Trees"

September 10, 1998

The route to Jackson, Nebraska was almost straight north from Holton, KS, passing through Nebraska City which has a strong connection in the history of tree planting. It was from here that J. Sterling Morton founded Arbor Day in 1872, which was adopted in all states by 1894. His legacy is sustained today in the National Arbor Day Foundation, headquartered in Lincoln, NE. We referred to information published by this organization in the planning of the project and encountered its nationwide presence in several locations through its *Tree City USA* initiative.

In 1994, our story was published by the Foundation in their July / August edition of *Arbor Day* under the headline *"Move Over Johnny Appleseed."* Later in the year, they awarded us a *"Certificate of Merit"* in recognition of our *"efforts on behalf of trees and environmental stewardship."* Although we had no affiliation with the Arbor Day Foundation, we felt that a certain kinship existed between their national scope and the objectives of The Jackson Legacy.

Visiting the Arbor Day Foundation's headquarters in Lincoln was a little off-route for us; instead, we decided to stop at the Arbor Day Farm / Lied Conference Center in Nebraska City which was right on the way to Jackson, NE. This complex is situated on what was once the agricultural estate of J. Sterling Morton. It is a designated National Historic Landmark. The construction of the conference center was made possible by a combination of grants and donations from Foundation members. It is the only education center of its kind in America with the staff and programs dedicated to tree planting and environmental stewardship. It's also a very impressive building constructed mostly of wood and incorporating the latest in environmentally-friendly construction features.

We stayed overnight in one of their earthy, timbered rooms. The surrounding grounds included various kinds of natural habitats and growing examples of different agriculture all laid out in an easy, walkable design. We enjoyed strolling through these gardens at twilight and the next morning, after meeting with Chris Aden, the General Manager at Arbor Day Farm.

He explained a lot about the Arbor Day Foundation. They fund themselves and do not accept donations in order to avoid pressure groups. It's refreshing to know that they are not a far-left tree-hugging organization but have a philosophy which balances off the aesthetic with the practical utility of wood. We showed him our scrapbook and he was very impressed. After speaking for an hour, we left to explore the gift shop. There we discovered the same tee shirt with the pictures of twenty-five trees that we had purchased on Cape Cod many years earlier which we wore to all of our plantings.

The Arbor Day Farm was a delightful place to visit. We lingered there as long as we could but after lunch it was time to begin the 150-mile trip to Jackson. An hour up the road was Omaha where we picked up interstate highway I-29. A couple of years earlier the owner of a trucking company had brought us out for a two-day visit in connection with a job interview which included a tour to all parts of the area. Since we weren't in any hurry, we spent some time revisiting a few of these sites such as Boys Town and places along the banks of the Missouri River.

That left us with about one hundred miles of travel to the place in Sioux City, IA which was recommended to us for purchasing the trees. Joe Fisher at the Better Homes and Gardens Nursery recommended Mayday trees (*prunus padus commutada*) although we weren't familiar with that species. He said it was related to the chokecherry. It's a low-growing tree that is the first to bloom in the spring. Birds are attracted to eat its fruit giving rise to its common name of European Bird Cherry. The trees were five to six feet in height which the trunk of the Pontiac Bonneville could handle for the ten-mile drive to Jackson.

Joyce called her contact Donna Hirsch from the hotel the night before the planting. Donna told us to expect quite a turnout at the community park near St. Patrick's church. Given the size of the town, we didn't expect any trouble in finding the location.

It may be a small village but it has an interesting history that typifies the common experiences of pioneers as they sought to establish their communities in an unforgiving land. In 1855, a Catholic priest led sixty, mostly-Irish people from Garryowen, Iowa, across the Missouri River into Nebraska. They established one of the first settlements in Dakota County which they named St. John City, in honor of St. John the Baptist. Half of them perished in the following severe winter. The survivors built a church in 1856 which was the first Catholic parish in the state only to see it destroyed by a tornado in 1860. Their priest, Father Jeremiah Trecy, traveled off to Washington, D.C. that year seeking permission to build a mission for the Ponca Indians living in Northeastern Nebraska. He was still there when the Civil War broke out and reassigned as a chaplain. He never returned to his people in Jackson. The village continued to grow, reaching two hundred in population in the early 1860's. By the middle of the decade, the river had shifted its course wiping out the entire village. The people still persisted by moving their settlement one mile south, this time naming it Jackson, named after Andrew Jackson after finding out that the name of Franklin was already taken. Over the next hundred or so years the village has remained at the same population level equally divided between those of Irish and German ancestry.

The first thing that caught our eyes in entering the village was the number of cars parked in what looked like a field. Then we saw the people and realized that this must be the park where our tree plantings were to take place. Several people came to greet us including the mayor of the village, Brian O'Neil, his wife Vicky, Donna Hirsch, and Tom Lynch who had just moved back from a sojourn in Dallas, TX. There were lots of other people standing and sitting in a picnic pavilion. Then a rush of children flowed out of the adjoining school building to join what was now growing into a small throng. Donna was right – there was quite a reception waiting for us, including television crews and newspaper reporters.

The holes were dug the previous day near the baseball field with a sign identifying the team as the Jackson Jackhammers. Two of them were placed near the bleachers and the other three along the first-base side of the field. Mayor O'Neill went right to work on the holes dressed in appropriate attire for the occasion, golf shirt and jeans. We measured, to make sure the holes were deep enough, then coaxed the trees out of their containers into each hole. All the while the children followed us in groups from tree to tree keeping up a constant chatter. They asked questions like: "*what kind of trees are they?; how high will they grow?; why are you doing this?; who are you, again?*"and all the other types of questions that kids are prone to ask. At each hole we chose a couple of them to help with pushing the dirt around the base of the trees.

The grown-ups mostly stayed around the pavilion where Joyce was kept busy darting back from the tree sites to show them the scrapbook and to do interviews for the media. We had gotten very comfortable with newspaper reporters who could refer to our press release as well as their interview notes in piecing together a story at their copy desk. TV was something altogether different because it made you simultaneously assemble your thoughts while talking at the camera. In the process you wonder if you're getting your point across and, of course, how am I looking to everyone out there in TV land. Two stations from Sioux City, KCAU Channel 9 with Jerry Gallagher and KTIV Channel 4 Evening News, did a good job editing together the pieces, according to what we saw on the video tapes sent to us from Donna Hirsch. Irma Foulks, reporter for the *Sioux City Journal*, sent us a copy of her article and photograph which appeared in the September 11, 1998, edition.

Mayor O'Neill conducted a ceremony at the conclusion of the plantings. He thanked us for coming to the village of Jackson for so worthy a purpose. The two of us each made short speeches in return. The audience clapped politely at the end of each speech which gave us short bursts of what it must feel like to be a celebrity. Then Father Michael G. Printy, pastor of St. Patrick's Church, made everything even more special. First, he recited, from memory, the poem *"Trees"* by Joyce Kilmer. He followed that with something that no one else had ever done before at one of our plantings – he blessed the trees. In calling on God's blessing he stated that *"A person who plants trees is always thinking about someone else."* What a nice thing to say and what a way for us to think about all those hundreds of people with whom we came in contact during our project.

Our stay in Jackson, NE wasn't over yet. All of us went back to the pavilion for juice, cookies and more fellowship. The kids wanted to stay longer but their teachers herded all fifty-four of them back to the classrooms for grades K through 8. Later, we visited the post office to get our postcards hand-cancelled by Darrell Hoover with the Jackson postmark, made a visit to St. Patrick's Church, built in the 1880's, and had lunch at the Sweet Tooth where Tom Lynch's sister showed us the note on the bulletin board calling all people to meet the Jacksons at the ballpark.

During our speeches at the end of the tree planting both of us said what a pleasure it was for us to be in their town. It really was. When practically the whole village turns out for the occasion, when the peace of the people and the place permeates everything and when God, himself, is invoked to bless our endeavor, what more could anyone ask?

Tragically, Jackson was to become another of the places we visited to be hit by a tornado. It occurred on August 17, 2001, at 5:45PM on a Friday afternoon. The twister destroyed some homes and the school as it touched down twice within the town. Fortunately no one was killed. Most of the houses have been rebuilt and a new school has been constructed. Mayor O'Neill reported to us, in 2009, that our trees were not affected by the storm. Most of them have survived and are living testimony to the efforts of a town and two strangers to create a little more beauty in a place named Jackson.

As the local TV Channel tapes the presentation , Mayor Tom Seifert presents a plaque to John and Joyce Jackson for planting five **Ash** trees in their local park.

Christine, North Dakota

North Dakota

"Not Far From Fargo"

September 11, 1998

One of the ironies of this four-state trip is that it began and ended in two places called the Red River Valley. Perhaps the more familiar one forms the border between Texas and Oklahoma which we crossed on the way to our planting site in Altus, OK. In fact, there's a statue in the center of the town showing a cowboy driving steers entitled "Crossing the Red." The one that we encountered in North Dakota is commonly called The Red River of the North, for obvious reasons, but it is as equally distinguished as its southern namesake.

The Red River Valley of the North extends into Manitoba, Minnesota and North Dakota. It was part of the consideration in determining the lands that would be included in setting the boundary between the United States and Canada at the 49th Parallel. Its rich, fertile soils were deposited from Lake Agassiz, the name given to the prehistoric lake which used to cover an area larger than the Great Lakes. The lakebeds of these prehistoric bodies of water resulted in the flat plains of the Midwest after they receded away.

Into these plains came the original Native American tribes such as the Ojibwe, also known as the Chippewa. They and their related bands were the most populous native people of the upper plains. Consequently they had to be reckoned with in the expansion plans of the U.S. government in the mid-18th century. That was resolved by the Treaty of Old Crossing in 1863 which extinguished the Ojibwe claims to the land and opened up the most fertile portions of the valley for later settlement by Caucasian people. Many of these new settlers were immigrants from Scandinavian countries who steadily moved into the area throughout the latter part of the century.

We got to see plenty of the plains as our little, thumping Pontiac covered the 320-mile drive from Jackson, NE to Christine, ND. The route was almost entirely along Interstate 29 and it made us wonder what the pioneers would have given for such a paved road. It reminded us of the frequent relocations of the Charles Ingalls family, especially when we passed through Brookings, SD, only forty-two miles east of their final homesite in De Smet, SD. It's amazing to think that the family lived in six different prairie states at a time when the usual mode of family travel was a Conestoga covered wagon.

In South Dakota we saw a sign for the town of Crooks, the same as Joyce's maiden name. She wondered whether there would be enough towns of that name around the country to support something like we we're doing with the Jackson name. After thinking about it some more, we decided there weren't too many places that would want to be identified with crooks.

There are no places named Jackson in North Dakota that we could find. The only choice that fit into our naming criteria was the town of Christine, our daughter's name. We could see that it wasn't far from Fargo, ND, which was where we decided to room for the night and purchase the trees. Even though it was nearing dusk, we had time to make our customary investigation of the town that was hosting our tree planting. Christine is a neat little town with a population around one hundred-fifty souls. In prior conversations arranging our visit, Mayor Tom Seifert informed us that the location for the trees would be the town park near the pavilion. It wasn't any problem finding the spot. No one was around to see us slip into and out of their town.

Fargo is the center of activity in this part of the Red River Valley. It had a heightened prominence this particular week due to being the home town of Roger Maris. Two days prior to our visit, as we sat in the timbered room at the Lied's Conference Center in Nebraska City watching the baseball game on television, we saw Mark McGwire hit his 62nd home run which broke the record that Roger Maris had surpassed from Babe Ruth in 1961. The whole Maris family was at the game in St. Louis, which was stopped so they could embrace McGwire. Everyone made touching remarks about Roger, a quiet unassuming man who died a few years earlier. It was with reverence that we went to the Roger Maris museum, set up in a shopping mall in Fargo, to see artifacts from his playing days with the New York Yankees and other teams. It's sad to think that such an honest, hard-working man's indelible mark on the game he loved has been supplanted in the record books by the likes of Barry Bonds, Mark McGwire and Sammy Sosa. Fortunately, there's another man from Fargo who embodies the character of Roger Maris in the person of Chris Coste, catcher for the 2008 World Champion Philadelphia Phillies. (As life-long Phillies fans, we had to find some way to insert a mention of our favorite team)

The morning of September 11th, we went to the Baker Nursery to meet with Eric Baker. He was very enthused about our project and suggested we plant ash trees. The ones he selected were seven feet tall and would grow to over forty feet in height. Ironically, ash is the most common wood used to make baseball bats, which seemed like another nice connection to the Roger Maris story. Eric was also very generous in pricing the trees to stay within our $100 budget. He even had his assistant, Cynthia, drive them the twenty-five miles to Christine for us and later came out to the planting ceremony.

We met Mayor Seifert and his wife, Judy, at their house in town, not far from the park. She was the President of the Park Commission in addition to being the "First Lady" of Christine. They led us over to the park where a large gathering of townspeople was forming next to the picnic pavilion, including Mort Berg, one of the Richland County commissioners. The mayor brought along shovels and Karen Ellingson, a Park Board member, provided a pike for turning up the dirt at each planting site. The soil was full of small pebbles but that didn't pose any problem in the face of the implements they provided. We kept our collapsible shovels out of sight for the time being. Everyone was just about ready to dig when several vans rolled up out of which poured cameramen and reporters from all three television stations in Fargo, as well as Karissa Lietz from the *Wahpeton Daily News*. The TV crews got up close and personal as the mayor and the two of us worked over the holes. Several times one of us had to pop up to be part of an interview while the other two just kept on digging away. The media would remain until all of the photo opportunities were exhausted.

The trees were set up in a semi-circle, well-spaced apart from each other. They became practically the only deciduous trees near the pavilion shelter which is one of the reasons why the townspeople were glad to receive our donation. The crowd had really grown; it was almost as if the mayor had a declared a local holiday. A lot of them began to set up for a picnic which they said would be in our honor.

Amidst all this activity, we steadily did the work of digging, adding peat moss to the holes, placing the trees, tamping down the soil around their base, building the earthen dams with our trusty trenching tools and then watering them. We didn't stop until the complete planting procedure was taken care of, no matter how close the cameras got or how many times the video camera's red light came on.

When all the planting work was completed, Mayor Seifert unveiled two inscribed plaques from the city of Christine and presented one to us containing the key to the city in appreciation of our contribution. The other one, identical except for substituting a shovel in place of the key, would hang in the Town Hall as a permanent commemoration of our visit. A TV guy held a boom microphone up to the group as the mayor made the presentation and we expressed our gratitude for such an outstanding reception. Finally the media had enough footage to take back to the station, so they folded their tri-pods, stowed their gear and headed back to Fargo, not far away.

That concluded what proved to be the first half of our time in Christine. Lunchtime was fast approaching but first the Seiferts took us on a tour of the town covering the Town Hall, the "Mall" and other notable structures. That gave the people back at the shelter time to set up for lunch which was waiting for our enjoyment when we got back from the sweep around town. The meal was accompanied by the easy conversation of people who laugh heartily and exude neighborly charm. They were continually amazed how far we had come and sincerely honored that we had chosen their town. They wanted us to stay on for the fish fry that night but our travel plans required us to get on the road to Minneapolis for the return flight home to Texas.

The headline in Karissa Lietz's preview article on September 10th referred to our project as "*Adventurous em(bark)ing*", saying "(*Christine) wasn't picked on a hunch, it didn't enter a contest, it was simply picked because of its name.*" She also reported "*It was a* BIG *day for the city of Christine and its community.*" It was for us, too. It would be hard to surpass the warmth and scope of the reception that the people of Christine accorded us.

Another person who helped us during the planning was Pat Pfingsten. She sent us a follow-up letter in which she stated that a neighbor was inspired by our visit to plant a flowering plum tree along with ours in memory of her deceased husband. Karen Ellingson also wrote two years later to let us know that the trees were doing fine.

The whole four-state tour was outstanding. Every community we visited was involved from the mayor on down. The participants appeared to grow in number at each succeeding stop, reaching its peak in Christine. It was quite a way to end up the 1998 portion of the program. Almost before we thought about it, there were now only nine more states left in a project that at one time seemed so formidable.

Joyce Jackson overseeing the planting of a twelve foot **Pear** tree that will grace an area in front of City Hall.
Aztec, San Juan County, NM

A lasting relic of the Anasazis Indians in the Chaco Canyon, New Mexico

New Mexico

"Westward Ho"

The eight western states we needed to cover in 1999 represented a wide expanse of geography. We decided to split them into four-state itineraries, one to be conducted in June and the other in September. The June timetable would take us to the states of New Mexico, Arizona, Utah and Nevada.

There was no community actually named Jackson in any of these states so we had to use the alternative naming criteria that we had developed for this type of situation. This resulted in our selection of Jackson County for one state and a mountain named Jackson for another. The names of the two other states were a bigger challenge to come up with and, for the first and only time, we had to incorporate the Spanish name for John, actually St. John – San Juan County in New Mexico and Utah, both named after the San Juan River which flows through the two states.

We literally inserted pins into a map of the U.S. to get a feel for the location of these four points. Surprisingly, we were able to determine that the planting locations in New Mexico, Arizona and Utah were generally within 200 miles of each other. That meant we could cover the first three states in one tour, beginning and ending at the same starting point of Albuquerque, before making a separate flight to Nevada which was out of easy geographic range to the others.

The June trip started with a flight from Houston to Albuquerque. It was our first visit to that city and we enjoyed the Spanish charm of its architecture and life-style. After spending a day there, we headed towards Aztec, county seat of San Juan County. En route, we came upon Chaco Culture National Historical Park, the ancient home of the Anasazi Indians. It was one of those encounters that we hadn't planned upon and it proved to be an enriching experience.

As an American, we don't often think of our country in terms of ancient history. Due to our mostly-European heritage, a majority of us feel that American history started in 1492. The physical examples of our earliest existence are often reconstructions of a settlement like Plymouth, Massachusetts or Jamestown, Virginia, or, at best, buildings from the 18th century. Few of us confront evidence of ancient life within the present-day boundaries of our own country and that is what's so powerful about Chaco Canyon.

The still-standing structures in this place can be traced to the period between 850 and 1150 A.D. The Anasazis built a network of masonry dwellings connected with each other into a city that housed over a thousand people. It was a center for Pueblo culture that became extinct for unknown reasons. It is striking to stand on our own soil to witness something from the same time frame of antiquity when the Vikings roamed the world and the signing of the Magna Carta was still centuries away. The time spent and the forty miles of travel over dirt roads to visit Chaco Canyon were well worth the effort.

The City of Aztec, NM is situated in the high desert at an altitude of over 5,600 feet. On the way there we passed through landscape that undoubtedly looks very different at other times of the year. When we were there, it was spring in the desert and the cacti and wild flowers were in bloom. Aztec was also greened up. The city is notable for the number of trees growing throughout the community which made it appear almost like an oasis to us, compared to the scenery outside of town. We later discovered that the city had applied for *Tree City USA* status.

The community of Aztec dates back to 1890, well before New Mexico became a state in 1912. It sits near some ancient Pueblo ruins which are known today as Aztec Ruins National Monument. With a population of over 6,400, it is an important center in the northwestern part of the state. It had everything we needed to choose it as a site for our tree planting, except Jackson in its name.

The city officials showed a lot of enthusiasm about our visit in previous talks with Joyce. In lieu of that, each new place always presented us with a little bit of apprehension until we actually got there. Eric Aune, City Planner, and Don Greenwood, Parks and Recreation Director, were two men who had worked with us on the advance arrangements. Don said that the city would provide the trees and help with the planting. The plan was to meet at City Hall which was within walking distance of the site.

Quite a few people were waiting for us when we arrived at City Hall around nine o'clock in the morning. The size of the reception committee immediately put us at ease and raised expectations for a better-than-average visit. Don and Eric were there to welcome us along with Mayor Mike Arnold, Mayor Pro-Tem Jerry Hanhardt and Debi Lee, the City Manager. They indicated that the trees would grace an area in front of City Hall next to the Desert Planters Garden Club, Memorial Rose Garden. A number of garden club members joined us as we walked out to the location, along with Judge Barbara Aldez, Police Chief Mike Heal and Roberta Roberts, secretary to the City Manager. The list of attendees also included Gary Spickelmier, Sherri Gurule, Shawnee Collins, Carmine Gay, Lori Hansen, Joanie Looney and Roberta Archuletta-Valdez. City employee Steven Parks was standing alongside one of the pre-dug holes in readiness for work. However, we noticed that there were only holes dug for three trees, not the five that go along with our project.

We gingerly brought up the subject, trying to avoid any semblance of disappointment. After all, the City had come out in force for our arrival, spent their own money on the trees and they were very proud of their efforts in our behalf. We could see a line of three widely-placed trees that occupied the entire space of available land next to the garden club. Could the other two be planned for somewhere else, as we had encountered in North Carolina or Indiana? Finally, we came to find out that the three were all they had purchased for the time being with plans to add two more at some future date. Again, no one could have detected any trace of disappointment from us but it was there nevertheless. Five is better than three, but three will have to do, for now.

It really didn't dampen any of the enthusiasm involved with the actual tree planting. Steve pitched in with us to complete the process. This is one of the few places where Joyce didn't have to fret about the depth and diameter of the diggings. The width of the holes could have accommodated much larger trees than the ones we had to deal with. One was a twelve-foot pear tree and the other two were seven-foot plum trees, obtained from San Juan Nursery in Farmington,

NM. The ground was very sandy but we used a good amount of peat moss to enrich the soil. As usual, Joyce shuffled in and out of the planting activities to show our scrapbook to those observing.

The television crew from KOBF-TV, Channel 12, in Farmington was late in arriving. They had been tipped off by a lady in the motor vehicle department upon our initial arrival. The crew covered the twelve miles from the station to Aztec quickly but all of the festivities were over by the time they arrived. They asked us to re-enact it for the benefit of the viewers of the afternoon and evening news programs. And, of course, we did. The re-enactment was easy for us to do since we had become accomplished stars on TV as a result of our many video performances during the project.

In the hustle and bustle, we didn't get much time to be alone with our trees. We were invited back to City Hall for more ceremonies and interviews for the newspaper. While there, Lori Cave, asked if we wanted to donate money for the planting of five trees at Chaco State Park. We gave her a check for $100.00. As it worked out, we didn't have to pay for the three trees planted by the City but we wound up paying for five trees to be placed elsewhere in the area. Sort of like three trees for the price of five.

The people of Aztec were very gracious to us. They went out of their way to provide a memorable reception. *The Aztec Local News* featured us in articles in their two June editions, the last of which was contributed by Eric Aune. He also sent us a picture one year later which showed how they had laid turf and boxed-in the areas around the bottoms of the healthy-looking trees. But there were still only three of them in the picture.

City employees of St Johns help plant **Red Maples** at the St Johns fairgrounds.

St. Johns, Arizona

Fertile valleys abound for grazing livestock.

Arizona

"John's Turn"

The three counties in which we planted our trees on this tour, comprised three fourths of the counties forming the famed "Four Corners" area, where the states of Arizona, New Mexico, Utah and Colorado meet. The journey from Aztec, New Mexico took us near the Four Corners but we decided to postpone that visit and hit it on the return drive to Albuquerque after planting in Utah.

The drive through San Juan County, NM, also took us through land in which 64% of the area has been assigned to Indian Reservations, predominately Navajo with a smattering of Ute. Apache County, Arizona, has a similar proportion of Navajo people, who make up the largest Native American tribe. It is one of only three U.S. counties where the most spoken language is neither English nor Spanish; 58% of the population speaks Navajo at home while the total makeup of the county is 77% Native American. The county is the sixth largest in the U.S. in total area, larger than eight states, the closest in size being Massachusetts. Apache County is the longest county in the nation at 211 miles in length. Within its borders, besides the Navajo Reservation, are the Fort Apache Indian Reservation, the Petrified Forest National Park and the Canyon de Chelly National Monument. We had to travel practically the entire length of the county to reach the county seat of St. Johns.

At about the half-way point in this drive sits Hubbell Trading Post National Historic Site. We stopped to see well-preserved stone and adobe buildings which gave us a real taste for what life was like out here in the late nineteenth century. It was a time when the native people were trying to adjust to life with the Anglos who had moved onto the land after the U.S. Army had relocated the Indian population. In Navajo circles this was known as the Long Walk as they were forcibly moved to new locations and then gradually let back in to live on reservations. The trading-post commerce allowed the Indians to exchange their wool, sheep and handicrafts for food, tobacco and other staples under a bartering system which lasted well into the twentieth century before money was introduced into the transactions.

The land in the north of the county is mostly stark, with mesas, red sandstone cliffs, valleys and canyons. Towards the south there are fertile valleys ideal for grazing livestock, so appealing that the Navajos sometimes allow their sheep and cattle to wander off the reservation to enjoy this rich grazing land. Since they make up such a large proportion of the county's inhabitants, it doesn't appear to bother the other ranchers in the area that much.

Driving south through the county we passed over Interstate 40 / U.S. 66, the famous Route 66 that's been sort of a legend even before the old television series of the that name. We also encountered it in Albuquerque during our visit a few days earlier where we took plenty of pictures and bought the obligatory souvenirs. There's something about certain old routes that captures certain people's imaginations, like the Lincoln Highway, the National Road and, of course, getting your kicks on Route 66.

Jackson Butte Recreational Area was the only place named Jackson in the state of Arizona but it didn't offer any facilities for hosting our visit. As stated earlier in the book, if there's no Jackson in the state, our substitute is the first name of a family member. In this case it became St. Johns in Apache County. It marks the first and only time that the name John was used in our project, not counting the two states where we used San Juan which is the Spanish translation of St. John.

Apache County was created in 1879 as an even-larger entity until Navajo County was carved from it in 1895. The city of St. Johns became the permanent county seat in 1892. It is also one of the highest places we planted in at an elevation of 5,725 feet. It is a town of nearly 4,000 in population living in an environment that would typify the old west to a lot of outsiders.

The first person we encountered upon arriving into St. Johns was an Indian, not an American Indian but an Asian Indian who called himself Mike and managed the Days Inn motel. After checking in we walked around the town to get a better feel for the surroundings. Our instructions were to show up at the City Hall in the morning which we had no trouble spotting the night before. We sat in the motel room that night thinking about how far we had come and how different the places were from what we were used to.

As was always the case, even the little bit of pre-game jitters that we felt was unfounded. It was dispelled immediately through the gracious reception we received upon our arrival at City Hall from Betty Clanton, the Administrative Assistant. Our primary contact in setting up the event was Ross Carpenter, Parks and Recreation Director. He greeted us and was joined a few minutes later by Geraldine Davis and James Goodwin, reporters for the *White Mountain Independent*. Jim was a recent journalism graduate from Nebraska working for his first newspaper. There's another reporter on the staff who uses the byline of Tom Jackson King, those first and middle names being the same as John's brother. But James Goodwin did a great job with his article and photograph that appeared on the front page of the June 11, 1999 issue of the newspaper, under the headline "*St. Johns part of couple's family tree.*"

The town was well prepared for us. To give us an idea of what was in store, Ross drove us to the two sites they had selected. Three trees were going to be placed temporarily at the fairgrounds to be later transplanted to the new health-care facility under construction. The other two would be placed next to the administration building at Aztec's general-aviation airport. During the orientation trip, Ross provided some more background regarding the two locations and about the city. Perhaps the purpose of the preview trip was to determine if we agreed with their plans before taking us out to the sites to do the actual planting. It's always best to avoid transplanting a tree, as they planned to do with the ones going into the fairgrounds, but that concern was off-set by our desire to cooperate with them in any way we could.

We returned to City Hall to pick up our rented van where the five red maples were waiting. The trees were purchased at Davis Feeds, in St. Johns, operated by Tommy and Nelson Davis. First we went to the City of St. Johns Fairground Park and the adjoining Apache County Fairgrounds. There our little entourage was joined by City Manager, Steve Anderson, city employee, Hank Hamlin, and Mike from the Rotary Club, not the Mike from the Days Inn. Thank goodness, Hank had brought extra shovels for us because we only had the little collapsible trenching tools. Admittedly, that was partially a ploy on our part to encourage the locals to help us with the digging but in practical terms, we couldn't afford to buy shovels, as we did in Minnesota, only to donate them at the last stop on each year's tour.

The quality of the ground looked poor but there were other trees growing in the immediate vicinity. On the other hand, the dead trunks of ones that didn't survive stood beside each of the three holes that were dug. The dirt seemed somewhat richer as we turned it out of the holes. To give it a boost we added some peat moss and fixed up the dirt at the base to hold in the water, which we figured would require copious amounts in this climate. We happily noticed that there was a sprinkler system within reach of the trees. The proximity of water hadn't helped the dead poplars adjoining each hole, whose trunks had been cut off about six up, to serve as tie-up stakes for the new trees.

Then we moved out to the airport. That was pretty exciting since John is a plane freak and this was the only time we were able to integrate an aviation location into the project. It was like a mini-testimony to the place that aviation played in The Jackson Legacy. It would have been impossible to cover the tens of thousands of miles involved without the use of commercial airlines, not to mention the added tribute to whomever invented the frequent flyer program, which we used to our advantage several times.

Gary Liston, the airport manager, was so happy to have our two trees at his site that he already had the holes dug before our arrival. Like the ones planted earlier, they were six to seven feet tall and made an immediate contribution to the otherwise sparsely-landscaped lawn of the administration building. Gary explained that the airport was a fairly-busy refueling stop-off for light aircraft flying between Texas and the West Coast. Naturally, as Texans ourselves, our chests swelled out at the mention of the Lone Star state.

Most of the group stayed with us throughout both plantings. As we departed at the end, Mike invited us to speak at the Rotary Club luncheon but we had to decline in order to start right out for the next destination. When everyone was gone we took care of our own dedication, even slipping back to the fairgrounds. We felt as if we had made another impact on another place, or as the newspaper quoted Joyce, *"So it makes a difference…and I think we're doing that."*

Monticello's City Manager digs a hole for one of five **Blue Spruce** to be planted outside the town Library.

Monticello, San Juan County, Utah

Utah

"Mormon Country"

June 9, 1999

As mentioned in the two previous chapters, the first three states on our initial 1999 tour were proximate to the "Four Corners" area. Two of them, in New Mexico and Utah, were within a hundred mile radius of that junction while St. Johns, Arizona was within two hundred miles, directly south. Consequently, the terrain traversed between these places was similar in a number of ways. Everywhere around us were sandstone structures carved out of the landscape by the weather over countless centuries. Some of these have been assigned names in accordance with their appearance like Ship Rock, Mexican Hat Rock and Chimney Rock. There are countless other formations without names but identified in such quintessential western terms as a chaparral, mesa, wash, canyon, gorge, arroyo or butte. We were never without this scenery the whole time although it varied in its range of earthy colors, texture and expanse.

Many national parks have been established in this region to provide people with access to their natural beauty. One of the most famous of these sits astride the border of Arizona and Utah not too far from where we crossed – Monument Valley. It's been the location for numerous movies and other commercial enterprises but serious movie buffs remember it most as the unforgettable background in John Ford-directed westerns starring John Wayne, like *Stagecoach* and *The Searchers.*

Most of these movies gave a certain negative characterization to the Indians that fit the stereotypical views existing throughout most of our history. Somewhere in the latter part of the twentieth century more of us began to seriously contemplate the place of the Native Americans in our culture and accord them the respect that they deserve. Even so, it's one thing to develop an understanding of Indian life through books and movies and quite another to actually experience, as we did, the not-too pleasant realities of life on the reservations that stretched throughout the three states we visited. It left us with the impression that more can still be done for these people.

The San Juan River plays a role in our story. It starts in southwestern Colorado in the San Juan Mountains, flows through northwestern New Mexico and enters Utah very close to the Four Corners. From here it meanders through southern Utah until meeting the Colorado River at Lake Powell, which is the second largest man-made reservoir in the United States. Both counties where we planted our trees, in New Mexico and Utah, take their names from this river. St. John being the English translation, and there being no communities named Jackson in these states, we elected to use the county seats in these alternatively-named places in connection with our project. Sometimes it took awhile for us to get that point across to the local people in explaining why we selected their town for our tree plantings when the name Jackson was not a part of their identity.

It was Joyce's task to enlist community support for the project in advance of our visit. When she called the office of the highest ranking official the call was usually taken by an administrative assistant. In the case of Monticello, Utah, it was Michele who first heard our story and, as other call screeners did, she referred us to someone who she thought could be of help. That turned out to be Rita Walker, City Recorder / Clerk. Rita was instrumental in guiding our request through the appropriate channels of government and stayed in touch all the way to the conclusion of our actual visit. She arranged the involvement of others including the Mayor, the Police Chief, the City Manager and the Director of Parks and Recreation.

Monticello is the county seat of San Juan County. It sits at an elevation over 7,000 feet with a view of other peaks in the county rising to 13,000 feet. Some members of the Church of Jesus Christ of Latter Day Saints, often referred to as Mormons, settled in the San Juan River Valley in southern Utah and had noticed the appeal of the area around what is now Monticello on their journeys north to Salt Lake City. They established a settlement in Monticello in 1888. Utah was the last state admitted to the Union in the 19th century gaining statehood in 1896 as the 45th state. Monticello has remained an important site of the Mormon faith. The year before we arrived, the construction of the Monticello Utah Temple launched the first generation of smaller temples of the Church.

We arrived in Monticello in the late afternoon of June 8, 1999, following a drive of 275 miles from St. Johns, AZ. Snow was still visible in the Abajo Mountains bordering the town. We observed a clean, very wide, main street and an orderliness of buildings and surroundings that gave the impression of a well-maintained community. A quick reconnoiter of the town established the building where we were to meet but no idea of the actual planting site. We went to bed at the Days Inn with the usual case of butterflies regarding the next day's activities.

At 9:00AM the next morning, we presented ourselves at the San Juan County government building. There to greet us was Rita Walker along with Trent Schafer, the City Manager. They took us to see Mayor Clyde Christianson, who welcomed us to Monticello but expressed regrets that other business prevented him from actually going out to the site, in the City Park directly behind the building complex. They explained that others would be joining us, including the local newspaper publisher, and gave us directions to the nursery to pick up the trees.

Hank Booher of High Country Tree Gallery, was waiting for us at his place with five blue spruces. They were bushy, two-feet tall beauties that he made available within our budget of $100, even though they were worth quite a bit more. Hank also followed us back to the site to help with the planting.

The planting location was near the library and apparently not too far from the school because some students and teachers came out to watch. They saw us mark off five plots in an arc on the embankment near the sidewalk, each about twenty feet apart from the other. Then everyone grabbed shovels to dig the holes. Eddie Allred, Director of Parks and Recreation, was one of those helpers joining in, along with Trent and Hank. Apparently, another building had previously been removed from the area which made it necessary to use a bar for digging down through a layer of crushed brick. But once penetrating through those impediments, the ground was generally good in quality, although we added some peat moss to further enrich the soil. Everyone seemed to enjoy the activities with plenty of conversation going on as we worked. Joyce helped in the planting while also doing public relations duties with the small crowd that had gathered, mostly made up of school kids but also including another City Council member, Julie Bronson.

They all seemed to feel a part of something distinctive going on right in their home town. The Mayor called to see how things were going and to invite us back to his office for a ceremony at the conclusion of the field activities.

The planting was wrapped up around 11AM and we headed to the Mayor's office. While waiting outside his office, Trent explained the reason why many western towns have an extremely wide main street. It dates back to the days when large wagons were drawn by a team of horses. They needed extra space in order to turn these wagons around to go in the other direction. The standard became a chain and a half or about 90 feet of road width. The sidewalks and buildings were set back accordingly.

Mayor Christianson presented us with the Key to the City of Monticello, Utah, in a ceremony attended by Police Chief Kent Adair, the other government officials that had accompanied us out to the site in addition to a few others from other departments. Bill Boyle, publisher of the *San Juan Record* arranged for photographs to appear in an article that we never did get a copy of. However, the same newspaper had published a preview story of our visit in the May 19, 1999 edition.

The reception in Monticello fulfilled all of our expectations. It produced a memorable experience involving people who combined hospitality with a sincere interest in the goals of our project. The visit reinforced our view of a West where you can depend on the word of down-to-earth people. We're sure that they have continued to nurture our trees into the symbols that will forever mark the day that the Jacksons came to town.

On the drive back to Albuquerque, we finally got to visit the Four Corners monument to experience the once-in-a-lifetime thrill of placing all four of our appendages in different states at the same time. Along with the Neldas from Medford, OR, we were practically the only people there, in a place of virtual silence, with the wind blowing across the desert. It was a reminder of the sights we had seen: the red sandstone creations of nature, the vastness of a land inhabited by few humans, most of whose ancestors having occupied the same ground for untold ages.

Standing (L-R) Raul Lara, John Jackson, Chuck Giordano (County Commissioner) Erich Hummel, Debbie and Mel Hummel and Brian Johnson.
Kneeling (L-R) Joyce Jackson, Billy Anderson (Nephew of the Hoencks), Bobby "Shorty"Hoenck" and Bob Hoenck helped plant fifteen trees at the Jackson Mountain Elementary School.

Photographer—Susan Hoenck

Jackson Mountain Elementary School was the site for planting five **Silver Maples,** five **Ash**, and five **Cottonwood** trees with the Jackson mountains as a backdrop.

Jackson Mt, Nevada

Nevada

"In the Mountains Still"

The four states we visited during June, 1999, could be collectively termed our "mile high" tour. And yet we don't ever recall experiencing shortness of breath, dizziness or any other altitude-related symptoms. Perhaps the gradual acclimation over the course of the week conditioned our bodies for the final stop in the Jackson Mountain Range of Nevada.

Getting there was an experience. It started out with a thousand-mile flight from Albuquerque to Reno. Basically that only entails traveling over one other state, either Arizona or Utah depending upon the flight path, but it again demonstrates the vastness of the western states. As an example, flying from New Mexico, through Arizona to Nevada, traverses through the fifth, sixth and seventh largest states in the nation, respectively.

Then, when you get to Reno, it doesn't want you to leave. *"The Biggest Little City in the World,"* does its best Las Vegas-like imitation using loads of glitter and neon to entice you to support the local economy. We had to put those temptations on hold for another twenty-four hours, along with it being Joyce's birthday, while we drove the remaining two hundred miles to Winnemucca, in Humboldt County, gateway to the Jackson Mountains.

You remember Winnemucca; it's the first place mentioned in Johnny Cash's rendition of the Hank Snow song *"I've Been Everywhere."* Almost a hundred other towns spill out in the lyrics, many of which match up to our own travels: *"I've been to Reno, Chicago, Fargo, Minnesota, Buffalo, Toronto, Winslow, Oklahoma…"* and later on in the song *"Jacksonville."*

But we couldn't find any community by the name of Jackson in Nevada. The only association we could find was the Jackson Mountain Range but the question became whether there was a place near the mountain that had enough people to help us out. The answer evolved as a result of Joyce talking with Linda in the Winnemucca City Hall who referred us to Barb Kelleher, recreation planner at the U.S. Bureau of Land Management, Winnemucca Field Office. Barb enlisted the support of local residents Bob and Susan Hoenck who lived near Jackson Mountain.

Joyce contacted Susan who came up with the idea of using the one-room Jackson Mountain Elementary School, near a place known as Desert Valley. That seemed like a good suggestion to us because it was based on a local person's knowledge of the area and because we always preferred schools as the site for our project. The school was actually on the property of the Giordano ranch but Susan took care of arranging their enthusiastic support.

The ranches out there cover extensive acreage in a very sparsely-populated region. Consequently, the number of attendees in the entire school averaged fewer than six students. Their teacher was Louise Garcia who stayed with a local family during the week and made the sixty-mile return trip to her home in Winnemucca on the weekends.

The neighboring ranchers were very receptive to the idea. The Giordano, Hoenck, Delong, Crouch and Hummel families had been meaning to beautify the school grounds with trees for some time but other priorities kept getting in the way. Our visit provided them with an incentive to combine their intentions with ours resulting in what promised to be a grove of trees amongst the sagebrush.

We left Reno early on Friday morning, June 11, 2009, for the long drive to Jackson Mountain. Our first stop was in Winnemucca to purchase the trees from Linda Schrempp, owner of Ron's Seed & Supply and a member of the Humboldt County School Board. She sold us five silver maple trees ranging between six and seven feet in height. She couldn't join us for the one o'clock planting but assured us that everything was in readiness and gave us detailed directions to the school. We packed the trees in the trunk of the rented Dodge Intrepid and started off on our own, carefully following the directions: 30 miles north on Route 95, turning west on Route 140 for 25 miles, left on Bottle Creek Road for 2 miles over gravel to the second cattle guard where we would find the school house. We looked at each other and wondered how we would tell the first cattle guard from the second one when we didn't even know what a cattle guard looked like. We didn't encounter a single person over the nearly sixty-mile ride who could have offered any further clarification.

Not to worry. The male instinct for navigation takes over in these kinds of situations; simply stated – when in doubt, keep driving while attempting to convey the impression that you know where you're going. It wasn't like there was a choice of several roads or numerous buildings to choose from. Eventually dead reckoning took us to what had to be the schoolhouse.

Waiting for us were Bob and Susan Hoenck, who Joyce had talked with during the weeks before our visit. While we were getting acquainted with them, County Commissioner Chuck Giordano and his wife, Debbie, drove up in their pickup truck followed shortly thereafter by their hired-hand, Raul Lara, on a backhoe. We started to unload our trees and noticed others were doing the same thing. The Hoencks brought out five ash trees and the Giordanos did likewise with five cottonwood trees making a total of fifteen trees to be planted including our own. There were no other stands of trees in the vicinity although some lone trees were growing on the other side of the building. We took that as a good sign that trees can survive in this harsh land.

Raul went to work digging holes with the backhoe as more people began to arrive. They were John and Judy Delong, Mel and Debbie Hummel with their son, Erich and his friend, Brian Johnson and Hoenck's nephew Billy Anderson. By our count there were thirteen people there who all helped with the tree planting in some way.

The holes the backhoe carved out were plenty big for the size of the trees. We had to backfill some dirt into all the holes to raise them up to where the top of the tree ball was level with the ground. Peat moss was added during this stage which made a great contrast in color between the rich material coming out of the bag and the dry, dusty soil into which it was spread. The holes were laid out in a straight line about twenty-five feet apart from each other, forming a sort of boundary around what served as the play yard. The kids, including the Hoenck's young son, Shorty, acted as water carriers on the heels of the adults as we concluded each planting. It was a real community effort by folks who appeared accustomed to helping each other out. In less than an hour all fifteen trees had embarked upon life at their new home.

At the conclusion of the work we all posed for numerous keepsake photographs. The most memorable ones show the two of us wearing our signature tree tee shirts standing with our deeply-tanned new friends. Next to us are the newly-planted trees poking up in the brown landscape with the snow-speckled mountain range in the background. It may not be everyone's vision of paradise valley but it's a scene that fills us with satisfaction on many levels and somehow inserts our presence into that land in a special way.

The Giordanos invited us to tour their ranch before departing the area. We gratefully accepted the chance to get a taste of a real western agricultural operation and we were careful to always refer to it as the ranch rather than the farm. Future son-in-law, Cory, drove us around in a pickup truck explaining the sights. We saw the alfalfa fields and where the grain was stored, the cattle grazing, the mule deer squatted down in the fields, the self-propelled irrigation wheels and even the abandoned gold mine (which was set to reopen when gold prices improved). All throughout the drive he patiently explained everything to us dudes in such a way that we weren't embarrassed to finally ask the question – what is a cattle guard?. The answer turned out to be a grouping of parallel metal pipes laid down across the road at the openings in the fence lines. The cattle are afraid to walk on these grates for fear of getting their hooves stuck and therefore stay on their side of the fence line. At least one of us Jacksons would probably have figured that out eventually. It's another one of the human male's traits that he will eventually come up with an answer for his spouse to every question even though he doesn't have a clue what he's talking about.

Back at the ranch house, we thanked the Giordanos for their hospitality and asked Debbie for one more favor. She agreed to make sure that Susan Hoenck received the fruit basket we had brought along for her in appreciation for all the work she did on our behalf. Susan was instrumental in setting up our visit to the Jackson Mountain Elementary School and in energizing the other neighbors to take part. Through our combined efforts five trees had become fifteen trees.

We stayed over in Winnemucca that night. The next morning we stopped by the newspaper office to leave information and photographs produced by using Walgreen's one-hour development process. Linda Shrempp also provided her input to reporter Mark Furman who wrote one of the better articles on our tree-planting project. It appeared, along with two photographs, in the July 1, 1999 edition of *The Humboldt Sun* in the middle of the front page under the headline "*Family helps "green" Jackson Mountain.*" One of the quotes is from Joyce describing the essence of our mission: "*We just decided we wanted to leave a legacy to our family name and also do something that is environmentally sound. Each time we plant one, you stand there when everybody leaves – it's just a really spiritual feeling to know that you have trees in every single state. It's just a real rooted feeling.*"

Another wonderful week of traveling-for-a-purpose ended with a cruise on Lake Tahoe on the paddle-wheeler M.S.Dixie II. That brought back memories from earlier tree planting trips viewing such boats along the Mississippi River and its tributaries. There's something uniquely American about a paddle wheeler. And there's something uniquely American about the gambling life that these boats typify in addition to what we experienced around Lake Tahoe and Reno. We looked upon that aspect with a sort of amusement park perspective. For a personal expenditure limit of $20 per visit, we can extract enough enjoyment from gambling to last us a long time.

It was time to save up our resources for the stretch drive. There was only one more extended trip remaining in our project and that would be upon us in less than three months.

The Jackson Legacy

Joyce and John Jackson with the help of a bobcat and long- handled shovels plant a **Canada Red Cherry** tree at the former Albert School property. The Ceremonial shovel sits on the left foreground.

Kadoka, Jackson County, South Dakota

South Dakota

"Faces and Places"

The makeup of our second circuit for 1999 was similar to June's itinerary insofar as three of the points were in close proximity to each other while the fourth location was a sizeable distance away. Since the singular state was South Dakota and it required flying into Rapid City, we decided to start the trip there allowing us plenty of time to visit nearby Mount Rushmore.

Seeing the faces on Mount Rushmore has got to be one of the top ten vacation sights that most Americans want to experience. However, reaching it can be a challenge for those living in the more populated areas of the country. As examples, the mileages from a few major cities are: Chicago – 931, Houston – 1,325, Los Angeles – 1,400 and New York City – 1,720 miles. That requires a lot of time cooped up in a van with the kids or making multiple airline connections with all of the associated hassles. Even the two of us had never been there after thirty-six years of marriage where we considered traveling as our number one hobby.

It's well worth the effort to get there. Being in the presence of the faces of Washington, Lincoln, Jefferson and Roosevelt excites a greater depth of emotion than what you can experience when contemplating them in other ways. Our strongest feeling standing there was gratitude to the Almighty for giving us these men, and others like them, who forged the best example of enlightened self-governance that mankind has ever known. The exaggerated size of their features serves to remind us of our own smallness within this realm but in a way that also emphasizes what all of us can accomplish when joined together as a collective force for good in the world.

Mount Rushmore is a memorable experience. We especially enjoyed it in the glow of floodlights after dark, in climbing nearer to the faces, in seeing the scaled-down models in Gutzon Borglum's workshop which served to calibrate the actual excavations on the rocks above. There were also plenty of other sites to see between here and our eventual destination of Kadoka, county seat of Jackson County. The Black Hills and Badlands have many entertaining attractions but our favorite was Wall Drug. We counted sixty-one signs along a forty-five mile stretch of Interstate 90 east of Rapid City promoting various enticing reasons for stopping at the Wall Drug Store. It's hard to imagine that any tourist passes it by. It stands out like an oasis on the plains with nothing around it for miles. You can get some appreciation for its magnetism in considering that its original pitch to travelers in the 1930's was *"Free Ice Water."* Today it is a haven for the sale of every possible kind of western apparel, trinket, memento, glitz, carvings, food, refreshment, jewelry and countless other bric-a-brac. It's so over the top that it's irresistible. Someday it will be a National Historic Treasure, if it's not one already.

Forty miles further east of Wall, and the only settlement along that entire distance, sits Kadoka, South Dakota, the new home for our five trees. It earned that distinction by virtue of turning up as the seat of Jackson County in Joyce's search for a suitable place-name alignment. Upon looking deeper into the local history we discovered that the county was named after John R. Jackson, a Dakota legislator when the county was formed in 1914 and that it was merged with Washabaugh County in 1979 (fortunately the name Jackson survived out of this merger or we wouldn't have had any place to plant our trees).

The name Kadoka means "hole in the wall" in Sioux. It bills itself as *"The Gateway to the Badlands"* through the nearby Badlands National Park; it has a museum of local artifacts displayed in an old railroad station, a distinctive main street of frontier-era buildings, and each Labor Day it hosts the World Championship Outhouse Races (no kidding).

The Pine Ridge Indian Reservation for the Oglala Sioux people spreads from Jackson County in the north through three other counties. It is the eighth-largest reservation in the country, larger than the states of Delaware and Rhode Island combined. In the southern part of the reservation is the site of Wounded Knee where the U.S. Cavalry is accused of massacring a band of Lakota Sioux Indians on December 29, 1890. Wounded Knee was also the site of a modern-day confrontation with the federal government in the winter of 1973 that resulted in two Indian deaths and other serious casualties. Today, over 47% of Jackson's total population of 2,900 is Native American.

Shortly after eight o'clock on Monday morning, August 30, 1999, we arrived at the Auditor's office to meet with Mary Jane Kerrick and Robin Jones. They had been in prior communications with Joyce in the process of coordinating our planting visit with Paul Briggs, the Public Works Director. They told us that Paul was already at the site, the former Albert School Property, digging the holes for our trees with a bobcat tractor. The Heritage Nursery in Rapid City told us that Canada Red Cherry trees would suit our purposes and the five-foot high trees they sold us were now about to be planted at the intended site.

City employee, Larry Johnson, led us over to the old school property and provided the introduction to Paul Briggs. The lot was vacant except for a few dead trees but they told us to envision that one day an ice-skating rink and other park improvements would grace the land next to our trees. They also pointed out that a water line from a nearby well would provide liquid nourishment. We noticed the moist, rich earth that the bobcat was turning up which stirred some confidence in us regarding the long-term outlook for fulfilling their ambitions and ours.

The four of us worked together on the tree planting. One of the nice things about getting help from municipal workers is that they bring the right tools. We always have our inimitable collapsible trenching tools in easy reach but for some reason the workmen never seem to need them. Joyce advised them to fill the holes to the proper height relative to the top of each tree ball and generally provided strong supervisory leadership to the return responses of *"Yes, Ma'am; Yes, Ma'am."*

Ronda Dennis, reporter for *The Kadoka Press*, snapped our picture standing alongside one of the planted trees. She took plenty of notes from Joyce's perusal through our scrapbooks, as well as taking a copy of the press release that we customized to each community in which we planted. The results of her news gathering appeared on the front page of the September 2, 1999, edition of the newspaper under the headline *"Jacksons plant five trees in Jackson County."*

At the conclusion of the planting, Larry Johnson took us back to the municipal building where one of the ladies delivered a proclamation to us that Mayor Harry Weller had authorized. Then Larry gave us a tour of the town museum. It was located inside an old railroad station that was built by the Chicago, St. Paul and Milwaukee Railroad about the time that Kadoka was founded in the first decade of the twentieth century. The old-west appearance of the town and its proximity to the Badlands has resulted in it being used as a location for numerous Hollywood movies. Most recently scenes from the film "*Thunderheart*" were shot on location and Larry was involved in the filming. He met the lead actors Val Kilmer, Sam Shepard and Graham Greene. Other movies filmed nearby were "*Starship Trooper*" and "*Armageddon.*" They both utilized the topography of the Badlands as moonscape simulations due to their peculiar rock formations.

All-in-all, we packed a lot of activity into less than forty-eight hours in southwestern South Dakota. We got to see Mount Rushmore and other nearby attractions, Wall Drug and Kadoka. We wanted to see the Corn Palace in Mitchell and the site of the annual Sturgis Motorcycle Rally but they were just out of our reach. Besides, we were limited to a maximum of 300 miles on the car rental and turned it back in at the Rapid City airport with the trip odometer showing 299 miles.

Joyce Jackson, second from left is sharing the Jackson Legacy album with the Roberts Town and County Garden Club.
L-R — Carmen Edelmayer, Deanna Wilde, Virginia Holtry, Donna French and Carol Harkness.
These ladies were instrumental in choosing the green space to plant the five **Aspen** trees.

Roberts, Idaho

Idaho

"Potatoland"

Amazingly, the next three planting sites were situated within close proximity to Idaho Falls, Idaho, which we decided would make a good base of operations. The closest destination from there was Roberts, Idaho just 17 miles away. After that there was Jackson, Montana at 145 miles, which was easily reachable on the second day. The third stop would be Jackson, Wyoming at 106 miles from Idaho Falls. As an extra-added bonus, two of America's premier attractions, Yellowstone National Park and the Grand Teton Mountains, were along our route of travel and easily includable within the five-day time span we allowed to do these three states.

It was more complicated and expensive to fly from Rapid City, SD, directly to Idaho Falls, so we opted for the more practical alternative of flying into Salt Lake City and then driving up from there. Salt Lake City was also a point of interest for us but we put off doing that until the end of the week after completing everything else on our agenda.

We arrived into Salt Lake City in the middle of the evening, ready to collect our luggage and rental car and then get a good night's rest. The next morning we started the 228-mile drive up Interstate 15 for the one o'clock tree-planting appointment in Roberts, ID. The journey also included a stop in Idaho Falls to pick up a total of ten trees for the next two planting sites. A tight schedule like that didn't allow any time for side trips but we absorbed as much local history as we could get from reading guidebooks and highway signs along the way.

In the writing of this book we have endeavored to reflect some of the noteworthy background stories that distinguish each area we visited. It would have been physically impossible for us to spend the necessary time to get acquainted with all of this history during our travels but writing about it, retrospectively, enriches both our understanding of the places visited and hopefully the reader's. We touched upon one of these side stories on the drive up Interstate 15 at the border of Utah and Idaho.

It was near here, on January 29, 1863, that the U.S. Army perpetrated a slaughter of the Shoshone Indians who had been aggressively resisting the encroachment of white settlers, mostly Mormon, on their tribal lands. The Indian death toll from the Bear River Massacre exceeded any other similar single incident in U.S. history, including Wounded Knee, SD.

The defeated Indians were relocated north to the Fort Hall Indian Reservation along the Snake River. The largest town in the vicinity was named after Shoshone Chief Pocatello who had led his people throughout their travails. Interstate 15 closely parallels the Snake River north through the city of Pocatello, the Fort Hall Indian Reservation, Idaho Falls and then to Roberts, ID.

Identifying with "Roberts" marked the third time we adopted some variation of our oldest son's name after failing to find a suitably-sized community named Jackson in the state. It became our most frequently-used, alternative place name in the ten states where Jackson didn't work out. The rest of the exceptions were: Christine – 2; Joyce – 1; Steven – 1, San Juan -2 and John – 1.

The population of Roberts is around 650, located in an agricultural area of Jefferson County where potatoes are the major crop. The state claims that it grows one-third of all the potatoes consumed in the U.S. and that the Idaho potato leads all other types in production. The name Idaho is of unknown origin. It's one state that has no reliable explanation where its name comes from.

We arrived in time for a quick lunch at the 1950's-style café before heading for City Hall. No one was there because they were all at Star Park waiting for us. We concluded that by looking down the street to where a bunch of people were gathered staring back at us. The people there welcomed us into their community with open arms. We met our original contact, City Clerk Carmen Edelmayer, who introduced us to Mayor Ben Poston and Rick Lamb, Public Works Director. They explained that three trees were to be planted in the downtown park cared for by the members of The Town and Country Garden Club while the other two trees would reside a short distance away across the other side of the Union Pacific railroad tracks. Then we went to our rented Dodge Caravan to unload three of the aspen trees bought from John Crook at the appropriately named Town and County Gardens in Idaho Falls.

The group was led by Virginia Holtry, who had just finished up a three-year term as president of the Garden Club. Others in attendance were Karol Poston, Donna French, Wayne Barnett, Carol Harkness, Deanna Wilde, a lady named Laverne and Terri Carr, reporter from *The Jefferson Star*. We became immediately immersed in telling them our story with Joyce, as usual, taking the lead with scrapbook in hand. Mayor Poston and Rick Lamb went to digging the holes. We quickly picked up shovels and started turning over the neatly manicured turf with them. The area was a green space set aside and fenced off for the enjoyment of the community. A Blue Star Memorial Highway plaque in tribute to our Armed Forces stood at one end *"Sponsored by the Idaho State Federation of Garden Clubs, Inc. in association with The Roberts Town and Country Garden Club and the Southeast District."* Virginia Holtry had also been a district director of the organization.

The ground was moist from a recent rain which helped with the digging. As soon as Joyce judged that the hole was of sufficient depth and width, we dropped in one of the aspens. They were about seven feet high with the sparse leafing that goes with a young tree. Peat moss was added to help them take root. According to our standard procedure, we formed an earthen dike encircling each tree trunk in anticipation of their initial watering. Deanna provided buckets for that purpose and assured us that she would personally watch after them. A water line was at the other site which also gave us promise of sufficient attention in the future. Then we stepped back to admire what all of us had just accomplished.

Before repeating the process for the two remaining trees at the other site, Mayor Poston presented us with a plaque which read:

The Jackson Family From Texas
In appreciation for your generous

Donation of trees to the City of Roberts
"A Living Legacy To Their Family"
Thank you from the Mayor, City Council
And Community of Roberts, Idaho
August 31, 1999

One of the ladies approached and gave us each "potato" pins to serve as a lasting reminder of what the area is known for. We received a couple of other lasting reminders in the form of a newspaper article and a poem.

The newspaper article appeared on page two of the September 1, 1999 edition of *The Jefferson Star* along with a photograph capturing the mayor and the two of us finishing up the planting of a tree. The story was continued onto another page which accurately reported the facts relating to our project as a "...*national decade-long living legacy.*"

All of that was nice but was in keeping with numerous other newspaper articles that we had received during the course of the adventure. Virginia Holtry gave us something that no one else ever did; she wrote us the following poem:

The Visitors

They trek across the country side
Doing good for the earth,
Making it a better place to live
Planting trees such as Aspen and Birch.

Their journey took them to Roberts, Idaho
Where they planted five trees,
In honor of their son Robert
So everyone who passed could see.

The town will surely appreciate these trees
They will be a bright spot, that can't be dimmed
Our lives will be much fuller and richer
And we will never forget who gave them.

So we thank these people from the bottom of our hearts
And hope they visit again some day,
We will always cherish the memory they gave
Because the Jackson family are special in every way.

Virginia Holtry passed away on September 28, 2005, at the age of 79. In the preceding six years, she kept in touch to tell us that the trees were doing fine, she invited us back any time for a cup of coffee and she left us with a memento from her heart.

Jackson Elementary School teacher, Theresa Murdock, John Jackson, Jay Nelson and Student Andrew Towery prepare to plant five **White Spruce** trees on the school grounds.

Jackson, Montana

An old Conestoga wagon adorns the front lawn of Jay Nelson, a prominent citizen of Jackson, Montana

Montana

"Our Most Memorable Character"

September 1, 1999

The next site would be in the Big Hole Valley, Beaverhead County, Montana. Most people wouldn't associate any special significance with that wide expanse of country just east of the Continental Divide and the Bitterroot Mountains but it's distinguished for Lewis and Clark, the Nez Perce Trail and Jay Nelson. The first two of these you'll find in the history books, the third is a slice of living history.

Jay was instrumental in setting up our tree planting at the Jackson Elementary School just across the street from the blue house he constructed for his family in this small hamlet. But there's so much more to be told about him and the valley he lives in before starting to tell the story of our visit there.

Interstate 15 continues northward from the Idaho Falls / Roberts, Idaho area, where we spent the day previous to starting out for Jackson, Montana. The highway ascends gradually until reaching the Continental Divide which forms part of the boundary between Idaho and Montana. Along the way we crossed the Nez Perce Trail over which Chief Joseph led his people towards Canada after engaging the U.S. cavalry in the Big Hole Valley. Further north along the Divide, Lewis and Clark had led their expedition through the Lemhi pass after also stopping in that same valley, in which Jackson, Montana is located today.

Lewis and Clark had navigated the Missouri River all the way to its headwaters in this part of Montana. They were hoping to discover another large river within easy reach of the Missouri which could serve as the northwest passage to the Pacific Ocean. Even in the first decade of the 19th century, the eastern side of the Continental Divide was looked upon as the watershed for major rivers flowing eastward and it was thought that the western side would be a similar watershed spawning major navigable rivers to the west. They had no way of knowing that the Rocky Mountains were an impregnable barrier to such a notion.

In July, 1805, the expedition came to that part of Montana where a female member of their party, Sacagawea, recognized what the natives referred to as Beaverhead Rock. She had been raised among the local Lemhi Shoshone people whose help she enlisted in guiding the party to the nearest mountain pass. In transit they went through the valley later known as Big Hole, over the pass and then on to the Pacific Ocean, several hundreds of miles to the west, ending their trip on the Oregon shore.

Modern-day Washington, Oregon and Idaho were the ancestral lands of the Nez Perce Indian Tribe. They lived on property assigned to them by treaties in 1855 and 1863. One band led by Chief Joseph lived in the rich Wallowa Valley of Northeastern Oregon which was coveted by white settlers. The government ordered the Nez Perce off this land in 1877 and into other reservations set aside for their tribe. Chief Joseph agreed to go in order to avoid bloodshed but angry members of the tribe took revenge by murdering some settlers. The Chief knew the cavalry would pursue them for these crimes so he decided to lead his people through Idaho, Wyoming and Montana over what is known as the Nez Perce Trail. Their intention was to unite with Chief Sitting Bull who had gone into Canada after The Battle of the Little Big Horn. The Army finally confronted the Nez Perce in the largest battle of the war in the Big Hole Valley of Montana. The Nez Perce moved on, again, but were finally subdued in the Bear Paw Mountains of Montana, less than forty miles from Canada. The words that Chief Joseph is reported to have uttered there is emblematic of the Native Americans' final desperation and submission to their fate: *"Hear me, my chiefs! I am tired. My heart is sick and sad. From where the sun now stands I will fight no more forever."*

Jay Nelson was born in the Big Hole Valley in 1923, less than fifty years after the Indian battle that bears its name. There were few modern conveniences in his youth; horses were still the main form of motive power and electricity was something that wasn't to come to the valley until after World War II. The war scooped Jay out of the valley in 1943 and deposited him in Belgium just in time for the Battle of the Bulge. His outfit, Company I, 395th Infantry Regiment, 99th Division saw heavy action in resisting the enemy counterattack and on into Germany. He fought at the Remagen Bridge and was wounded in action at Linz on March 14, 1945. He was one of only 12 men left from the original company complement of 187 soldiers that landed in France.

He returned to Jackson and the Big Hole Valley after the war and never lived anywhere else. In a region where fewer than a couple hundred people live, nearly everyone is interdependent on their neighbor and leaders are critical to the common welfare. Jay Nelson is that consummate leader. The lights finally came on in Jackson for the first time in 1947. Jay's father was on the board of the regional electrification authority and Jay served after him for the balance of the century. Jay was also a craftsman who exclaims *"There's less than a handful of houses in the valley I haven't put a nail into at some time."* He's been multi-term Chairman of the Board of Western Montana Electric G&T, Chairman of the Jackson Water and Sewer District, a state-wide leader against new grazing and logging restrictions, a proponent of enlightened environmentalism and Post commander of the VFW for more than twenty-five years. And that just scratches the surface of what he means to the people of his community.

Despite all of that, Jay comes across as that rare human being who is without pretense, comfortable in their own skin, cognizant of the broader world around them and appreciative of the place that each of us plays in the grand scheme. He displayed all of that in talking with Joyce about the arrangements and in hosting our visit to his town. The night before, he spent two hours with us in his home telling stories of life in the valley, finishing up a handmade gift basket for us and generally treating us as if we were visiting royalty. He told us that the town was named after Anton Jackson, an early postmaster from a family that spans several generations in the town, one of whom, Robert Jackson, was on the school board when they opened the present school in 1964. It replaced the one that Jay and his brother had attended by riding their horses to class every day.

Jay is one of those individuals who want to be involved in whatever he can do to make life better for as many people as possible. There was not a hint of self-importance at any point in our time together. We had no idea about the details of his life until receiving a 150-page book from one of his children upon our departure entitled, *"Love, And a Prayer."* It's the story about his growing up and service in the Second World War.

We left Jay's home after his son, Bob, gave us two jars of home-made pickled cauliflowers taken from their greenhouse which is warmed by water from the hot springs that run through the area. It was a short walk down the street, in near-freezing weather, to the Jackson Hot Springs Lodge. Our lodging was a two-room cabin in which we promptly got a fire going in the fireplace. We swam in the naturally-heated pool, had a nice dinner and then retired for the evening.

We're not normally early risers but something in the air roused us out of bed at 6:30AM. That still probably marked us as tenderfoots compared to the local citizens but pioneer blood doesn't run deep in our DNA. Jay had already opened up the school and prepared the four teachers, eighteen students and his dog, Riley, for our arrival at nine o'clock. The adults included Theresa Murdoch, a teacher whom Joyce had talked with in planning our trip, Jay's daughter, Ruth Ann Little, and teachers Jacque Brissette and Dianna Peterson, along with reporter Kim Albea from *The Dillon Tribune.*

We unloaded the mini-van of the trees we had brought along from the Town and Country Gardens in Idaho Falls: three Bosnian Pines and two Colorado Blue Spruces. They were eagerly snatched up by the kids who went right to work on the planting while the adults looked through our scrapbook in the near-freezing weather. Looking beyond the town we could see that snow had already coated the mountain peaks in the distance even though it was only September 1st.

It wasn't easy planting the trees. The ground was hard but they didn't have to dig down too deep because the trees were only two feet tall. Jay used a pike to loosen the soil and we did our part. The kids scurried about, vying for their stint with the shovel, tamping the dirt down around the holes, raking up the left-over pebbles and grasses, bringing water to the plants and posing for the camera. It was always a lot of fun to get children involved with the plantings for all of the unbridled joy and excitement that they always brought to the occasion.

 The trees were placed in a line perpendicular to the road about twenty-five feet apart. This allowed plenty of space for their eventual growth to thirty or forty feet, if the climate conditions permitted them to survive to maturity. Regardless of the eventual outcome, we had done our part in bringing a piece of our family to this outpost on the old frontier.

The town reflected that aura through its architecture and sparse complement of buildings. Directly across from the school in front of Jay's house stood a Conestoga wagon with its canvass top rolled back half-exposing the ribs beneath it, the general store with its classic western slab-front design containing the name Jackson Mercantile in the raised portion above the entrance, the post office where we got our postcard hand-cancelled with the Jackson postmark, the Jackson Hot Springs Lodge constructed of logs with an oak interior graced by countless antler racks, then there was Shepherd's garage, Rosie's Cantina, a smattering of houses and a church.

The Dillon Tribune ran a nice feature in their September 8, 1999 edition covering the upper half of page 13 with four captioned photographs accompanied by a story. One of the photographs shows the students, teachers, the Jacksons and resident Jay Nelson. A lot has been written about him and by him. The book which we received on our visit entitled *"Love, And a Prayer"* is an account of his war-time service as taken mostly from letters he exchanged with family members. In 2006, Jay wrote another autobiography entitled *"Big Hole Memories"* which is *"A Collection of Jay Nelson's Stories and Family Photographs."* Author Nadine Epstein wrote a wonderful four-page biography of him for the November, 1994, edition of *Rural Electrification Magazine* entitled *"Chairman of the Valley"* which we referred to in writing our book.

It was with regret that we had to leave our new friend after so short a time. But in his indomitable way Jay said he was looking forward to seeing us when we returned, and assured us that he would still be there.

The Jackson Legacy

Joyce Jackson, Tim Young, Pathways Director and John Jackson sizing up the area where they will be planting five **Aspen** trees.

Jackson, Wyoming

Wyoming

"Here at Last"

After planting on three successive days we needed a breather before tackling the final stop in Jackson, Wyoming. So after the visit to Montana, we backtracked the 145 miles to Idaho Falls for our second night at the Comfort Inn. Idaho Falls was a pleasant place to collect ourselves. We enjoyed sauntering along the River Walk as it wandered next to the Snake River rapids through the heart of the city. The relaxation gave us time to store up energy for the remaining four days of the trip which were packed with planting activities and major sightseeing venues.

There were four sites that we always wanted to see out this way but never had the opportunity to be in this part of the country to experience them, until now: Yellowstone National Park, the Grand Tetons, Jackson Hole and Salt Lake City. The plan was to take care of the planting, first, which left the rest of the time for vacation-type endeavors. As it turned out, three of the four sights would fulfill all of our expectations.

It's a drive of a little over one hundred miles from Idaho Falls to Jackson, Wyoming but it's no walk in the park. The elevation is already over 4,000 feet as you start out and continues to gain altitude up into the Teton Range. The highway eventually finds its way through the mountains at Teton Pass, at an elevation of 8,431 feet. At the summit is a sign pointing towards Jackson Hole eleven miles beyond and 2,200 feet below. The sign reads *"Howdy Stranger, Yonder is Jackson Hole, The Last of the Old West."*

People named Jackson played important roles in this part of Northwestern Wyoming. First to arrive was David Jackson, one of the earliest-known trappers attracted to the region after news emanating from the Lewis and Clark Expedition revealed a plentiful population of beaver and other valuable fur-bearing animals. Before the arrival of Caucasian trappers the valley was the hunting grounds for numerous Indian tribes including the Shoshone, Crow and Bannock. Initially Jackson and his fellow mountain men plied their craft and traded with the natives only during the temperate months, spending their winters in more hospitable climes. But in 1829 he supposedly stayed the winter at the base of the Grand Tetons. Consequently his partners referred to this mountain valley as "Jackson's Hole" and the lake came to be known as Jackson Lake. Then came William Henry Jackson in 1871-72, as part of the Hayden Expedition. He took the original photographs of the Grand Tetons and Yellowstone which would help persuade the government to establish the world's first national park in 1872. Now, another couple of Jacksons, John and Joyce, arrived to leave their mark here at the end of the 20th Century.

We had finally come to the place that seemed to be at the top of everyone's list when asking us questions about the project, as in *"Have you been to Jackson Hole yet?"* There's something captivating about that name, something that stirs visions of majestic mountains and modern-day, snow-resort people existing side by side with stereotypical old west inhabitants. It's an impression that is challenging to live up to, on a par with your prior expectations of Disney World, Hawaii or the Indianapolis 500 before actually going there. Like most things, the degree of fulfillment of the vision lies in the eye of the beholder.

We had high expectations not only of the town itself but of the caliber of reception that we anticipated it would accord us. It was so prominent in our minds that, at one time, we had decided that it would climax our entire project as the 50th and final tree planting site. Unexpectedly, that plan got sidetracked when we somehow couldn't seem to ever work the state of Oregon into another of our itineraries, forcing it into the final spot on our schedule.

The Town of Jackson sits in the mountain valley known as Jackson Hole. It is renowned as an alpine resort, for its scenery, wildlife and as a winter residence for the rich and famous, including Harrison Ford, Tiger Woods, Sandra Bullock and former Vice President Dick Cheney. Befitting it's prominence as one of America's poshier addresses, the town of 8,600 permanent residents is replete with toney boutiques, restaurants, lodges and lounges catering to the well-to-do. Not that it doesn't also have provisions for the less wealthy, but the two seem to exist in separate but parallel universes.

Joyce's exploratory call to the office of Mayor Barney Oldfield, months before, resulted in gaining contact with Tim Young, Pathways Director, who would serve as our coordinator for the visit. Friends of Pathways is a non-profit organization and community advocacy group for promoting safe and convenient recreation within the Jackson Hole region. The group was developing an eight-mile trail system that was expanding every year and opportunities existed along its route for enhancements such as our tree plantings. Tim decided that our trees could grace an area where new funding had been raised the year before. Bringing all of these factors together, we planned for September 3, 1999, as the date on which we would journey to Jackson to plant aspens at the juncture of the Russ Garaman trail with the Crabtree Lane pathway.

After postponing our appointment by an hour, Tim met us in the lobby of our hotel just before ten o'clock in the morning. He said that Mayor Oldfield hoped to come out to the site later but that no one else would be joining the three of us at Russ Garaman Park. It's located on the western edge of the town backing up to the Bridger-Teton National Forest just off Powderhorn Lane. The improvement work that the group had been providing was immediately evident. The trails were paved and marked with signs, a newly-constructed foot bridge spanned the picturesque Flat Creek near where the two trails joined. That would be the planting grounds for the trees. On either side of Crabtree Trail were containers of magnificent aspen trees ranging in height between twelve and fourteen feet. They were to be arranged in stands of multiple trees placed closely to each other; one three-tree clump and one of two trees. Before coming out to the site we had purchased peat moss at the same nursery which supplied the trees – the Sunrise Home Center. By prior arrangement, the Friends of Pathways agreed to accept our donation of $100 to help defray the cost of the trees.

The ground was somewhat hard and rocky, something like you might find in the bottom of a river bed. Tim had anticipated this by bringing along a pick, a pike and shovels for digging. With his guidance, we positioned the appropriate number of potted aspens at each of the two locations. He helped with the initial digging but then informed us that he had to leave.

We were by ourselves for awhile digging and thrusting into the soil and working up a sweat until newspaper reporter Mark Huffman showed up. We had sent our press release in advance to *The Jackson Hole News.* They published a nice article in the September 1, 1999 edition on page 3 which notified the community of our impending arrival and where the planting would take place. The sub-heading for the story was *"Husband and wife mark the millennium with 10-year tree-planting project in Jacksons around the country."* It was a very well-written article but it didn't attract any other onlookers except the reporter himself.

Mark was very interested in our adventure and took note of as much information in our scrapbook as he could. In the process he also gathered numerous quotes from us which appeared in his follow-up story in the September 8, 1999 issue.

After Mark departed, we went back to working on our own. Some people out for a walk on the trail stopped to see what we were doing. We exchanged pleasantries but tried to stay focused on the planting chores. The size of the trees required deeper and wider holes than we were accustomed to. In other cities where we had planted, we normally had the help of workmen or community attendees to deal with the larger trees. The picture that accompanied the second newspaper article shows John lugging a multi-trunked aspen out of what appears to be a twenty-five gallon container held down by Joyce. It took all of our peat moss and most of our strength to finish the job but the effort was well worth it. In its own way, the site along the pathways near the creek, with post and rail fences nearby and a grand view of the mountains, was one of the prettier places that we planted. It made it all the more pleasing to savor what we had done when it came time for our personal meditation.

Mayor Oldfield never did show up. We went to his office just to see if we couldn't get a few minutes with him but he wasn't there. We did stop at Tim Young's office to express our gratitude for his help and to inform him that the trees were all nicely planted. A few weeks later the Executive Director of the Friends of Pathways, Margie Lynch, sent us a letter expressing thanks for our $100 donation. After leaving Tim's office we lingered for awhile in Jackson to experience some more of the sights and then left town to begin the vacation part of the trip.

We didn't have to go far. Within four miles we were into Grand Teton National Park. The three major peaks and other views of the Teton Range were every bit as striking as the pictures everyone has seen of them, especially when reflected upon the waters of Jackson Lake. The drive along the lakefront was a constant series of starts and stops as we pulled over to absorb the latest evidence of nature's beauty.

Then it was on to Yellowstone to experience first-hand why this is one of our country's leading attractions. It offers so much of what is exotic and compelling in nature. Expansive vistas of mountains and trees roll endlessly across the landscape, bears and elk and buffalo ramble unaffected by the human on-lookers, geysers blow, sulfur pits bubble and everywhere there's the feeling of being in a special place. We spent the good part of a day ambling around Yellowstone and surely could have enjoyed spending more time there but for the necessity to keep moving.

The final day was spent in Salt Lake City, Utah. We had been moved by the beauty of the Mormon Temple outside of Washington, DC and expected that the home temple would be an even grander site. And it was. Not just for its architectural style but for the opportunity afforded us to get more familiar with the religion and to witness a practice session of its world-famous choir in its home environment. It was also memorable that once seated inside the sound-proof observation room inside the temple we weren't allowed to leave until the choir was done rehearsing. John had sung with important choirs in New Jersey and Texas, once even making the front page of a section in USA Today through a photograph showing John and Joyce at the choir's performance in Vienna, Austria, but nothing compares with the Mormon Tabernacle Choir.

For sure, it was too short of a trip to properly experience all that these places have to offer but it was long enough to make a lasting impression. We feel like we made a lasting impression in other ways as Mark Huffman quoted John in the second article in response to the question why we plant trees: "*It's a statement that fits our objectives. What can you do, what lives on after you?*" What indeed!

The Jackson Legacy

Stephanie Horton, President of Jacksonville Chamber of Commerce reads a welcoming letter to the Jacksons. Alan Horabin (not pictured) a retired landscape architect helped select the **different species** of trees that were planted at the Beekman House Arboretum.

Jacksonville, Oregon

As a tribute to the final planting of the trees for the Jackson Legacy Project, homing pigeons, owned by Judy Taina were released for good luck.

Jacksonville, Oregon

Oregon

"The Final State"

March 20, 2000

The 20th Century ended with the year 2000. The last decade of the 1990's likewise ended with the year 2000. It had always been our plan to journey throughout the United States in the last decade of the twentieth century to plant our trees and that goal was going to be realized. At the start of the year the only remaining tasks were to plant in the final state of Oregon and conclude the project with a ceremony in the Nation's Capital.

The turn of a millennium is something that very few people in history ever get to experience. Consequently, it carries a special appeal to celebrate in some memorable way. Most people were so anxious to mark this occasion that they even accelerated the millennium starting date not willing to wait for its official commencement on January 1, 2001. As with the rest of the world, we were drawn to the date of January 1, 2000, because that's when all the festivities were going to occur and nothing anybody could do was going to stop it. Adding to the focus on that date was the Y2K scare which forecast untold horrors in the world's computer systems because software wasn't pre-designed for the implications of using dates other than for years beginning with 19--. That compelled a lot of people to gather on December 31, 1999 to witness the possible end of life as we knew it.

For all of those reasons it seemed like a good time to assemble the family so that we could be there together when our fates played out. It was Joyce's idea to rent a duplex beach house on South Padre Island, a Gulf Coast resort just north of Brownsville, Texas. The last decade was noteworthy to us for other things than the tree project. Over those ten years the original five Jacksons had grown to eleven through our children's marriages and the births of grandchildren. The expanded size of our brood deepened the meaning of our tree-planting legacy even more. Now there would be more heirs to track the adventurous story of their patriarch and matriarch in the years to come.

Even before the end of 1999, Joyce had been in constant contact with the people of Jacksonville, Oregon. Somehow the state never quite fit in with our efforts to include it in earlier itineraries. It wasn't a conscious attempt on our part to single out Oregon for the ultimate honor of being the last state but we're sure glad that it worked out that way.

An October 4, 1999 letter from Larry Smith, President of the Jacksonville Woodlands Association, gave some promise of things to come. The letter was a follow-up to one which we sent to Mayor Jim Lewis. Mike's comments left no doubt that the town was behind our effort because it fit right in with their own dedication to tree planting. He promised an important site for the plantings, the City's help in paying for some of the costs and indicated that they wanted to secure plenty of press coverage. He even sent us a copy of a video that the City had prepared entitled *"If Trees Could Talk,"* narrated by actor Kevin Hagen who played the part of "Doc" on the television series *"Little House on the Prairie."* It wasn't the first time that we had run into a connection to the story of the Laura Ingalls family during the tree planting project. It had to be an omen, right?

Our cadre of early supporters spread to include Maryl Cipperly, Office Manager of the Chamber of Commerce, and Terri Geig of the Movers and Shakers. Through Maryl we received the endorsement of the Chamber of Commerce President, Stephanie Horton, who would play an important role in facilitating many aspects of our visit.

The feedback we received from the community leaders was very encouraging. We kept their momentum going by providing examples from visits to previous states, such as selected newspaper articles from the numerous ones we had received. The list of awards and recognitions that we provided was extensive; just by its content it revealed the variety of ways that communities had chosen to note our presence. We revised the press release to best describe all of the pertinent aspects of our project and updated the printed list which displays our chronological progress through all the other states to this final culmination point. We wanted to provide every possible incentive to drive their enthusiasm as well as stimulate our own dedication towards making this the best visit of them all.

The planting date was set for the first day of spring, March 20, 2000. We started out three days earlier on a flight from Houston to San Francisco to spend a few days with our priest friend, Larry Finegan, before flying from there to Medford, Oregon. On the day that we departed, a story in the *Medford Mail Tribune* announced our visit to the public in the following words: "*Joyce and John Jackson, of Kingwood, Texas, will plant alders, hemlocks and a white fir at 10 a.m. Monday at Beekman Woods, behind the Beekman House at the corner of Laurelwood and California streets. During the ceremony, 20 to 30 white homing pigeons…will take flight. Guests will include students from the Jacksonville Elementary School, an actor who plays the part of Jacksonville pioneer banker Cornelius Beekman, and a prize-winning llama from Pleasant Valley Farms. Tree-shaped cookies will be served.*"

We arrived in Jacksonville around dinner time the night before the planting. The town is a carefully-preserved remnant of late 19th Century Americana which has resulted in its designation as a National Historic Landmark. Gold was discovered along Jackson Creek in 1851, followed by additional discoveries the next year. The influx of people quickly established a burgeoning settlement which was named Jacksonville after the nearby creek. The Territorial Legislature created Jackson County in January, 1852, in honor of Andrew Jackson, naming Jacksonville as the county seat. Native Americans opposed the encroachment of the new settlers but were finally subdued in 1856. The gold strike played out before too long and Jacksonville began a steady decline in population although it managed to sustain some prominence as a trading center. This commercial activity enabled the town to hold itself together avoiding the fate of other boom towns that wound up as ghost towns. Eventually, the neighboring city of Medford outpaced Jacksonville in importance and after resisting the inevitable for many years, Jacksonville finally had to relinquish its status as the county seat to Medford in 1927.

The historical atmosphere of the town certainly made an impression on us as we drove around the streets to get our bearings and to find a place to eat dinner. There were several nice places to choose from but we decided on Aldofino's. The next day we discovered that we shared the restaurant with some other people who would be at our tree planting but there was no way for us to have recognized each other at the restaurant. After dinner we went back to the Stage Inn to make last-minute preparations, relax and to await the big day.

Maryl Cipperly came to the hotel around 9:00 AM. Our meeting with her was the connection point between all of the preparatory work that went before and the events to come. All of us were anxious to get to the site but first Joyce presented her with a plant and a box of candy from See's Candies, in South San Francisco, as tokens of our appreciation. Then we followed her to the Beekman Native Plant Arboretum, part of the Woodlands in Jacksonville.

There were lots of people from many different sectors of the community waiting for our arrival. Introductions went on for some time. As we went from person to person we noticed that the holes had been dug and the trees had been laid next to them. Otherwise it would have been difficult for us to converse with all those people and attend to the plantings at the same time.

Stephanie Horton, Chamber of Commerce President, officially welcomed us to Jacksonville in her opening speech. She noted that we had chosen their town for our final planting because it was twice-identified with the name Jackson through the name of the town and the county, not to mention that the namesake creek also carried the name of Jackson. Stephanie introduced the others in attendance which included another person who had helped us with the planning, Terri Geig; in addition there were the following: Nick Williamson, Chamber of Commerce Vice President, Alan Horobin, the horticulturist for Woodlands Park who had chosen the site and the types of trees, the President of the Woodlands, Phil Gahr and his wife Kelly, an actor in a stove-piped hat and 19th century garb portraying renowned citizen Cornelius Beekman, Mr. and Mrs. Francis Nelda, Medford residents who had met us at the Four Corners Monument on June 9. 1999, Robin Taina, with her white homing pigeons ready for release, Lou and Camille Myersky who had brought a prize-winning llama from their farm outside of town, school children from Mrs. Reisinger's class at Jacksonville Elementary, numerous other onlookers, reporters from the *Medford Mail Tribune* and the *Jacksonville Review* and a camera crew representing Medford TV stations KTVL and KOBI, with on-air reporter Aubrey Aquino.

After Stephanie's opening remarks we made a brief speech outlining the project emphasizing the importance of our visit to Jacksonville as it concluded our planting in all fifty states. Stephanie presented us with a letter of appreciation from Mayor Jim Lewis, who was in Washington, DC at a conference of mayors. We informed the crowd that the Governor of Oregon, John A. Kitzhaber, sent us a letter expressing regrets that he couldn't attend and that we would soon be in Washington, DC, ourselves, to commemorate one more tree to our cause.

Then Jody Taina, of Applegate, handed each of us a white homing pigeon. Each bird nestled quietly in our hands as its heart calmly beat against our fingertips and, upon a command to release, the entire flock fluttered into the sky, circled over our heads and headed off for their roost. Chalk up another first. Along with the llama, it's the only time that we had non-humans invited to participate at one of our planting ceremonies. We don't count the gopher in Iowa or Riley the dog in Montana because they just happened along.

The Beekman Arboretum is a three-acre plot that features many trees, shrubs, plants and other flora native to the Siskiyou Mountains surrounding Jacksonville. It is located behind Beekman House which was built in 1875 by a prominent local banker, Cornelius Beekman. The design of the arboretum was supervised by semi-retired landscaper, Alan Horobin, in collaboration with the Jacksonville Woodlands Association organized in 1989. By the time of our visit, the area was well-established with plantings and trails winding throughout its acreage. Our trees were carefully placed to blend in with the others but each was to be identified with a small wooden plaque resting on a trail-side marker.

We had help from the onlookers in maneuvering the trees into their holes. The trees averaged about seven feet in height and included white alder, mountain hemlock, western hemlock, red alder and white fir. The ground was a nice loam covered with pine needles. Neighboring trees produced ample shade making a nice habitat for survival. The grounds appeared well tended giving us no reason to expect anything but a long, serene life for our trees.

The two of us attended to the tree planting procedures with a little tinge of extra significance because this was our final state. Only one planting remained, in Washington, D.C., after which we would never have to worry again whether the hole was wide enough to allow the roots to spread freely, whether the soil was rich enough to provide nurture or needed additives, whether they were straight and spaced far enough apart to accommodate their girth at maturity, or whether nature would treat them kindly after they were left on their own.

The excitement in ourselves and those gathered around us brought back fond memories of other places in other times. To hold a sapling in your hands for placement into the ground is to hold a piece of life for which you are responsible. Every aspect was important to us from the selection of the species with the best chance for survival to gauging the likelihood that the community would look after them in the future. We felt very confident in entrusting the people of Jacksonville, Oregon, with their part of our mission as we handed it over to them.

After it was all done, Terri Geig presented us with a basket of goodies donated by town merchants. In turn we passed out fifty cookies we had especially baked for the occasion from a shop in Atascocita, TX, as well as two bags of See's Candies lollipops for the school kids. People slowly drifted away a few at a time. It seemed like we had spent a long while at the scene, with all that was going on, but actually it was still mid-morning by the time everything was finished.

Terri, Stephanie and her mom invited us to the Good Bean Shop for bagels and coffee, after which we visited Terri's shop. Our plans included staying another night in Jacksonville so we spent the rest of the day touring the sites around town. Joyce did a little bit of shopping but we also visited historic buildings, the cemetery (where we saw our first-ever tombstone with the year 2000 carved on it) and accepted the Myersky's invitation to see their llama farm. Here we discovered that they are originally natives of New Jersey. One of them is from Summit which is only a few miles from Madison where we lived for the first six years of The Jackson Legacy. Back at the hotel we saw ourselves on the six o'clock news but the day wasn't done yet.

The Jacksonville Chamber of Commerce invited us to dinner that night at the Mediterranean Restaurant. Our hosts were Stephanie Horton, Terri Geig, Nick Williamson and Lee and Marilyn

Lewis, Board members who we hadn't meet before. The two of us sat on opposite sides of the table to better mingle with our hosts in telling them more about the wondrous project that had just concluded in their town. We told them how happy we were to hold Jacksonville, Oregon until our last stop because it epitomized all that we could hope for in the way of community response and warmth of reception.

The newspaper coverage was great, too. Woody Hunter of the *Jacksonville Monthly Review* caught the essence of the occasion in five group photographs published in the April, 2000 edition. The photos show all the diverse people who attended the ceremony from school kids to town officials, with a stove-pipe hat, a llama and a flock of birds thrown in for good measure. He even published the letter we sent to thank the town in the May, 2000 edition. In a story written the day after our visit, Paul Fattig, of the *Medford Mail Tribune,* lead with the headline:"*Family leaves a legacy of trees*" and drew heavily from his interview notes, including the following quotes:

> Joyce: "*The people we met across the whole country are really great. Everybody in each town we visited loved their town.*"

> John: "*I'm kind of sorry to see it end. We had a lot of fun doing it. We met a lot of people. We've been to about every Jackson there is.*"

And then it was over. Not just one state or one group of states but all the states were done. "*The circle is complete now,*" Joyce said. Ironically the last flight home, at the conclusion of the project, happened to occur at the same airport that received our first flight in starting the adventure – Seattle, Washington. The intervening ten years experienced all the wonders described in this book but the written word is not powerful enough to capture everything. Those other indescribable memories exist only in our hearts, along with the inexpressible gratitude we have for every single person who entered our lives along the way.

The National Park Service delivered the twelve foot **Red Oak** tree to be planted at Grant's Plaza.

Photo courtesy of Mary Ann Gatty

A USA Navy bugler played Taps in honor of the late Joseph Jackson at the planting ceremony in Washington, DC

Photo courtesy of Mary Ann Gatty

Erin Adams, a sixth generation of the Jackson bloodline is getting ready to release the butterfly in memory of her grandmother's father, Ray Crooks.

Photo courtesy of Mary Ann Gatty

Standing under the National Memorial to Ulysses S. Grant situated at the foot of Capitol Hill were family, friends and work associates of the Jackson clan who came to witness the planting of the **Red Oak** tree.

Washington, DC

240

District of Columbia

"The Grand Finale"

At the Nation's Capital in Washington, D.C.

May 1, 2000

Connections to Andrew Jackson abounded throughout the course of our project and he would surface again with regard to our final planting in Washington, D.C. Most of the Jackson places that we visited were named in his honor for one reason or another. His political legacy has been exceeded by few other Presidents much less the other aspects of his life that also left their mark: he was a legendary war hero, a judge, a senator and a tree planter.

Sometime during his presidency, which lasted from 1829 to 1837, he had a magnolia tree planted on the south lawn of the White House. It was planted near the mansion, itself, just below the windows of the state dining room, within easy view of anyone who ever gazed out that part of the building. In the early morning of September 12, 1994, that magnolia tree was all that prevented an errant aircraft from penetrating into the White House after an intentional crash landing on the south lawn.

A suicidal man stole a small plane in Maryland late on the night of September 11th and headed for DC. Radar picked him up as he circled the city and observed him as he banked over the Washington Monument in a collision course with the White House. The plane impacted the ground, slid through a holly hedge and came in contact with Andrew Jackson's magnolia tree which helped to halt its progress only feet from the building.

President Clinton and his family were temporarily living across Pennsylvania Avenue in Blair House that night. It's not believed that the pilot intended to do harm to anyone, other than himself, but the event exposed vulnerabilities in the Secret Service's protection system that were more than embarrassing to them.

The year of 1994 was significant to us for the following reasons. Joyce's father, Ray Crooks, passed away in March; in June we were invited to Andrew Jackson's estate, The Hermitage, to plant a tulip poplar tree not far from his mansion; the White House plane crash into Jackson's magnolia tree occurred in September; and in October, we completed a planting in the twenty-fourth state which meant we were one state shy of the halfway point to our goal of fifty states.

From the outset of our project, it had always been our intention to conclude with a planting at the Nation's capital in the year 2000. The involvement of Jackson's White House tree in the plane crash seemed to add another aspect of symbolism that turned our attention to the possibility of planting our tree there. The big question was whether the Secret Service would consider that enough of a reason to permit us on the grounds of the Executive Mansion?

In 1999, Joyce began to work on the actual plans for our final planting in Washington, D.C. Her dream was still to plant our last tree on the White House grounds. She contacted all kinds of agencies in pursuit of that goal to no avail. Officials expressed positive reactions upon hearing a brief outline of our legacy story, including the connection to Andrew Jackson's magnolia tree, but not to the point of providing any access to the most guarded house in the country.

Included in our effort was an attempt to enlist help from the National Arbor Day Foundation. We figured that our past history with them could qualify our mission for their support. After all, they had given us an award, featured our story in their newsletter and treated us like dignitaries when we stayed at the Arbor Day Farm in Nebraska. We wrote a compelling letter to them detailing the reasons why we thought their support would be beneficial to them and ourselves. But their help was not forthcoming.

It's not in Joyce's nature to give up. She continued to research possible avenues on her own and one day mentioned the quest to our next-door neighbors, Jeff and Denise Lochore. It was their suggestion that started the ball rolling in the right direction; they knew our local state representative, Joe Crabb, who would pass our request through to U.S. Congressman, Kevin Brady (R-TX). In other words, a little bit of lobbying was in order.

Representative Brady's response to our letter was to pass the request on to the National Park Service under his letterhead. There's nothing like receiving the backing of a sitting congressman in an effort to stimulate action from a government bureaucracy.

Suddenly the National Park Service saw more merit to our request than perhaps they had recognized before. They informed us that conditions weren't right for securing access to the White House grounds but perhaps they could arrange something on the grounds of the U.S. Capitol Building.

In 1903, a large appropriation was made to erect a national memorial to Ulysses S. Grant situated at the foot of Capitol Hill. It was to be a grand outdoor sculpture befitting the memory of our most prominent Union General and beloved President. Commissioned only forty years after the end of the Civil War, it was expected to share equal importance with the Lincoln Memorial and the Washington Monument across what is now the National Mall and reflecting pool. It never achieved that level of prominence but it remains the third largest sculpture of its type in the world, encompassing Grant on his charger, mounted cavalry, artillery soldiers and four recumbent lions. It is 250 feet wide and took twenty years to build. When President Barack Obama made his inaugural speech from the steps of the Capitol in 2009, he was looking over the Grant Monument across the Mall towards the Lincoln Memorial. When Dr. Martin Luther King made his immortal *"I Have a Dream Speech,"* he was facing in the opposite direction from the steps of the Lincoln Memorial, across the reflecting pool, over the Grant Memorial towards the U.S. Capitol on the Hill. It was here, within the shadow of the Grant Memorial, that the National Park Service granted us space for our tree.

The achievement of such a prominent site motivated Joyce to greater heights in preparing the ceremony to mark such an occasion. This time it would be completely up to us to celebrate in whatever ways we thought appropriate, within the restrictions imposed by the Department of the

Interior, National Park Service (NPS). This agency required us to file for a permit to conduct a "Special Event." In granting the permit they assigned Steve Lorenzetti as our event coordinator but most of our contact was through Julie Long. The date and time was set for May 1, 2000, from 10 am to noon.

Having dealt with the Department of the Interior, Joyce next went to work on the Pentagon. She wanted to open the ceremony with "Taps" being played by a Navy bugler, in honor of our deceased patriarch, Joseph Jackson, a Navy veteran of World War II. In a letter received only three weeks prior to the event, the Director of Ceremonies & Special Events advised us, on official U.S. Army stationery, *"Regrettably, due to official requirements, the support you have requested cannot be provided."* In closing he stated *"I regret a favorable response is not possible, but trust you understand our limitations."* Joyce had also been in direct contact with the Navy Department and somehow we held out hope that the bugler, whose name had already been provided to us, would show up. We decided to keep him in the program.

It was going to be quite a ceremony in front of more than fifty invited guests, comprised of relatives, friends and associates. The program encompassed the actual planting of the tree, opening and closing remarks by the two of us, presentations by each of our three children, a song by a professional singer and special participation by our oldest granddaughter together with nine other grandchildren, grandnieces and grandnephews, with several surprises in store for the attendees. In essence, it was to be a fitting *"Grand Finale"* to a memorable adventure.

The family members left their homes on Friday, April 29th to travel to the D.C. area. On Saturday we all assembled in Chestertown, Maryland, 75 miles away from the Capital, to celebrate the 85th birthday of Joyce's mother, Madge Crooks. On Sunday we returned to the D.C. area to make final preparations for the next day. That included picking up a dozen butterflies at "Butterflies on the Potomac" in Dickerson, MD. These were for release during the ceremony, symbolizing the twelve members of our immediate Jackson family and in honor of Joyce's father. The butterflies had to be kept in the refrigerator overnight which slowed down their metabolism to be reawakened by the warming rays of the sun just prior to their release at the ceremony.

We all stayed at a hotel in Lanham, MD, on Sunday night and next morning took the Metro train into Washington. Everything we needed was packed into carrying bags, which included: butterflies, blanket, karaoke machine (for voice amplification), special cookies, albums, water, shovels, camera, film, gloves, tape recorder, video camera, batteries and the programs.

It was a perfect springtime day as our little group walked from the Metro stop to the west lawn of the Capitol on Monday, May 1, 2000. Strung out behind us were all of our children, Rob, Chris and Steve, their spouses, Mike Adams and Debbie Jackson, all of our grandchildren. Katie, Erin and Matthew Adams and Bryan Jackson, and the memories of all the experiences we had encountered in progressing to this final stage of our project.

Waiting for us at the Grant Memorial were more relatives and friends that we had invited to share the occasion with us. They included both of our mothers, Helen Jackson and Madge Crooks, Bill and Barb Coffey, Cheryl Cummins, Lisa and Dave Lewis, Bill Crooks, Jeff and Sue Zern with Ellie, Lisa Grim with Meghan and Caraline, Carrie Lynn Robinson with Olivia,

Jennifer Brinsfield with Katherine and Sara, Angelo and Bambi Colonna, Bunny Dunleavy, David and Irene Balazek, David and Barb Cvengros, Bob and Marie Anderson, Nancy Jones and sister-in-law Ruthie Gray, Bernie and Sue Perella, Carolyn Meeker, Cliff Harvison, John Conley and John Grimm.

Also waiting were Julia Long, of the National Park Service, Lois Young, an entertainer we engaged from Newark, DE and our photographer, Mary Ann Gatty, from Sterling, VA.

Three workers from the NPS were poised to remove a 12 foot red oak from the bed of their pickup truck at the right moment in the ceremony.

And then, walking around the corner of the monument in a dress-white uniform, came Navy bugler, Musician First Class John Schroeder. We were overjoyed that the Navy had found a way to honor us with his presence. Everything was now in place for the ceremony.

THE END

Note: The transcript of the D.C. ceremony can be found in the Appendix

The Jackson Legacy

Final Tree Planting
U.S. Capitol
Washington, D.C.
May 1, 2000

Welcome .... John Jackson

*"Taps" .... Major General Daniel Butterfield
Musician First Class John Schroeder, Bugler

Invocation .... Steven Jackson

History of the Tree Project .... Joyce Jackson

Planting Ceremony .... Julia Long, NPS

Tree Planting... Red Oak
John Jackson
Joyce Jackson
Robert Jackson
Christine Adams (Jackson)
Steven Jackson

Arbor Day Comments .... Robert Jackson

The Tree Song .... Lois Young
Lois Young, Children's Recording Artist,
Songwriter and Puppeteer

"Secrets Revealed" .... Christine Adams
Christine Adams, Poetess

Butterfly Legend .... A Native American Legend
Kathryn Emily Adams

**Butterfly Release...................................... The Great Grandchildren
Kathryn Adams   **Erin Adams**
Matthew Adams   **Bryan Jackson**
Sara Brinsfield   **Katherine Brinsfield**
Caraline Grim   **Meghan Grim**
Elizabeth Zern   **Olivia Robinson**

Epilogue .... John Jackson

*In Memory of Joseph Jackson
**In Memory of Ray Crooks

Secrets Revealed

In the tranquil embrace of an early dawn,
A tree stands tall.
Its strong trunk and graceful branches
A symbol of God's magnificent work.
The richness of its bark and gleam of shiny leaves
Boast of vigor and life.
A haven for creatures seeking protection and rest.
Its calm and silent presence brings peace.
The tips of the highest tree brush the clouds
Like a passage to heavenly lofts.
One has only to glance at a tree to unlock life's simpler mysteries.

Christine Adams

The Jackson Legacy

We've finished our journey, planting five trees in each of the fifty states.
*All of the selected places contained the name **Jackson** or one of our first*
names representing a family member.
In this way we have commemorated a lasting legacy which will also help to
protect, beautity, cleanse and provide habitat for nature.
We encourage you to join with us, wherever you live, by planting a tree.

The Jacksons
John, Joyce, Robert, Christine, Steven

Questions and Answers

Over the years, we've been asked a lot of questions about our project. Following are some of the most-frequently asked with our responses:

Q. How did you think up the idea for the Legacy project?

A. It was Joyce's idea. She wanted to create something at the end of the 20th Century that would survive after we were gone. She came up with the idea to plant trees because we had made a practice of doing this for special occasions wherever we lived.

Q. How did you get permission to plant in each state?

A. Joyce wrote to the chief political officer in each community that we selected. That person either helped us directly or cleared the way for someone else to work with us. It took hundreds of phone calls to hold this all together.

Q. How long did it take you to plant all the trees?

A. It took us 10 years, from 1991 to 2000.

Q. How much time did you spend planting at each site?

A. Normally, the physical act of planting the five trees took about an hour but we could spend four times that in interacting with the local people and talking with the media.

Q. How many trees did you plant?

A. All told, we planted 252 trees; five in each of the 50 states and one each at The Hermitage and on Capitol Hill.

Q. What kind of trees did you plant?

A. We always asked the local people for suggestions on what trees were indigenous to their area with an eye out to planting the ones with the best chance at survival. Initially, we bought all of the trees, ourselves, but later on many communities purchased them in advance of our visit.

Q. How many miles did you travel?

A. Our best estimates are: 48,330 by air, 15,823 by car, 34 by boat and 32 by train, for a total of 64,219 miles.

Questions and Answers (continued)

Q. Have all the trees survived?

A. Unfortunately, No. Newly-planted trees have a casualty rate under the best of conditions. We take comfort in knowing that we did the best we could for them and that the vast majority have sprouted into assets for the communities we visited.

Q. Did your children go with you?

A. Our children went with us on a number of occasions but the majority of the time we traveled by ourselves. Ohio and New Jersey were the only places that all of us gathered at the same time, but there were six other states where at least one of our three children was present.

Q. How did the public relations process work?

A. After about five states were done, we developed a media kit describing our project, listing awards and citations, excerpts from newspaper articles and anything else we could come up with to inform the community representatives and local newspapers.

Q. How much news coverage did you get?

A. At least forty-five newspapers ran some portion of our story, along with seven television appearances, two on live radio, two magazine articles and mention in a book on family traditions.

Q. Did other people help you plant the trees?

A. Usually there was someone to help us plant. Our experiences ranged from a couple of places where we were alone to situations where a substantial number of people turned out from the community.

Q. Why did you plant a tree at *The Hermitage*?

A. Because The Hermitage has been preserved as Andrew Jackson's home and he was the primary Jackson person after whom places were named all over the country.

Q. Why did you plant a tree at the Nation's Capitol Building?

A. As a final tribute to all the townspeople we encountered during the project. Also, as a commemoration to our deceased fathers, Joseph Jackson and Raymond Crooks, for the sacrifices that they and all others made during World War II to allow us to live the way we do.

Questions and Answers (continued)

Q. Do you go back to see the trees?

A. We have been back to many sites and will always try to continue doing that. In places that we can't physically visit, we ask our local contacts to send us pictures. One way or another, we keep up on how the trees are doing.

Q. What is the most-asked question regarding your project?

A. The most-asked question was "*Have you been to Jackson Hole?*" We didn't cover that location until our 49th state, so it was a question that we heard over and over again during the course of the project.

Q. What is the most lasting impression you got from the project?

A. That no matter where they live, most people are proud of their home town and want you to know how great it is to live there.

List of Awards, Gifts, Notices and Recognitions

Letter of Recognition from President George H.W. Bush, May 17, 1991

Key to the City of Jackson, Alabama, presented by Mayor Norma Beard, January 15, 1992

Declaration of Jackson Family Day, New Castle County, Delaware, presented by Dennis Greenhaus, County Executive, on August 17,1992

Friend of Recreation plaque from the State of Delaware Recreation and Parks Society, presented by Zachary C. Carter, DRPS President, February 16, 1993

Letter of Appreciation from Mayor Kane Ditto, Jackson, Mississippi, March 26, 1993

Letter of Recognition regarding our trip to Alaska, from Governor Jim Florio, New Jersey, May 19, 1993

Mention in *Celebrating Family Traditions, an Idea and Keepsake Book*, Helen Baine Bland and Mary Seehafer Sears, authors, A Bullfinch Press Book, Little Brown and Company, 1993

U. S. Department of the Interior, Volunteer Service Award, for stewardship of America's public lands, 1992-1993, by Bruce Babbitt, Secretary of Interior

Letter of Recognition from Vice-President Al Gore, July 6. 1993

Proclamation presented by Mayor Donald R. Capen of Madison, New Jersey, honoring the Jackson Family at Arbor Day Celebration, May 7, 1994

Honorary Citizen of the City of Jackson, Kentucky, presented by Mayor Franklin E. Noble, June 6. 1994

Key to the City of Jackson, Tennessee, Declaration of Jackson Family Day, presented by J. Alex Leech, County Mayor and Charles Farmer, City Mayor, June 8, 1994

Certificate of Merit, National Arbor Day Foundation, November 30, 1994

Feature article in *American Forest* magazine, Cheryl Baisden, author, November/December, 1994, issue

Commemorative plaque from the Town of Jackson, North Carolina, shirts and logo patches, May 10, 1995

Jackson logo shirts and badges, Jackson, Minnesota, June 10, 1996

List of Awards, Gifts, Notices and Recognitions

Department of the Army Commendation, presented by Major Robert F. Martinsen, Executive Officer, FSCC, Honolulu, Hawaii, February 19, 1997

Proclamation of the Town of Walden, Jackson County, Colorado, presented by Mayor Kyle Fliniau, May 26, 1998

Certificate of Appreciation plaque, from City of Altus, Jackson County, Oklahoma, presented by Mayor T.L. Grambling, September 7, 1998

Jackson Day Proclamation from the City of Holton, Jackson County, Kansas, presented by Mayor Richard J. Mulroy, September 8, 1998

Key to the City of Christine, North Dakota, presented by Mayor Tom Seifert, September 11, 1998

Proclamation from the City of Aztec, San Juan County, New Mexico, presented by Mayor Mike Arnold on June 7, 1999

Key to the City of Monticello, San Juan County, Utah, presented by Mayor Clyde Christianson on June 9, 1999

Commemorative plaque from the community of Roberts, Idaho, presented by Mayor Ben Poston, on August 31, 1999

Letter of Appreciation from Mayor James W. Lewis of Jacksonville, Oregon, a Jacksonville blanket and a basket of goodies presented by the merchants on March 16, 2000

Citation from the National Park Service acknowledging the planting of our tree near the U.S. Capitol Building on May 1, 2000

Mention in *Family Circle* magazine article by Margaret Jaworski, June 2, 2000, issue, page 11

Sources

The Columbia Lippencott Gazetteer of the World. Ed.Leonard E. Seltzer. New York: Columbia University Press, 1952.

Epstein, Nadine. "Chairman of the Valley." *Rural Electrification*.(*Vol.53, No.2*) Nov. 1994. 14-18.

Harder, Kelsie B. *Illustrated Dictionary of Place Names*. New York: Van Nostrand Remhold, 1976.

Jackson, Halliday. *Civilization of the Indian Natives*. Philadelphia: Marcus T.C. Gould, 1830.

Kane, Joseph Nathan. *The American Counties*: *Origins of Names, Dates of Creation and Organization, Area, Population including 1980 Census figures, Historical Data and Published Sources*. 3rd ed. New York: Scarecrow Press Inc, 1983.

Rand McNally...Commercial Atlas and Marketing Guide. 119th ed. Chicago: Rand Mc Nally And Company, c1988.

Smith, Alice. "Virtual Nebraska, Jackson, Dakota County." *CASDE |Jackson- -Dakota County* http://www.casde.unl.edu/history/counties/dakota/jackson/.com.

In writing the book, we are indebted to *Google* and *Wikipedia* which often directed us to websites operated by each town, Chamber of Commerce, state or other municipal-type site. These sources helped in a number of ways to get our facts straight and to help embellish the description of our journey. They helped us to blend source material into a summation that is uniquely our own account.

www.city-data.com
www.epodunk.com
www.jacksonhotsprings.com
www.native-languages.org
www.stjohnsaz.com

APPENDIX

Transcript of the Final Planting Ceremony in Washington, D.C. on May 1. 2000

Welcome (John)

Welcome family from Pennsylvania, Maryland, Ohio and Indiana. Friends from Florida, Ohio, New Jersey, Virginia, Maryland and Pennsylvania. Guests from Delaware and D.C. We are here today to dedicate our final tree-planting to the memory of my father, Joseph Jackson, WWII Navy veteran, and the name Jackson. We are honored to have **Musician 1st Class John Schroeder of the U.S. Navy Band** to begin the program with the playing of "Taps". Please rise.

Invocation Introduction (John)

Thank you, sir (*to the bugler*). Please remain standing while our son, **Steve**, leads us in prayer.

Thank you, Steve, that was very moving and now Joyce will summarize the Jackson Legacy project.

History of the Tree Project (Joyce)

Hello, everyone. In the last ten years, the Jackson family has, sometimes as a unit and sometimes just John and I, visited every state to plant five trees in each town named Jackson and there were forty such areas. In the remaining ten states, we used our first names so we could account for all fifty states. For example: St. Johns, Arizona, Joyce, Washington, Roberts, Idaho, Christine, North Dakota and Stevens Village, Alaska. We were given special permission to plant the state tree, tulip poplar, at President Jackson's mansion at The Hermitage outside of Nashville, Tennessee. However, the most important tree planted is the one here at the Capitol. It symbolizes the completion of a great journey by the Jackson family during the last decade of the 20th Century. This Red Oak will welcome in the new century and stand as a reminder to the name Jackson, not only as a great President of the U.S. but also to Joseph Jackson, husband of Helen, father of John, grandfather of Rob, Chris and Steve and great grandfather of Katie, Erin, Bryan and Matthew. As this Red Oak grows to its full potential of 60 feet and a life span of 100 years, we hope that many visitors to the Capitol grounds see its beauty and majestic presence and appreciate God's gift of a tree through the Jackson Legacy project. We have made a difference; 252 trees stand all around this country as a result of our efforts. We thank the many people from around the country who helped us achieve our goals and to everyone here we give thanks for your interest and support over the last 10 years. Joining us today are 2 staff members of Congressman Kevin Brady, Carol Thobar and Amy Thornberry. Regrettably, Congressman Brady is en route from Texas and is not able to be with us but sends his regards. Our next guest was instrumental in selecting this spot for our tree planting. She has been with the National Park Service for many years. May I introduce Julia Long.

Presentation of NPS Commendation by Julia Long

Citation from the National Park Service presented by Julia Long (*wearing her NPS uniform; we also received a letter from NPS Superintendent, Arnold Goldstein, expressing appreciation for our donation of $250).*
The Citation reads:

Blossoms in Our Future
The National Park Service gratefully acknowledges
John & Joyce Jackson and Family
for your living gift to the Nation of
A Red Oak in Memory of Joseph Jackson, Veteran, USN, WWII
your contribution will help ensure the beauty of
our Nation's Capital for future generations
visitors to Washington, D.C. will be reminded
of your generosity and good will.

Tree Planting (Joyce)

Thank you, Julia. We appreciate all your help. It is now time for the tree planting. Would Rob, Chris, Steve and John come up?

(*The three workers from the National Park Service moved the red oak from the bed of their pick -up truck to the hole that had already been dug into the ground at the back of the Grant Memorial. The tree was located to the right of the sculpture, in front of some other trees, back from the sidewalk that circles the Memorial. The tag on the tree reads "GR016", signifying "Grant Reflecting, tree number 16". All five family members participated in the planting and spreading of the dirt around the tree, taking turns using the two collapsible trenching tools that had accompanied us throughout all the other tree plantings. At the conclusion of the planting, all of the NPS representatives departed, leaving us to continue with the program*)

Arbor Day Comments – (John)

Our oldest son, Rob, will share some thoughts on Arbor Day and how the Jackson Family Legacy complements this day.

(*Arbor Day is observed in most states on the last day of April, which was the day before our tree-planting ceremony in D.C. Rob recited the many ways that we came in contact with the concept of Arbor Day during our project, even though we are not directly associated with the National Arbor Day Foundation*)

The Tree Song – (Joyce)

Thank you, Rob. I want to thank my sister, Barb, for introducing me to the music of our next guest. She is a classically-trained singer and actress, who has performed in New York, on TV shows and scores of commercials. She has written over 70 children's songs and has been delighting fans for 10 years on the East and West Coast with her popular albums and interactive performances with life-sized puppets. Today we will have the pleasure to hear her sing *"The Tree Song"*, so appropriate for today's planting. Will everyone please join with me to welcome this very talented and versatile young lady – Lois Young. *(The kids gathered around as she performed for them and the rest of us)*

(John) Thank you, Lois, that was just wonderful and the kids loved it. I can see why the elementary schools rave about your extraordinary voice, Thanks again.

Poem *"Secrets Revealed"* by Christine Jackson Adams (John)

The Jackson family takes great pride in its poetic abilities. My father passed this gift to me and my daughter carries on in this tradition. It is my pleasure to present Chris Adams reciting her poem entitled *"Secrets Revealed."*

(the text of the poem is reproduced on page 3 of the program)

(John) Thank you, Chris. Joyce will speak about the butterflies.

Butterfly Symbolism (Joyce)

We have chosen 12 Monarch butterflies to release because they are lovely ambassadors of good will from the insect world and the 12 Jackson family members, too, have been ambassadors of good will by bringing the trees into selected towns and beautifying them. The release of the butterflies also is in memory of my father who always cheered us on during our journey. Thank you, Daddy. Our next guest speaker is our oldest granddaughter, Katie, form Ohio, who will recite the Butterfly Legend.

Native American Butterfly Legend - read by Kathryn Emily Adams

"If you have a secret wish, capture a butterfly and whisper your wish to it. Since butterflies cannot speak, your secret is ever safe in its keeping. Release the butterfly, and it will carry your wish to the Great Spirit, who alone knows the thoughts of butterflies. By setting the butterfly free, you are helping to restore the balance of nature and your wish will surely be granted."

(this story came from the providers of the butterflies – Butterflies on the Potomac)

Butterfly Release (Joyce)

That was just great, Katie. Thank you. Now for the release of the butterflies. Will each child bring a parent or grandparent up please; Mom Crooks and Mom Jackson. When you open your envelope, the butterfly will be sleepy. You can gently pick them up by their folded wings and place them on your hands or arms or even right in the middle of your nose for a fun photo. They should fly away in a minute or two.

(Every butterfly was a performer. They rested on their hosts until the sun warmed their bodies for flight. Some took off and then hovered or returned temporarily to another human resting

place. That gave everyone ample time to appreciate the beauty that nature has bestowed in these tiny creatures)

Our program will come to an end with some closing comments from John.

In Closing (John)

We're so grateful to have so many people here today.

When we first started in 1991, in Joyce, Washington, there was an elderly postmistress and a couple of patrons from their general store.

California was the next state, and no one attended our planting of five seedlings.

That didn't bother us a bit because the whole project was conceived as something personal to our family. We weren't looking for fanfare or notoriety.

But that began to change at the next planting in Pennsylvania. We had started to name each of the five trees and when we pointed out our daughter's tree to the little girl who was standing there, she went over and hugged the blue spruce saying *"I love you Chrissy."*

The reception got a little better in New Jersey, then the Mayor of Jackson, South Carolina, turned out to help us dig the holes and at our seventh stop, we got the key to the city of Jackson, Alabama, with a nice write-up in their local paper.

It just continued to grow from there: the trees got bigger, the reception committees grew larger and our press releases generated more media coverage.

So many warm and wonderful people have helped us, all around the country. I thought I would pick out five of them for special mention:

The mountain man in Montana served as our host took us into his home for some pickled cauliflower. On the way out of his town, we discovered a book written about his experience as a combat soldier in WWII, where he was wounded and decorated for action in Germany.

The Athabascan Indian assistant chief, who was filling in while the chief traveled to Vienna, Austria, and who arranged for us to stay overnight in a salmon fishing camp, frequented by grizzlies. Remember, Steve?

The mayor of Jackson Junction, Iowa, who interrupted his digging to grab a shotgun and dispatch a gopher.

The ranchers of Jackson Mountain, Nevada, who tripled our number of plantings because they'd been waiting for motivation to beautify their one-room schoolhouse.

And the priest in Nebraska, who was the only clergy to bless our tree-planting effort.

Of course, there's a lot more interesting people and interesting venues to mention, but we'll cover that in our book.

It's been a wonderful journey: figuring out plane schedules, nursery purchases, all of Joyce's set-up work, long trips in rental cars, whistling over the miles and sometimes other emotions, dodging a hurricane, torrential rains and seeing, up close, the fearsome aftermath of a tornado.

On the sad side, our family lost two patriarchs over the ten-year span, Joe Jackson and Ray Crooks. Both were very supportive of our efforts on this project. We honor both of them today.

Thanks for coming today. Thanks for the little things that kept us going, such as your interest.

Especially, I want to thank Joyce for turning a humble idea into a fantastic journey that touched not only our lives but untold others.

Now please join us across the street at the Rayburn Building for lunch.

-The End-

John and Joyce Jackson are co-authors of their first non-fiction book, *Trail of Trees*. John is a graduate of Villanova University, Villanova, Pennsylvania. Joyce attended West Chester University and graduated from Kingwood College, Kingwood, Texas. After spending more than twenty years moving around the country, the Jackson's now reside in Delaware, Ohio where they can be near their three children, spouses and five grandchildren, Kathryn, Erin, Matthew, Bryan and Noah.

Future tree planters
Grandchildren of John and Joyce Jackson

41/500